ENCHANTED IRELAND

ENCHANTED
IRELAND

Published by The Reader's Digest Association Limited

LONDON • NEW YORK • SYDNEY • MONTREAL

ABOUT THIS BOOK

I T MAY CONCEIVABLY STRIKE some readers as odd that a series called *Exploring the British Isles* should include a volume on Ireland. Unless and until a new term is thought up, however, the British Isles include Ireland, geographically speaking at least. North and South, Ireland has much in common with the rest of the British Isles, but it also has a distinct and fascinating identity.

One quality of the Irish people that visitors remark on universally is their hospitality. Robin Neillands, author of the book that forms the centrepiece of this volume, found himself toasting many new friends during his epic walk from the far north to the far southwest. His reflections on the island's rich history and culture, and the customs and passions of her people, are enhanced with informative features on a wide range of subjects. First, though, is an introduction to the island by travel writer John Kahn, who paid a more recent—and less arduous—visit; and rounding off the volume is a 'Highlights' section, which contains the editors' pick of the best the Emerald Isle has to offer.

ENCHANTED IRELAND was edited and designed by The Reader's Digest Association Limited, 11 Westferry Circus, Canary Wharf, London E14 4HE

Walking through Ireland Original full-length version by Robin Neillands, published by Little, Brown & Company, 1993, paperback edition published by Warner Books, 1994
© Robin Neillands, 1993
The moral right of the author has been asserted.
British condensed version © The Reader's Digest Association Limited, 2000

CONTRIBUTORS

Series Editor Steve Savage

Volume Editor Charlotte Rundall

Assistant Editor/Researcher Miriam Sharland

Associate Editors David Blomfield, Hugo de Klee

Copy Editors Morag Lyall, Barbara Roby

Editorial/Picture Research Assistant Kate Michell

Art Editor Karen Stewart

Designer Carl Meek

Picture Researcher Helen Ashford

Additional material by James Harpur, Henrietta Heald, Lindsay Hunt, John Kahn

Cartography Anthony Sidwell (page 9), Malcolm Porter (pages 136–137)

Index Brian Amos

FRONT COVER *Gortahork's sweeping bays, lush pasture and whitewashed cottages make an idyllic rural scene.*
BACK COVER (TOP) *A love of music runs in the blood and moves the feet of even the youngest Irish folk.*
BACK COVER (BOTTOM) *Clerke's grocers in Skibbereen presents a bright and cheerful front to local shoppers.*
TITLE PAGE *The Giant's Causeway is one of the most spectacular sights along the Northern Irish coast.*

THIS PAGE *Unlike their red Northern counterparts, letterboxes in the Republic of Ireland are emerald green.*
PAGES 6–7 *The shimmering light of the Ring of Kerry picks out a lonely rowing boat in the misty scenery.*
PAGES 24–5 *An aerial shot captures the drama and huge scale of the limestone plateau known as the Burren.*
PAGES 134–5 *A night view of Dublin, a lively and bustling metropolis studded with star-like lights.*

CONTENTS

EXPLORING IRELAND

with John Kahn

IRELAND

with John Kahn

THE LINE OF LATE-EVENING TRAFFIC had been moving smoothly, but it slowed down as the lights of a town came into view. What town could it be? According to my road atlas, there was no town at this point. Perhaps I'd managed to take a wrong turning, and some time ago too—quite in keeping with the notorious signposting on Irish roads. At last, on the outskirts, a sign announced the town's name: Newry... Just a minute! Newry's in *Northern* Ireland! But how...? I'd crossed the border without realising it.

A DIVIDED AND UNDIVIDED ISLAND

Even during the daytime, you may not realise for a good while that you've crossed the border—not perhaps until you notice that a village postbox is painted red rather than green or vice versa, or you see a note on a shop door reading 'WE ACCEPT STERLING'. Until then, the transition is imperceptible. No glaring changes in terrain. No road blocks across the highway. No passport or customs officers, let alone security patrols. Not even a 'YOU ARE NOW ENTERING THE UK' sign—at least, none that I noticed. To the casual visitor, Ireland gives the inescapable impression of being, in most respects, a single place. It may be divided between two countries. There may be two (or more) traditions, as they say. There are, without question, political conflicts of great complexity. But the entire island has a coherence or consistency about it—a spirit of place, and a distinctive Irish temperament.

An island off an island off the European landmass, so remote that the Romans never got round to colonising it, Ireland has been characterised as Europe's satellite, her lighthouse keeper, and her love child; and also, in view of its heart-wrenchingly sad history (and perhaps its climate), as Europe's teardrop.

In fact, its independent geographical life goes back only about 10,000 years, when the last Ice Age ended and sea levels rose, cutting it off from Britain just as Britain was cut off from the Continent. The island of today has a surface area slightly more than one-third the size of mainland Britain's (though its population

is less than one-tenth as large). And it has its own satellite islands, chiefly off the west coast: the famous old-world Aran Islands off County Galway, for example, or, confusingly, Aran Island off County Donegal (quite unrelated, being 150 miles further north).

As for Ireland's political geography, that too can be highly confusing without some orientation. Four ancient kingdoms became, in the Middle Ages, four traditional provinces: Ulster in the north, Connaught or Connacht in the northwest, Leinster in the east and Munster in the southwest. These provinces inspire some loyalty or sense of identity in their residents, thanks to provincial newspapers, sports teams and divergent personalities. Then there are various vaguely defined 'regions'—based on a characteristic landscape or history, perhaps—such as the Burren, a vast limestone plateau in County Clare, or Connemara in County Galway. But it is the counties themselves that inspire the greatest sense of local identity. They number thirty-two in all, six of which make up Northern Ireland.

Northern Ireland is often referred to as Ulster, but the traditional province of Ulster consists of nine counties, not six. The extra three are part of the Irish Republic. And one of them, Donegal, actually contains the northernmost point of Ireland as a whole. So 'the South' of Ireland reaches further north than 'the North' does.

The island's terrain is comparably perverse. Instead of rising in a more or less orderly way from the shore towards the centre, the land often rears up sharply near the coast and then subsides into plains and bogs as it moves inland. In the east, the Wicklow and Mourne Mountains peer over the Irish Sea, while lengthy stretches of the winding north and west coasts are dramatically rugged, and backed by mountain ranges of their own.

Not that the interior is short of fine scenery. It has its share of modest mountains too, with gorgeous drives through the passes. It can offer, as a contrast, the austere beauty of a bog-land nature reserve such as Clara Bog in County Offaly; or the Shannon, the longest river in the British Isles; and the myriad lakes, a parting gift from the ice cap at the end of the last Ice Age: in each case, a paradise for boaters, anglers and ramblers.

But for most visitors, it's the coastline that casts the strongest spell, and in particular the wild western seaboard. There is something singularly exhilarating about standing on a wind-blown cliff top, in Kerry or Galway or Donegal, and gazing out across the Atlantic. You are on the very edge of the Old World. Due west lies the New World—not the United States, but the chill Labrador peninsula of Canada—deep-frozen in the winter, whereas Ireland stays fairly mild, thanks to the warm caress of an arm of the Gulf Stream.

Whether this landscape can continue to remain unspoilt for much longer is debatable, when so many foreign tourists are now thronging its roads and pathways. Such popularity is a great recommendation, of course, though also perhaps a reason to choose an off-peak season for your own visit. Given the whimsical climate, you take your chances almost as plausibly in late autumn as in high summer. Atlantic clouds blow in at any time of year; without them, the Emerald Isle would not be emerald. And they blow in at any time of day— the weather can turn on a sixpence, as the Irish would say—but they blow over just as unpredictably.

OPPOSITE *The magical beauty of Ireland's coast is typified by the Dingle peninsula in County Kerry, where fields sweep up to the brink of rugged cliffs.*

ABOVE AND RIGHT *Archaeologists believe that the impressive Stone Age passage tomb of Newgrange also served as an observatory. But they remain baffled by the mysterious pattern of spirals and semicircles that adorn the site's massive entrance stone.*

ANCIENT HISTORY, RECENT HISTORY

At the time of my unwitting border crossing, I was heading for Belfast after visiting one of the oldest buildings in Ireland: the ancient passage tomb at Newgrange in County Meath. It's a famously evocative spot, rich in symbolism. The Celtic god Aengus supposedly lived in the vicinity, and the great mythical hero Cuchulain was conceived here. The setting of the tomb is breathtaking. On a gentle slope, a sweeping arc of pale granite walling (a reconstruction, it turns out) fronts a huge grassy dome—the artificial mound hiding the tomb building itself. That in turn is an extraordinary piece of primitive engineering, with massive stone slabs creating not just the burial chambers and the long corridor but also a kind of arched ceiling at the far end, and astronomically aligned to admit the rays of the rising sun at the winter solstice. And all constructed before Stonehenge and before the pyramids, some 5,200 years ago!

Of all the symbolic associations that the place suggests, one above all appealed to me: a very recent one too. To get to the tomb nowadays, you take a shuttle bus from the visitors' centre, an airy, welcoming, up-to-the-minute building, in starkest contrast to the tomb itself. What struck me was what a nice symbolic pairing the two buildings make: the old and the new. That phrase could be the slogan of today's Ireland, so aptly does it sum up the paradoxical impression that the island as a whole conveys.

Within the visitors' centre, what's more, the exhibition hall, with its enthralling multimedia display, is the very model of a modest modern museum. It's heartening to see how often the new and the old complement each other in this thoughtful way—mutually enhancing rather than undermining. Ireland is lucky, it seems, in having come late to the mass-tourism industry, and, after studying the mistakes and successes of other parts of the world, it appears to be getting things right first time.

My first impression of Belfast, when I saw it the following morning, was heartening in its own way. The city belies its reputation. It seems the opposite of demoralised and beleaguered. A cheerful bustle prevailed, though that was, I was told, always in evidence, even during the height of the recent Troubles. But by now the Good Friday peace agreement of 1998 was signed, security measures had relaxed considerably, and you couldn't help feeling that there was an extra spring in the step of all the shoppers and passers-by.

Belfast came of age during the Industrial Revolution: linen and cotton mills sprang up, and then engineering factories and shipyards. In common with most industrial cities, it doesn't put on any airs. It makes no pretence of being beautiful. There are several striking buildings, certainly, from the majestic new Waterfront Hall conference centre and the enormous palace-like 100-year-old City Hall to the ornate Crown Liquor Saloon, a perfectly restored Victorian pub, down to its gas mantles and wooden snugs and mosaic-tiled floor, owned by the National Trust. But the overall Victorian grandeur that the city centre presumably once enjoyed is difficult to discern nowadays.

Not that it's a dour city. Heavy subsidies, from the European Union (EU) and from British central government, have preserved its prosperous air. The leafy area around the Queen's University is full of cafés, secondhand bookshops, small theatres or clubs and other bohemian touches, and during my visit was gearing itself up for the annual Belfast Arts Festival. On the northern outskirts of town, a broad tract of parkland embraces a fine zoo, two small nature reserves, a Victorian castle, remnants of prehistoric forts, and a hill more than 1,150 feet high—Cave Hill, or 'Napoleon's nose' as it's known locally—affording wonderful views on a clear day not just of Belfast itself and Belfast Lough but all the way across the sea to Scotland.

All the same, Belfast is hardly a tourist magnet in its own right. When I called in at the central Tourist Information Office, it was only to learn that no guided tour of the city was available that day—whether by bus or on foot. 'Not enough demand,' the lady at the enquiries desk admitted. 'The tours are running just three days a week now; that's as much as we can justify in the winter.' Tourism in Belfast had certainly increased in recent years, but not enough: it was still to some extent a casualty of the Troubles. The popular image of the city (a highly unpopular image with locals) derives from old TV scenes of bomb damage or of the gigantic menacing murals in the Falls Road and Shankhill Road areas of West Belfast—the front lines in the sectarian

BELOW *The newly built Waterfront Hall—a modern conference centre and concert hall—symbolises Belfast's attempt to redefine itself as a positive and forward-looking European city.*

ABOVE *Northern Ireland's sectarian divisions are defiantly expressed in murals in West Belfast.*

conflict. But these are surely places where few tourists would wish to present themselves. (If you do want to study these areas, the local cab drivers will gladly take you on a tour of inspection, apparently, though they may baulk at joining you for a political discussion in one of the pubs thereabouts.) In fact, Belfast and other Irish cities, both North and South, are considered comparatively safe for tourists, far more so than most continental and American cities.

One great virtue of Belfast is its location, making it a convenient launching pad for day-trips to some serious beauty spots. In the words of an Irish compliment, it's a good place to be for getting to other places: westwards to Lough Neagh (pronounced 'loch nay'), the largest lake in the British Isles; eastwards to Strangford Lough, a sheltered sea inlet with a profusion of wildlife; southwards to the rest of County Down, where, just as the song says, the stately Mourne Mountains really do sweep down to the sea; northwards to the Glens of Antrim, along the stupendous cliff-top coastal road, perhaps pressing on as far as the Giant's Causeway, the unique rock formation that Robin Neillands—author of our featured book—chose as the starting point for his epic walk through Ireland.

ARMAGH AND BEYOND

My route out of the North back into the Republic passed through Armagh, city and county. A year earlier, before the signing of the Good Friday peace agreement, I'd probably have given it a wide berth. That was the advice one was getting, as Robin Neillands reports at the very start of his book. By the mid-1990s there had been several attempts to end the terrible game of 'atrocity snap' that Catholic and Protestant paramilitary groups played. The Anglo-Irish agreement of 1985 gave the Irish Republic some say in Northern Irish affairs. The Downing Street declaration of 1993 offered Sinn Fein (the IRA's 'political wing') a role in future peace talks if the IRA declared a truce. Following the ceasefires of 1994, two Anglo-Irish framework documents in 1995 proposed a new Northern Ireland assembly, and outlined a possible new kind of relationship between the North and the South.

But all that was not enough. South Armagh remained 'bandit country'. The impression endured of a constant undertone of violence, punctuated by intermittent outrages and regular provocations by the Provos—the activists of the Provisional IRA. None of that was likely to confront me now. The Good Friday peace agreement of 1998, with its imaginative attempt at rethinking sovereignty and citizenship, had brought an increased feeling of reassurance. Even the outrage of the Omagh bombing later in the year could not dispel the new tone of optimism, and my long-brewing interest in the region could now be satisfied. The chance to see the city of Armagh was not to be missed.

Armagh is hilly, in marked contrast to Belfast; down at heel but holding its head high; disclosing some fine Georgian terraces, and full of quaint corners and curiosities, such as the antique Observatory, the Shambles and the visitor centre's model of Gulliver tied to the ground by the Lilliputians. But its peculiar

LEFT *Armagh, the ecclesiastical capital of Ireland, has two St Patrick's Cathedrals— the Church of Ireland's with a sturdy tower, and the Roman Catholic one with twin spires.*

BELOW *One of Armagh's attractions is the Observatory, which houses this antique telescope made in 1885. The Observatory itself was founded almost 100 years earlier, in 1790.*

fascination rests in something more abstract—a kind of political resonance. It is here that the great warrior-king Brian Boru, a prototype Irish national liberator, and scourge of the Vikings in 1014, is buried. It was here, five and a half centuries earlier, that St Patrick, Ireland's patron saint, had reputedly built his church headquarters. And it is here that the two paramount Irish cathedrals stand today—both called St Patrick's Cathedral—on two nearby hilltops. These cathedrals are the seats of the two Irish primates: the head of the Church of Ireland (broadly speaking, the counterpart of the Church of England) and the head of the Roman Catholic Church in Ireland. *All* Ireland, in each case. Whether as a political act or a non-political act, both Churches appear to disregard the partition of Ireland that came about in 1921, and to treat Ireland as a single entity. The border, once again, seems insubstantial.

Such a reflection is unlikely to impress many of the Protestant 'loyalists' or 'unionists' in the North, it's true. Their loyalty to union with Great Britain, and their opposition to a united Ireland, persist with a fervour that goes quite against current trends. On the one hand, Wales and Scotland are progressively loosening the unity of the United Kingdom, and on the other the EU is increasingly blurring the old national loyalties and divisions in Europe. But in Northern Ireland the long history of sectarian strife is not something easily set aside—that relentless round of disrespect, distrust, antagonism and violence. The Northern Protestants retain various suspicions, superstitions, and possibly fears, in regard to the Republic. Their bugbear vision of the South, in its intensest form, harks back to the old caricature of a blighted and benighted land, impoverished, ignorant and vengeful, oppressed by grim priests and enchained by tradition and intolerance. As the next few days of my travels would confirm, the reality could not be more different.

ABOVE *Tax concessions and EU subsidies, which have improved Ireland's infrastructure, have encouraged many international companies, such as this computer manufacturer, to open factories there.*

THE NEW AND THE OLD

Over the last twenty-five years, and particularly the last ten years, the economy of the Irish Republic has been transformed. Agriculture no longer dominates. Generous subsidies have been won from the European Union; overseas companies have been attracted to set up operations; tourism has surged; local talent has kindled and fanned a roaring computer industry; and the Irish flair for business is at last steaming along at home rather than just abroad. A few years ago, British and Irish newspapers reported a wondrous historic reversal: English labourers were travelling to the Irish Republic to work on the building sites there!

Social changes have almost kept pace, except in notably controversial matters such as divorce and abortion. Family ties are looser; censorship is now very light. Both the current and the former presidents of the country are women, and have—informally, and in their different ways—continued to shake up old habits and attitudes. The power of the Roman Catholic Church, so scorned or feared by traditional Northern Protestants, has waned conspicuously. Certainly there are social problems—unemployment, drug-related crime, lingering poverty—but they cast only a small shadow. In general, the youthful population is well informed and tolerant, forward-looking and outward-looking. The old stereotype Irishman—gormless and feckless—is even more of a travesty figure now than formerly. Those tedious old Irish jokes ring utterly hollow today. Modern-day

Ireland is very much a modern Ireland: easy-going, progressive and prosperous; and not as oppressed or hampered by its traditions as one might suppose.

Not that it rejects the traditional for the sake of the modern, or expels the old for the new. As far as possible, it takes advantage of both: pop music and folk music; golf and Gaelic football; a go-getting business-minded disposition and a devil-may-care, fun-loving outlook. The Irish enjoy betting at the racetrack, or fishing for trout, or gossiping in the pub just as much today as they've done in the past.

The trick is to keep the past in perspective, not to sweep it aside. To dismiss it like that would be impossible anyway: in Ireland, more than most places, the past is ever present, as tourists immediately discover: prehistoric stone circles or tombs, as at Newgrange; old picture-postcard country towns, with their brightly painted shop fronts, such as Carrickmacross in County Louth; unspoilt villages such as Inistioge (pronounced 'innish-teeg') in County Kilkenny or Avoca in County Wicklow (where the popular television series *Ballykissangel* is filmed); above all, the ruins.

Ireland is blessed (if that is the right word) with a wealth of ruins, the legacy of the Vikings, of troops sent by Elizabeth I or Oliver Cromwell, of uprisings and reprisals, and of impoverishment or official vandalism. They range from extensive monastic complexes such as Clonmacnoise or Monasterboice, to Norman castles such as that at Trim in County Meath, to some anonymous mossy

LEFT *Trim Castle, one of Ireland's numerous ruins, is the country's largest Norman castle and testimony to Trim's ancient ambitions to be the Irish capital.*

medieval masonry in a field, used as a windbreak by sheep. So abundant are the ruins in Ireland that you sometimes tend to overlook the smaller ones, as if mistaking them for a natural part of the landscape, alongside dead trees or heaps of rock. For my taste, the romance of Ireland lies in its ruins far more than in its myths and mysteries—the heroes and spirits and 'little people' of folklore. Any banshees or leprechauns you chance upon are likely to be human beings dressed as banshees or leprechauns. But Irish ruins, glimmering in the mist or silhouetted in the distance at sunset, are unchallengeably real, and often provide a fine romantic shiver, evoking as they do that wistful sense of loss that pervades Ireland's history.

THE OPEN ROAD

The balance between the old and the new cannot always be perfectly maintained. In one or two respects, the modernising of Ireland is happening too fast for most people's liking. The traditional donkey carts and thatched cottages are becoming a rarity, for instance. And although the old vivacious high streets haven't yet been supplanted by the out-of-town shopping centres, they are occasionally spoilt in a different way… by traffic jams.

Ireland's new prosperity has meant a surge in car ownership, and the road system, though improving, cannot keep pace. If you are on a driving holiday, then, set a modest daily mileage when planning your itinerary. Progress can be slow. All the more so in view of the several wrong turnings you're likely to take. That signposting! I drove through one small Kilkenny village no fewer than four times, having headed out along one exit road or another briefly before losing my nerve and doubling back.

The thing to do, of course, is to ask your way. And there perhaps lurks the reason for the strange signposting malaise throughout Ireland. Not pranksters… not incompetent civil servants… not self-absorbed and inconsiderate local residents. Quite the contrary, in my view: the local people are very keen to help outsiders, and very concerned to direct them accurately, but they believe in the personal touch. It's a matter of hospitality. Motorists aren't just passers-by, they're visitors; and they deserve a personal greeting on arrival and a friendly handshake to send them on their way. Why bother with efficient signposting then? So if you stop to ask a pedestrian the route, quite possibly he or she will insist on hopping into the car and accompanying you to the turnoff. (I was twice helped in this charming way on my recent trip: in each case, curiously, the passenger's own destination happened to be very near the turnoff in question!) Flag down a tractor driver, or a villager out taking the air on horseback, and quite possibly he or she will insist on changing route and leading you (slowly— but it would be churlish to object) to the exit road you need.

Even travelling at a modest pace, you can cover a lot of ground in a day. The country is

BELOW *There's no need to take a taxi in Ballyvaughan: just hop on a donkey cart driven by an local and his pipe-smoking dog. The uninflated price adds to the nostalgia.*

compact enough to provide a sumptuous variety of sightseeing within a leisurely drive. Consider the timetable of just one memorable day's motoring during my recent trip. Morning: a sequence of three famous ruin sites in County Tipperary—Holy Cross Abbey (now largely restored, alas; why did they have to ruin such fine ruins?); the marvellous Rock of Cashel, a limestone outcrop swathed in 12th- to 15th-century fortifications and church buildings; and the Norman castle at Cahir (pronounced 'care'), setting for some of the scenes in the film *Excalibur*. Early afternoon: a splendid, twisting, panoramic drive through the Knockmealdown Mountains. Midafternoon to dusk: down to the sea, for an invigorating walk along the beach of Ballycotton Bay, and across to Cobh, on an island in Cork harbour, in time for sunset.

HISTORY LESSONS

Cobh (pronounced 'cove' and meaning the same) is a delight, as my explorations the following morning would reveal. From the pastel-painted parade of shops along the harbour road, the town rises steeply up a hill, with tiers of neat houses and a spectacular Gothic Revival cathedral gazing down over the harbour. Known

LEFT *In the 19th century Cobh took the name Queenstown in honour of Queen Victoria, who took her first steps on Irish soil here in 1849. In those days it was a bustling port, serving emigrant ships to America and British naval vessels.*

as Queenstown in Victorian times, it was formerly the port for the city of Cork, just across the bay, and boasts a remarkable maritime history. It was the starting point for the first-ever steamship crossing of the Atlantic, in 1838. It was the last stop made by the *Titanic* in 1912, before that ship's fateful mid-Atlantic encounter with an iceberg. It was the base for the rescue and salvage effort when the *Lusitania* was sunk near by in 1915. And it was for a long time the country's major emigrant port—the tearful point of embarkation for millions of Irish people driven by hunger and despair to seek a new life in America. The town's eventful history is vividly celebrated in an exhibition entitled 'The Queenstown Story', which is housed in the old railway station and customs hall.

My stay in Cobh was all too short. I had to be in Dublin that evening, some 160 miles away, and had set my heart on a detour, what's more, to the parish of Ring, or An Rinn, in County Waterford. Just a couple of quiet villages on a tiny peninsula, and a few fishing boats bobbing in a small harbour—far off the beaten track. That is what makes An Rinn special. Being so remote, it has remained a Gaeltacht, or Gaelic-speaking region, the best-known such region outside the far west, with a renowned college and a proud heritage.

It's a never-failing pleasure to hear Gaelic being spoken in the street, and to know that this musical, ancient language has been saved from extinction. It is, in fact, the primary official language of the Irish Republic, and an official EU language. Many television programmes are broadcast in Gaelic, and there is an all-Gaelic radio station. But there are fewer than 80,000 people today whose first language is Gaelic and, although it is a compulsory school subject and can boost one's career, fluency in it is fairly rare among Ireland's English-speakers.

I asked a local schoolteacher how it was that this small pocket of Gaelic had managed to survive here in the southeast. 'Partly through being in a cul-de-sac,' she told me (in a most beautiful English), 'partly through being a self-sufficient fishing community and so needing few dealings with outsiders, but mainly because we were not going to let you English be having your way with us.' She broke off to chat in Gaelic to her toddler grandson, and then resumed her teasing of me in English. It might have gone on in this fashion all afternoon, but I had to take to the road again to get to my appointment in Dublin.

A GRACIOUS CITY

Where Belfast leaves an impression of Victorian vigour, Dublin shows a Georgian lightness of touch. And if Belfast is industrial and industrious, Dublin feels cultural and cultivated. It has a continental air about it: jaunty yet gracious, businesslike yet buoyant. Grafton Street, for pedestrians only, with its mix of smart stores and buskers; O'Connell Street, like an august boulevard that's seen better times, with its sequence of heroes' statues; the chic district of Temple Bar, known as the 'Left Bank Quarter'; the dignified complex of Dublin Castle; the haven of St Stephen's Green, the twenty-two-acre park right in the heart of town, oblivious of all the hurrying and perturbation on its periphery.

To get my bearings, I bought a day pass on one of the double-decker sightseeing buses that ply the main routes through the central precinct—no lack of guided tours here, as there had been in Belfast—and sunned myself for an hour and a half on the open upper deck, enjoying the driver's irreverent commentary, and making a note of highlights to return to on foot later for a close-up look.

The city looks admirably spruce—free of litter, and scrubbed clean of grime. Its Georgian squares more than live up to their reputation: each finely proportioned

ABOVE *A statue of the Catholic 'Great Liberator', Daniel O'Connell, presides over O'Connell Street, one of Dublin's main thoroughfares.*

LEFT *Dubliners while away a sunny afternoon beside the ornamental pond in St Stephen's Green, at the heart of the city.*

BELOW *The elegant Long Room of Trinity College Library—fully 210 feet long—is home to many national literary treasures.*

window, each flawlessly painted front door, each gleaming knocker and peacock fanlight—the word 'elegance' hardly does justice to it all.

Dublin is a city of secular shrines. Depending on your interests, you can make your pilgrimage to the grave of Jonathan Swift, in St Patrick's Cathedral, where he was dean for the last thirty-two years of his life; to the General Post Office, focal point of the fateful Easter Rising in 1916; to the Abbey Theatre; to the delightful statues of James Joyce and George Bernard Shaw, two of the city's many great literary sons; to the banks of the River Liffey; to one of the pubs featured in Joyce's epoch-making novel *Ulysses*; to the museum at the Guinness brewery…

If you have time for nothing else, do at least drop in to Trinity College (where Swift studied, and Oscar Wilde too, and many another famous Irish author), to see the library's magnificent Long Room, book-lined and wood-panelled like the inside of a barrel, and especially to visit the gallery beneath it to glimpse the *Book of Kells*. This copy of the Gospels, dated about AD 800, is arguably the finest artistic creation of the Dark Ages. Only a couple of its large elaborate pages can be displayed at any one time, but they convey more vividly than any other work you'll ever see the full meaning of the phrase 'illuminated manuscript'. It's as if the pages are illuminated from within: they seem to glow in the subdued lighting of the gallery, and to testify still to the fervent faith as well as the artistry of the monks who wrote and illustrated them so painstakingly all those centuries ago.

If you're lucky enough to be staying in Dublin for more than a few days, it would be worth your while to take one or two day-trips out of town. As with Belfast, the surrounding countryside has many exceptional attractions on offer, scarcely an hour's drive away in each case: northwards to that stunning Stone Age tomb at Newgrange; westwards to the horse races at the Curragh racecourse,

RIGHT *Barely an hour from the hubbub of Dublin, a tumbling waterfall breaks through lush green woodland on the flanks of the Wicklow Mountains.*

perhaps, or to the National Stud just outside Kildare Town; south to the Wicklow Mountains, and specifically to Glendalough, an idyllic blend of lakes, background mountains, woods, waterfalls and ruins—history and geography offsetting each other in a glorious composition.

THE NATION'S OTHER CAPITAL

My last evening in Ireland was spent deep in conversation with friends, four assorted drinking companions…who had never met me before. The Irish can be somewhat reserved with strangers, briefly, before taking them to their heart, but any such reserve on this occasion was so brief as to pass unnoticed. A second drink was bought for me before I could protest. My accent was promptly made fun of, as were those of the two non-Dubliners among the four friends (one from 'the North', one from 'out west'; to the Irish, there is of course no such thing as a mere Irish accent). Amid the crackle of the 'crack' or *craic* (witty fun, teasing chat, good-humoured gossip), they engaged eloquently in an earnest political argument. That easy switching between light-hearted and earnest is very common in Irish conversation. Each of the four friends had kissed the Blarney Stone, metaphorically at least.

The evening crystallised for me a sobering realisation, if that's the right term to use when the setting is a jovial pub in central Dublin. The realisation was that, of all Ireland's great attractions for the visitor, the greatest of all is its people. Some remark of mine about Dublin as 'the nation's capital' had prompted the old rejoinder that 'The nation's capital is its people.' That's true of any nation from its own point of view, of course, but in the case of Ireland, it's true from the tourist's point of view as well. In Ireland, the people have always been part of the sight-seeing, as it were. In the old days, it was often doubtless in a condescending way: Irish folk were seen as quaint and endearingly antiquated, in addition to being genuinely warm and welcoming. Today the genuineness and the hospitality shine on undimmed, but there's no overlooking the modern outlook and self-confidence alongside.

The infamous melancholy that one always used to associate with Ireland—the melancholy of all the old song tunes: 'Galway Bay', 'Danny Boy', even 'When Irish Eyes are Smiling'—that melancholy is almost indiscernible now, it seemed to me, at least among the younger generation. And the days have long gone when the typical wish of an ambitious or inquisitive young Irishman was to get out of Ireland as soon as feasible. The people seem extremely buoyant in the Republic, and moderately so in the North. Turbulence could return, of course, brought on by shifting tides in EU policy perhaps, or by tremors and upheavals in the peace negotiations. But with luck—the luck of the Irish, long overdue—fair wind and calm water lie ahead for Ireland as a whole.

INTRODUCING *WALKING THROUGH IRELAND*

The travel writer Robin Neillands likes to visit places in a far more leisurely way than most travellers—'leisurely' in the sense of 'unhurried' rather than 'indolent'. He travels on foot. Anything but indolent, his marathon walk through Ireland sounds daunting to the point of heroic, though you would never think so from his modest account of it. That account, together with many fascinating detours into the history of Ireland, forms the substance of the book that follows.

It was written after the 1994 ceasefires in Northern Ireland but before the 1998 Good Friday peace agreement, and it concentrates on the rural rather than the urban areas, both North and South. All the same, it is probably one of the most perceptive portraits of the region and the people that you can find, and certainly one of the most engaging.

WALKING
THROUGH IRELAND

A condensation of the book by Robin Neillands

SETTING OUT

ABOVE *The author, former soldier Robin Neillands, who chose to test his endurance by walking across Ireland, from north to south.*

LATE ONE AFTERNOON, halfway up the side of the waterfall that passes for the track up Ireland's highest mountain, Carrauntoohil, with water pouring up my sleeves, I had a sudden thought: why am I doing this? People had been asking me that for weeks, but only now, with the end of my walk across Ireland in sight, did I ask the question myself. The answer is that it seemed like a good idea at the time. I felt like it; it was my fancy; and given the time I might even do it again.

So how was the decision arrived at? Slow and easy is the answer, by considering factors, by a process of elimination. I am a professional travel writer, and working writers do not believe in the sudden flash of inspiration. I was looking for a country where they spoke a tongue I could speak, and a country that I could walk across in about six weeks. Ireland swam slowly into my mind and stuck there, nagging. How little I really knew about Ireland! The North had been in the news every day for twenty years, and I knew and liked a lot of Irish people, but Ireland itself I hardly knew at all. Before long I went out and bought a map and sat brooding over it and scribbling on a notepad.

Ireland is not very big—about one-third the size of mainland Britain. The distance north to south is just over 300 miles, and that allows for getting round some lakes and rivers. I studied the map for a suitable starting point and eventually came up with the Giant's Causeway, in the northeast. A straight line across the country gave me an axis of advance to Valencia Island in the southwest, just off the Atlantic coast of Kerry. Then I began to underline on the map places I simply had to see, and my direct route began to wobble a bit.

During this planning phase, practically everyone I spoke to mentioned the IRA—the Irish Republican Army. There seemed to be a general idea in England that the Provos were just waiting in the hedgerows for me to come ambling by and cause an international incident. I had already been to Ireland and knew it simply isn't like that, but since I was planning not simply to walk but to walk on my own, a little advice might still be useful.

'I think you should avoid south Armagh,' said an old commando friend of mine. 'The Provos have a nasty habit of setting up their own roadblocks down there, and if you bump into one of those and they don't like the look of you, it might get…well, difficult. Otherwise you'll be all right. There are some very nice people over there…Just remember not to sing "The Wearing of the Green" in Union areas, or "Killing Billy Slew the Papish Crew" in Catholic ones, and you should be all right.'

'How do I know when I'm in a Protestant area or a Catholic one?'

'You'll know,' he said grimly.

Happily my planned route across Northern Ireland took me well clear of south Armagh. From the Giant's Causeway it went first along the Antrim coast to Coleraine and then south and west across the Sperrin Mountains to Omagh and Enniskillen, and so out of the North and into the Republic. This route took me through the only gap between the two arms of Lough Erne and out towards Sligo, the Yeats Country, and the beautiful west coast. I did my sums again and found that the distance had gone up to 451 miles without the inevitable diversions, so I added fifty miles for those. Things never go as intended. Nor do I wish they should.

My most urgent concern, as the day of departure drew near, was the weather. In Ireland it rains. On the west coast they get over fifty inches of rain a year, which keeps the ground wet but supplies the country with those 'forty shades of green' and creates that Emerald Isle the poets sing about.

ABOVE *The Antrim coast, first leg of the author's journey, soaks up the rich colours of the setting sun.*

I duly acquired some state-of-the-art rain gear. One friend I consulted told me that if I was lucky on my journey it would be coming down like stair rods for only 90 per cent of the time.

Then there were maps. The Northern Ireland maps are fine. Elsewhere you must still cope with maps that should have '*Here be leprechauns*' written on them; they are set to a very small scale. There is also the snag that many Irish maps are out of date.

Time was pressing as winter gave way to spring, but I still had to furnish my mind. There is a saying that if you want to learn anything about a country you have to take a lot of learning with you. This is true of any journey, but it is particularly true of Ireland. I emptied the shelves of the London Library and read everything I could find about its history. I ended up confused, but I knew I could sort it all out piece by piece as I trudged across the country. That indeed was now the object of my journey: to discover and identify all those people who rose from the pages of the history books and went parading through my mind. Who were W. B. Yeats, Daniel O'Connell, Patrick Pearse, Wolfe Tone and the rest? What really happened during the Great Hunger, and why did the English push into Ireland with such tenacity when all the Irish wanted them to leave? I didn't know, but I would find out. I would drink in the pubs and sleep in the bed and breakfasts, and hear the old tales and make some sense of it.

I decided to go in June. That fell back a bit, but when I eventually got to the airport I was as ready as I could be. I even felt quite intrepid standing there at Heathrow in my weather-beaten Rohan clothing among all the suits; but before we begin this journey, a final word of warning.

There is quite a lot of conversation in this book. The Irish are a talkative people and I spent a lot of time in their pubs, resting my feet and drying my clothing. When you do that you soon get into the 'crack'. The crack is an Irish institution, but it is one of those local words it is hard to put your finger on. The implication is that there will be witty or amusing, or at least worthwhile, conversation. I love listening to good conversation, and nowhere is it better than in Ireland; so it may help if the reader can imagine at least 50 per cent of the speech with an Irish accent.

FIRST IMPRESSIONS

Northern Ireland is quite a small province, roughly ninety miles square, a green and fertile farmland which cradles Lough Neagh, the largest lake in the British Isles. The River Bann flows out of Lough Neagh in two directions, to the north and the south, and the destination on my first day's walk was the town of Coleraine, which lies on the River Bann as it flows into the Atlantic on the Antrim coast.

In very little time we were crossing the coast of Northern Ireland and beginning our descent. As the aircraft began to circle Belfast, a voice in my ear said, 'There's the Maze,' and there indeed lay the unmistakable H-block roofs of Ulster's most secure and notorious prison.

'There's a lot of hard men penned up in there,' said my companion, but his tone was noncommittal. In Northern Ireland you don't commit yourself until you know who you are talking to. That apart, he was friendly. He was also very pleased that I had come to Northern Ireland and wished me all the best on my journey. He even gave me his phone number in case I should get stuck. My first impression of the Ulster folk was favourable, and it remained so.

The people of Northern Ireland are very friendly because that is the way Ulster people are, but also because they feel themselves traduced by the media and neglected by their fellow countrymen on the mainland. As a result, anyone from the mainland who comes wandering among them is sure of a welcome.

ABOVE *The distinctive H-blocks of Belfast's high-security Maze prison have held numerous convicted terrorists, both Loyalist and Republican.*

I collected my rucksack from the carousel and made my way out to where Philippa Reid was waiting for me. Philippa was with the Tourist Board and had volunteered to drive me up to the start of my journey on the Antrim Coast.

'Where do you want to go first?' she asked. 'A quick tour of Belfast or straight up to the Glens?'

I decided to pass on the city. Belfast is a splendid town which became rich in the 18th and 19th centuries from the flax and linen trade, and then from shipbuilding and engineering. As a result it has some fine public buildings and parks, and

LEFT *The still waters of the United Kingdom's largest inland lake, Lough Neagh, cover 153 square miles. The lough is an abundant source of eels, and a thriving fishing industry has operated there for centuries.*

BELFAST: A TOWN BUILT ON LINEN

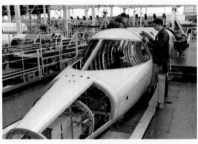

LEFT *Belfast's imposing City Hall was completed in the early 20th century and reflects the wealth of the city at that time.*

ABOVE *Among the aircraft fuselages manufactured by Bombardier Aerospace-Short's is that of the Learjet 45 business jet.*

OVER THE COURSE of the 19th century, Belfast, a neat provincial town of 20,000 people, was transformed into a great bustling city of 350,000. It was a city typical of the late Victorian age: on the one hand wealth and confidence, exemplified in the grand merchants' houses along Malone Road and extravagant public buildings such as the City Hall and the Grand Opera House; on the other, insecurity and exploitation, in the red-brick terraces of the poor workers' quarters. Dominating all stood the huge mills, their chimneys belching smoke, and the teeming port with its buzzing quays and shipyards.

Two assets underpinned Belfast's development: its extensive docks, and, above all, linen. The spinning and weaving of flax, a cottage craft in Ireland since ancient times, became an Ulster speciality when Huguenot refugees from France introduced the art of making damask, a richly patterned linen, around 1700. During the 18th century linen production—and for a while cotton, too—thrived in Belfast. Then, in about 1830, mechanisation of linen manufacture began. Huge mills sprang up as Ulster damask and embroidered linen became household essentials in every well-appointed British home.

In the wake of linen came new services and industries—tobacco processing, rope-making, banking and especially shipbuilding. The Harland and Wolff shipyard, established in 1862, employed at its peak a work force of over 12,000, launching from its slipways such ships as the ill-fated *Titanic* (1911) and the P&O liner *Canberra* (1960). It is still the largest shipyard in the British Isles. Among other famous engineering works is Short Brothers, the oldest-established aircraft manufacturer in the world, now part of Bombardier Aerospace.

Belfast's industrial heyday waned after the Second World War. Most linen mills closed. And many of the great factories, by virtually excluding Catholics from jobs, damaged their own prospects by fostering sectarianism and thereby discouraging investment. The city's media image became one of a war zone, and this too blighted the economy. In recent years, however, development grants from the European Union and British government have stemmed the decline, and attracted new industries in sectors such as electronics and synthetic textiles. Prospects for peace have also improved, fuelling residents' hopes for a return to better times.

ABOVE *In the 19th and early 20th centuries, many of the women of Belfast were employed in flax mills such as those owned by Thompson's, advertised here.*

RIGHT *The seemingly invincible* Titanic *dominates the Harland and Wolff shipyard. It was from here that she was proudly launched in 1911.*

nothing could less resemble the Irish Beirut of popular imagination. However, it was forbidden to leave cars unattended in the centre of the city, and this restricted the opportunities for a quick stroll about. Besides, I wanted to get started; so we set out at once for the Glens of Antrim.

As we drove north out of Belfast, I had my first lesson. Northern Ireland has its problems, but it is a prosperous place, and it shows. It is also very beautiful. Like the rest of Ireland it endures a fairly relentless rainfall and is therefore noticeably lush. It is well cared for too, a tidy land, patchworked with farms.

There was indeed, however, no difficulty in telling which were the Catholic villages and which were the Protestant ones. The former flew the tricolour and had green, orange and white stripes painted on the pavements. The Protestant ones flew the Union flag and had red, white and blue stripes on the pavements.

As we drove, Philippa explained the root causes of the present Troubles.

THE TROUBLES

The Irish date the Troubles back to 1170, to the English invasion of Leinster by the mighty Strongbow, Earl of Pembroke. He was brought into Ireland by Dermot MacMurrough, King of Leinster, and offered the hand of the King's daughter if he would help MacMurrough in his local wars. Strongbow came over with a force of bowmen and mailed and mounted knights, and having married Dermot's daughter he became King of Leinster when MacMurrough died in 1171. Thus the English gained their entry into Ireland.

For a time it seemed likely that the incomers would intermarry with the local people and become 'more Irish than the Irish', but then two events occurred that drove a Protestant stake into the Irish heart: the 'plantations' of Elizabeth I, and the coming of the Puritans, who won the English Civil War under Cromwell.

The purpose of the plantations was to drive the native people off their lands and replace them with loyal Protestant settlers, largely Scottish Presbyterians, whose descendants live in Ulster to this day and still maintain strong links with their distant connections in Scotland. 'Planting' continued throughout the first half of the 17th century and reached its peak in the bloody years after 1649, when Oliver Cromwell came to Ireland and drove the Irish west into Connaught.

The Act of Union of 1800 then abolished the Irish Parliament in Dublin and effectively made England and Ireland one country. For the next 100 years Ireland struggled to free itself, in the teeth of poverty, evictions and an appalling famine. Many of the leading advocates for Irish independence during the 19th century were Protestant, but when it came to the point of emancipation, the Protestant majority in the North would simply not consent to live in an independent, Catholic Ireland. They still won't, and that is the root and branch of it.

A Home Rule Bill was introduced in the English Parliament of 1886 by Charles Stewart Parnell, but the House of Lords swiftly rejected it. In 1893 the Irish members tried again with similar results, and yet again in 1912. By now, however, the tide of opinion had turned and after two years of debate the Home Rule Bill finally went through in the summer of 1914.

The Protestants of Ulster, however, had decided to fight Home Rule long before the first Home Rule Bill, and by 1913 they were importing arms. In 1914, in the 'Curragh Mutiny', officers of the British army stationed at the Curragh near Dublin made it clear that they would resist any attempt to use them in coercing the North. Though hardly a mutiny at all, it was evident that the army could not be relied upon to suppress a Protestant rising in the North, and the British government found itself on the horns of a dilemma. If they did not grant Home Rule there would be a rebellion in Ireland. If they did grant Home Rule there would be civil war between Protestants and Catholics. Their solution to the problem would be Partition.

At this moment came the First World War and implementation of the Home Rule Bill was suspended until the end of hostilities. There was no conscription in Ireland, but when the war began Irishmen flocked to the Colours in their tens of thousands, assured of their own country after the war; but some did not believe this promise, or could not wait, and in 1916 they rebelled. The Easter Rising of 1916 was vastly unpopular with the Irish people, at least until the British executed sixteen of the leaders. After that, the independence movement began to press for immediate Home Rule, and there was a brief but bloody Anglo-Irish war, between the British irregulars, the notorious 'Black and Tans', and the Irish Republican Army. During this time the leaders of the newly formed Irish Parliament came to accept that they could not hope to gather in the intransigent Protestant community of the North and they therefore agreed to the Anglo-Irish Treaty, which involved Partition.

In 1921 the Government of Ireland Act established the six counties of Ulster with Protestant majorities among the population as the UK Province of Northern Ireland and the other twenty-six counties as the Irish Free State. The Free State then had dominion status, and remained closely linked to the British Crown until 1937, when it passed its own constitution and became Eire. Eire became the Republic of Ireland in 1949.

I now had an outline of the facts behind the Troubles. The cost of founding the Free State was Partition, and the consequences of that fact we live with to this day, because the IRA and sections of the Republic's government have always refused to accept Partition. Indeed, as soon as the Free State was established, the IRA started a civil war against those who had agreed to the treaty. Michael Collins, one of the heroes of the struggle for independence, and one of the signatories to the treaty, said at the time, 'I have signed my death warrant.' This turned out to be true. The Irish Civil War was brief but bloody and when the government won the IRA went underground.

Enough of this for now, except for one final point. The present province of Ulster is usually referred to in the Republic as 'the Six Counties', which is inaccurate because the original province of Ulster had nine counties, not six. The current Six Counties are Antrim, Armagh, Down, Fermanagh, Tyrone and Londonderry—or at least Londonderry to the Unionists; the Republicans or Catholics call it simply Derry, and that name applies to the city as well as the county. In former times,

ABOVE *Charles Stewart Parnell, son of a distinguished Anglo-Irish landowning family, fought vigorously for Irish Home Rule and tenants' rights. His political career was cut short by a divorce scandal and his early death at the age of 45.*

before Partition, the province of Ulster also included the counties of Monaghan, Cavan and Donegal, which now lie in the Republic. It is therefore more correct to refer to what the English call 'Ulster' as 'Northern Ireland' in the North and 'the Six Counties' in the South. So too, if someone refers to the Republic as 'The Free State', in the North this probably indicates someone of a Republican persuasion, since this implies that Northern Ireland is not free. Safer then to refer to it as 'the South', or, more correctly, 'the Republic'.

For a local person these names are a way of identifying where the speaker stands, confirming his political opinions, even his religion. We may live in an ever more secular world, but in Ireland religion is a force to be reckoned with, a fact to consider.

On an earlier visit to Northern Ireland, I remember propping up a bar, deep in one of those long, rambling conversations with the barman. He told me he could always tell a Catholic from a Protestant.

'Well, it beats me,' I said, 'but then I've never understood religious differences anyway… maybe that's because I'm an agnostic.'

The barman shook his head. 'You couldn't be one of those up here, so you couldn't. You'd either have to be a Catholic agnostic or a Protestant agnostic.'

ABOVE *The original province of Ulster, pre-1921 and Partition, spread over nine northern counties.*

THE COAST OF ANTRIM

There are nine glens in Antrim, a rippling mixture of rounded, moor-topped hills and lush river valleys. Two of these glens, Glentaisie and Glenshesk, run out at Ballycastle on the north coast.

The main road to Ballycastle skirts to the west of the glens. Then it flows round the smooth bulk of Knocklayd Mountain and so down to the coast. Three long-distance footpaths converge hereabouts: the Moyle Way which comes over Knocklayd, the province-circling Ulster Way which follows the spectacular east coast of Antrim and, to the west of Ballycastle, the North Antrim Coast Path which runs for forty-two miles along the cliffs and beaches from Fair Head to Magilligan Point, and which I would follow on the morrow towards the Bann estuary. Meanwhile there were places to see hereabouts.

Ballycastle is a pretty fishing port and a resort town, one of those places with pubs and tea shops and whitewashed houses with B & B signs outside. Just out to sea lies the boomerang shape of Rathlin Island and away to the east the soaring cliffs of Benmore, or Fair Head, which drop 600 feet sheer into the sea. This is a spectacular and beautiful coastline, and the path runs right along it.

Beyond Fair Head and well out to sea lay a loom of blue and purple hills, mysterious in the heat haze. 'What's that over there?' I asked Philippa, pointing.

'That's Scotland,' she replied. 'The Mull of Kintyre.'

'My God… it's very close.'

'Only thirteen miles,' she said. 'They say that in the old days the Puritan people used to row across to church…but the North Channel is very wild when the wind gets up, so I rather doubt it.'

With Scotland that close, it is no wonder that the Presbyterians found it so easy to leave their heather-clad hills to cross the narrow sea and take up residence in the rich farmlands of Ulster. In fact, the Scots were coming here long before that. In the early part of the 14th century, the would-be King of Scots, Robert the Bruce, fled across the sea to Rathlin Island, just off the Antrim coast, where he hoped to avoid the English. It was while he was sheltering in a cave on Rathlin that he saw a spider trying to spin its web and was thus encouraged to return to Scotland and try, try again, until he defeated the English at Bannockburn in 1314 and gained the throne of Scotland. So legend has it—and legend is a potent force hereabouts.

Rathlin Island lies in plain sight from Ballycastle and there is a daily ferry in the summer which takes visitors out to see the gulls and seals or spend an hour or two ashore. The population of Rathlin is around 100, most of them fishermen, and there is a notorious whirlpool off the southern tip of the island known as the Swallow of the Sea, which nearly swallowed St Columba when he set off to convert Scotland in the 6th century.

Ballycastle has other claims to fame. The big event of the year hereabouts is the Ould Lammas Fair which began in 1606 and used to last a week or until the pubs ran dry, whichever was the sooner. Now it lasts just two days and is mainly devoted to selling sheep and ponies, for the Ulster folk are great horse lovers. The Lammas Fair is so famous there is even a song about it:

> *Did you treat your Mary Ann*
> *To dulse and yellow man*
> *At the Ould Lammas Fair in Ballycastle—O?*

'My husband loves dulse,' said Philippa, 'but I can't stand it. It's a sort of seaweed and you chew it… ugh! Yellow man is toffee, hard as rock. They have to smash it to bits with a hammer before they weigh it out…it's terrible for the teeth but people love it.'

I felt like a walk and I especially wanted to walk across the rope bridge to Carrick-a-rede Island. There are marvellous views from here: east to the sheer drop of Fair Head and west towards the Giant's Causeway. Carrick-a-rede actually means the 'rock in the road', which is said to refer to the route taken by salmon on their way home from the Atlantic.

The island is a hump of rock set in the shallow waters just offshore and the salmon fishermen hang their nets from it during the annual salmon run along this coast. They put up the rope bridge in the spring and take it down in the autumn, and the visitors just love crossing it.

To get to the island means a jittery walk along the two-plank-wide bridge, eighty feet above the sea. We had a climb about the rocks before setting off again west for the little town of Bushmills.

ABOVE *Dulse and yellow man—dried seaweed and hard toffee—are local delicacies sold at the annual Lammas Fair in Ballycastle.*

OPPOSITE *At Carrick-a-rede a precarious rope bridge, 80 feet above the clear waters of Rathlin Sound, links a small island to the mainland.*

Bushmills sprawls. Most Irish towns, North or South, support or have supported a weekly market, with the result that the main streets always seem unnaturally wide, though not so wide that the locals find it unnecessary to double-park their cars. These wide streets give the towns a helpfully spacious air, helpful because, by and large, Irish towns are not pretty. The shop fronts tend to be narrow, though the interiors, especially the pub interiors, are frequently vast. The blues and pinks, purples and bright vermilion with which the Irish love to paint their shops and houses may strike the visitor as garish for a while, but you soon get used to it.

Bushmills is the home of Bushmills whiskey—note that Irish whiskey is the one with the 'e'. The Old Bushmills Distillery opened for business as long ago as 1608 and claims to be the oldest legal whiskey distillery in the world. Philippa gave me a bottle to cheer me on my way, and a glass of Bushmills would mark the end of many a day in my tramp across Ireland.

My destination that evening was the Auberge de Seneri, a curious name for a hotel in this part of the world. The Auberge was owned by a Frenchman,

CATERING FOR A HEALTHY APPETITE

MOST TRADITIONAL Irish dishes originated as peasant food, and so tend towards the hearty rather than the delicate. They were cooked on the griddle or in the pot, seldom in ovens. Hence the prevalence of stews: bacon and cabbage; Dublin coddle (sausage, bacon, potatoes and onions); and above all the mutton-based Irish stew. Vegetable dishes include champ, a Northern Irish speciality of buttery mashed potatoes with chives or spring onions, and the boxty, a kind of potato pancake. Then there's Irish bread: soda bread, made with sour milk or buttermilk, and a yeasty currant bread called barm brack.

One would expect seafood to figure large in the Irish diet, what with the national passion for angling, and Molly Malone's cockles and mussels, but fish was long considered 'penance food', and avoided. No longer: salmon and trout consumption is booming, and Ireland's famous oysters and lobsters are now enjoyed in Ireland itself, not just abroad. Game, too—hare, venison, wild duck and pheasant—has become more widely appreciated, and local gourmet cheeses are increasingly in

LEFT *Irish shops and restaurants now offer a tempting and delicious array of local, homemade farmhouse cheeses.*

RIGHT *Purists argue about the exact ingredients of an Irish stew, but it is always hot and filling—and welcome after a rainy day out in the country.*

demand. In general, a food culture seems to be developing, with two oyster festivals taking place in the Galway Bay area each September, and an international gastronomic festival each October at Kinsale in County Cork.

Pub culture remains dominant, however. A pub is the ideal setting for

Jacques Defres, who was waging a campaign to put some spark into Irish cooking. Jacques offered to drive me up to the start of my walk next morning, and helped me into my room with the rucksack, grunting under the fifty-pound weight in a most gratifying fashion.

THE GIANT'S CAUSEWAY

In spite of all the warnings I had received about rain and mist and sudden storm, I began my journey on a beautiful day. It was already warm at nine thirty in the morning, and with the sun shredding the sea mist below the cliffs it promised to be a good deal hotter by the end of the day.

The Giant's Causeway and the coast round about it is owned by the National Trust, who manage the access to the Causeway from the cliffs to the sea. The Causeway is Ireland's first World Heritage Site, a fact I learned in the visitors' centre at the top.

This part of the Antrim coast would be remarkable enough even without the Causeway, for the cliffs run up to 300 feet and are topped with jutting pinnacles or

LEFT *The boxty, a type of savoury pancake often cooked on a griddle, makes good use of Ireland's most popular vegetable—the potato.*

BELOW *Soda bread takes its name from the baking soda used as a raising agent in its production instead of yeast.*

LEFT *Irish malt whiskey is made using barley and crystal-clear spring water; Bushmills is one of the best-known brands.*

a Guinness (*see feature on page 90*) or a whiskey. Irish whiskey differs from Scotch whisky not just in spelling but in manufacture as well: the barley is malted without peat smoke; and the liquor is distilled three times rather than just twice. Among the famous brand names are Paddy, Powers, Jameson and Bushmills. There are famous Irish liqueurs, too, notably Irish Mist and Bailey's Irish Cream. And, served the world over, Irish coffee: sweetened black coffee laced with whiskey, topped with cream and served in a heated goblet. The story goes that Irish coffee was

invented by a barman at Shannon International Airport half a century ago to keep delayed passengers warm—or perhaps docile. But according to a rival theory it was just a means of getting round the Irish licensing laws.

ABOVE *Seafood, for a long time scorned by the Irish, is now considered one of the highlights of Ireland's national cuisine.*

stacks. To the east lies the headland called Port na Spaniagh, where the *Girona* galleon came to grief in 1588. This was one of the many losses sustained by the Spanish Armada.

The captain of the *Girona*, don Alonso Martinez de Leiva, was heading for Scotland, hoping for shelter and fresh water, but he ran onshore and his ship broke up in the storm. Over 1,000 men were lost. Instead of receiving a warm welcome, those who got ashore were knocked on the head for their possessions. The wreck of the *Girona* lay offshore until it was excavated in 1967.

The Giant's Causeway is an equally remarkable natural sight. It is composed of about 40,000 grey hexagonal blocks and columns, and looks rather like a giant's Lego set, clumsily fitted together. When he came past here in the 18th century, Dr Johnson remained unimpressed. 'Worth seeing, but not worth going to see,' he said grumpily, but his verdict hardly seems valid. This morning, with the oystercatchers '*peet-peeting*' about among the rocks, the blue sea crashing in and the blocks standing up in fluted columns, the Causeway looked well worth visiting.

THE WRECK OF THE *GIRONA*

THE MOST FORMIDABLE naval force the world had ever seen—130 ships and over 30,000 men—set sail from Spain in July 1588 on the orders of King Philip II. Its mission: to invade and conquer Protestant England. But when the Spanish Armada reached the English Channel, the fleet was scattered and half its ships were destroyed by Queen Elizabeth I's navy. The other half made their escape northwards, via the North Sea and round Ireland.

One of the Armada ships, the *Girona*, floundered in Ireland's unfamiliar, stormy waters and was driven aground at Killybegs in Donegal. From there, damaged but salvageable, she set sail to Scotland where her captain, Commander don Alonso Martinez de Leiva, hoped to find sanctuary with the Catholic King James VI.

But on a dark October night, the heavily laden ship struck a reef off Lacada Point and was smashed to pieces. Of the 1,300 souls on board, only five

made it to shore, and the *Girona* herself sank to the seabed.

Nearly 400 years later, in June 1967, at Port na Spaniagh ('the port of the Spaniards'), a Belgian underwater archaeologist discovered the resting place of the *Girona*. He returned a year later to excavate the wreck, and his explorations unearthed a major haul,

ABOVE *A gold salamander brooch, once belonging to a Spanish nobleman, from the wreck of the* Girona.

LEFT *A diver recovers an astrolabe—a navigational device—from an underwater forest of kelp.*

including precious jewellery, silver coins and, perhaps most beautiful of all, a gold salamander brooch, studded with rubies. These treasures are now on display in the Ulster Museum in Belfast, a poignant reminder of the devastating loss of life and priceless riches given up to the deep on that fateful night in 1588.

There are various theories as to how the Causeway got there. The 'Vulcanists' believe that it is the result of volcanic action about 60 million years ago, when a volcano spread lava out to form these basalt formations and cut out the deep channel, which is now filled by the Irish Sea. A second scientific explanation comes from the 'Neptunists', who hold that the columns are the result of chemical reaction on the sedimentary rocks.

I prefer a third, or Irish, version of how the Causeway was created. Long ago, the giant Finn MacCool lived hereabouts. Finn was a feisty fellow who greatly enjoyed his daily slanging match with the giant Fingal who lived across the water in a cave on the island of Staffa, off the coast of Scotland. Then matters escalated. The two giants stopped hurling abuse and started hurling stones.

One day, Finn MacCool picked up a handful of land—the cavity thus created became Lough Neagh—and hurled it at Fingal. He missed by quite a margin, for the handful fell in the sea to the south and became the Isle of Man.

MacCool then decided to build a Causeway across to Staffa and settle Fingal's hash once and for all. Work began and the Causeway gradually crept out across the sea, but as he got closer, MacCool realised that Fingal was a lot bigger than he had appeared from a distance. He therefore fled back to Ireland with Fingal in hot pursuit and took shelter in his mother's cottage.

Now this Finn MacCool was not just a mass of brawn. He had a brain about him and so, putting on baby clothes, he leapt into a handy cot. He had just stuck the dummy in his mouth when Fingal came hammering on the door. There was a lot of hammering and bellowing before Fingal thought to peer through the window… and there was MacCool lying in his cot.

Dear me, thought Fingal—or thoughts to that effect—if the babies hereabouts are as big as *that*, I can't imagine how big that bastard MacCool will be… so I'm off back to Scotland.

ABOVE *Polygonal columns form the geological phenomenon known as the Giant's Causeway. Similar columns are found across the sea on the Scottish island of Staffa—hence the notion of a causeway.*

Well, it's a good tale. The Causeway may perhaps have extended right across to the Western Isles at some time, because there are vestiges of it on the Scots' side, but whatever the truth of it, Volcanic, Neptunic or legendary, it remains a most remarkable sight.

I made my way back up to the visitors' centre, and off over the wind-tugged grass out onto the North Antrim Coast Path, heading west for Portrush.

Drifts of sea pinks cascaded down the cliffs, and the grass under my feet was soft and springy. Gulls, terns and kittiwakes zoomed about my head or sat nesting in the crevasses of the rocks below, so I had plenty to entertain me as I made my way to Dunluce Castle.

THE PLANTATIONS

Dunluce Castle is a romantic-looking place. It began as a 13th-century medieval keep which belonged to the de Burghs—or Burkes—but it came to prominence in the 16th century when it was the home of Sorley Boy MacDonnell, chief of the MacDonnell clan, who ruled most of northern Ulster. Sorley Boy eked out his rents with cattle raids on his neighbours and piracy off the coast. He paid little heed to the laws of his liege lady, Elizabeth I of England, and ignored all her edicts. Therefore, in 1584 Elizabeth's Lord Deputy in these parts, Sir John Perrott, marched against Dunluce, pounded the castle with artillery and forced the MacDonnells out. Sir John installed an English garrison and departed.

Sorley Boy brooded over this for a year or so and then attacked the castle in his turn. He gained access by getting half a dozen men onto the seaward ramparts, from where more MacDonnells were hauled up the cliff in baskets. The garrison was slaughtered and the English commander hung from the walls in a cage. However, all this fighting had left Dunluce in a very dilapidated state, and it remained that way until the *Girona* galleon came to grief on the rocks to the east. Those of the crew who staggered ashore were killed by Sorley Boy and his men and some of the loot from the ship helped to repair the castle.

This slaughter of their Spanish enemies enabled Sorley Boy to make his peace with the English. The MacDonnells lived on in Dunluce for another fifty years until 1639, when one night a portion of the cliff fell into the sea, taking with it the outer walls, the kitchens, the dinner in the oven and most of the cooks. Sorley's descendants, the Earls of Antrim, hung on to what was left until the mid-1600s, since when Dunluce has stood empty. It has now been partially restored and is a fine sight, standing on the wild green cliffs of Antrim.

Looking at Dunluce took my thoughts back to the 16th century. The Irish had always been seen as a source of rebellion and disaffection by the English Crown. They had supported the House of York during the Wars of the Roses, which did not endear them to the Tudors, but matters took a more serious turn after the Protestant Reformation. The Irish people remained stoutly Catholic, and the Protestant tide never swept far up their beaches. The Irish were therefore seen as a base for the Counter Reformation, the western arm of the Franco-Spanish pincer that could crush the English like a nut.

The English remit in Ireland then did not extend very far. In practical terms it existed only within a few hundred square miles around Dublin, generally known as 'the Pale'. This name arose from the word 'paling' for the planks of a fence. Life 'beyond the Pale' in the mid-16th century was nasty and brutish, but free. Irish lords ruled and paid only nominal allegiance to the English King. Fearing a Catholic rebellion, Henry VIII decided to change all that.

In 1541 Henry decided that *all* Irish land was to be surrendered to the Crown, which would then redistribute it to loyal adherents. Naturally the Irish lords resisted. Henry had too many problems at home to apply his will in Ireland, but his daughter, Elizabeth I, would not tolerate defiance. Her support for the Dutch fighting the Spaniards in the Low Countries made her very sensitive indeed to unrest or rebellion in Ireland. A succession of her best captains and favourites was dispatched to keep the Irish in order, and when they returned one after the other, with only failure to report, she decided on a drastic solution. If she could not

BELOW *The ruins of Dunluce Castle stand on the precipitous cliffs of Antrim. In 1639 a violent storm washed part of the cliff and castle into the sea, but several years passed before the stoic occupants finally quit their coastal stronghold.*

change the Irish lords, then she would change the Irish people. Thus began the plantations: the planting of Irish land with English and Scots settlers.

The Plantation of Ulster—and many other parts of Ireland as well, but particularly Ulster—is often cited as the worst offence in the long list of Irish grievances against the English Crown. The planting took place in the 17th century, but the effects endure to this day.

Elizabeth did not trust the Anglo-Irish lords, the O'Neills and MacDonnells and the rest, and her lord deputies were English peers who went to Ireland to do her bidding and make their fortunes. The result was rebellion. There were three major risings in Ireland during Elizabeth's reign, each put down with growing ferocity.

The result of this conflict was to establish a permanent division between the Protestant English and the Catholic Irish, which came to a head in the person of Hugh O'Neill, the Earl of Tyrone, who then ruled most of Ulster. After forging an alliance with another Ulster earl, Hugh O'Donnell, the Earl of Tyrconnell, he rose against English domination in 1598 and defeated Elizabeth's forces at the Battle of the Yellow Ford, near Armagh.

Three years later, the war still continuing, a Spanish fleet arrived at Kinsale, landing Spanish soldiers to aid the rebel earls, but this disparate collection of soldiers proved no match for the English army of the new Lord Deputy in Ireland, Lord Mountjoy. Mountjoy smashed the Spanish–Irish army, and the earls were forced to submit in 1603. They were pardoned by the Queen, and Hugh O'Donnell died soon afterwards, but O'Neill found it impossible to live happily under English domination. In 1607 O'Neill and the new Earl of Tyrconnell, Rory O'Donnell, took a ship for France and never returned.

After this 'Flight of the Earls', O'Neill's lands were given away or sold to English settlers. This time those invited to start plantations saw a profit in it. Chief of the planters were the guilds of the City of London. They were granted land in County Derry, which then became Londonderry, and distributed that land among their livery companies—the goldsmiths, the innkeepers, the drapers, the fishmongers—who were directed to find and settle Englishmen on Irish lands. There is still a Draperstown in Londonderry. But though the English came the native Irish did not leave. They stayed on as workers or tenants on the land they had previously owned. By the 1630s about 20,000 Scottish and English settlers had arrived, all Protestant, and the seeds of the present conflict had been sown.

A WARM WELCOME

After Dunluce I followed a rough track along to the river that curves round between the links of the Royal Portrush Golf Club. This is just one of a dozen golf courses along this coast. I went over the dunes, pulling myself up the slopes with

BELOW *In 1603 Hugh O'Neill, Earl of Tyrone, whose family had ruled in Ulster from the 5th century, submitted to Lord Mountjoy, the English Deputy in Ireland, after British troops successfully put down his rebellion.*

ABOVE *This 17th-century plan of Londonderry illustrates the areas allotted to various livery companies of the Corporation of London.*

handfuls of marram grass, and down onto Portrush beach, which was crowded on this sunny Saturday afternoon, then on, along the coast, towards the rushing estuary of the River Bann by Portstewart. The heat was quite shattering and the sea was therefore pulling the crowds down onto the long beach of Portstewart Strand, where there is some good surfing to be had. I had been trudging along for five hours now, and decided it was time for a decent drink.

Portstewart is a Victorian resort, and rather snobby. In the last century the townspeople even rejected the offer of a railway station in case it let the vulgar people in. It still looks reserved but rather charming, its streets lined with pastel-painted houses.

I left the coast and set off along the River Bann for Coleraine. The place I had arranged to stay in lies just across the river from Portstewart, but the only bridge was at Coleraine.

Coleraine is not a pretty town, and it has seen more than its share of Troubles in the last few years. Six months after my visit a huge IRA bomb devastated the heart of the town.

There was no sign of any trouble now. When I came limping in about tea time there was not a soldier or a policeman in sight, even around the crowd enjoying the regatta by the bridge.

They have held an annual regatta on the River Bann at Coleraine for almost 150 years, and rowing eights and coxed fours were zipping about the surface of the river like so many aquatic insects. My night stop at Norrie and Billy's Bed & Breakfast was two miles out of town; so on I went, ever slower now, towards the Bann estuary, stopping every so often to check my map. While I was doing this a ramshackle Land-Rover pulled up alongside.

'You must be Rob,' said the lady driver. 'No one else would carry a pack like that on a day like this.'

'I am,' I replied, 'and you must be Norrie.'

'I am,' she said. 'So hop in and we'll away to the regatta.'

Norrie was a smiling, busy lady of a certain age and she drove the Land-Rover with the ease of Boadicea handling her chariot. In other words, rather fast. Within minutes I had been co-opted into helping her tow away the finishing-line box from the lawn on the far side of the river. This box also served as the finishing-line box at the local horse races. It was well after six o'clock before we were back at Norrie's house.

I was just settling down in my socks for a pot of tea and some scones when her husband Billy came in, a big, fit, jovial man.

'Billy was in the police,' said Norrie. 'I'm glad he's out of it now, I can tell you. I was worried all the time.'

I asked the usual question: how or when will it end?

HORSES: A NATIONAL OBSESSION

LEFT *A tightly packed field thunders along Laytown sands, in the only official meeting in the world to take place on a beach.*

BELOW *Galway Races, where all Ireland, it seems, comes together in a celebration of horses and horsemanship.*

T HE IRISH AFFECTION for horses is legendary. Cynics jest that it is gambling they love rather than horses *per se*—and they do have a point, with some IR£90 million bet on racing every year. Even the Church seems to turn a blind eye: popular myth has it that it was a priest who first organised the Laytown beach races back in the late 1800s.

Whether for money or simply for the love of it, people have been racing horses in Ireland since before the birth of Christ. Race meetings now take place on more than 230 days a year, at any one of 30 racecourses. Most of the horses running will have been bred and trained locally, the majority in a

region known as the Curragh, west of Dublin, where lush pasture grows on calcium-rich soil, thought to give the horses strong bones. The epicentre of Irish racehorse breeding is the National Stud, near Kildare, founded in 1900 by an English colonel, later Lord Wavertree. His methods were eccentric—he decided whether to keep or sell new foals on the basis of their horoscopes—yet he succeeded in laying the foundations of a breeding stock of Irish thoroughbreds that is the envy of the world.

The Irish have, in fact, excelled at breeding the perfect horse for every equestrian activity. For hunting and showjumping there is the Irish hunter, a strong, agile cross between the Irish draught horse and the thoroughbred. The stocky Irish cob, meanwhile, mixes the blood of these two, plus that of the resilient, good-natured Connemara pony, to make an ideal general-purpose riding horse. The native Connemara appears to have refined itself purely by accident, interbreeding, legend has it, with Arab horses that escaped from ships of the Spanish Armada when these were wrecked off the Irish coast.

All these breeds, plus assorted less aristocratic nags, change hands at

any number of horse fairs up and down the country. Top breeders and trainers from around the world flock to the great bloodstock sales at Kill in County Kildare, while at lowly Smithfield Market in Dublin wily traders do deals with streetwise kids, who keep their ponies on scraps of land between the tower blocks.

BELOW *Smithfield Market in Dublin is an informal affair, held monthly. The expert equestrian could find himself a bargain here.*

RIGHT *Colonel Walker, later Lord Wavertree, who laid the foundations of Ireland's famous bloodstock industry.*

BELOW *Irish draught horses are prized in their own right and as an ideal type to cross with thoroughbreds.*

'I can see no end to it,' said Norrie. 'There's so much hate here, so little under-standing. Billy is a Protestant and I'm a Catholic, you know. When we got married the families were upset. My folks soon got to like Billy, but you feel the hate, the distrust, everywhere. My sister-in-law swore she would never buy a car from a Catholic... now isn't that daft? The car doesn't have a religion. She said the car was fine and the man was honest, but she just wouldn't feel happy about it. How can it end when even good people feel like that?'

God knows, but, as they say in Ireland, He's not telling.

It is also curious that while the distrust between the communities is certainly there and the extremists thrive on it, outsiders like myself are hardly aware of it. On that day, and all other days, everyone I met was charming.

I slept like a log that night, and woke up to another warm day. All was bustle at the B & B, for Billy and Norrie were off to a horse show—every other house seemed to have a horse or two in the paddock and a horsebox in the yard. First though, an Ulster Fry.

The Ulster Fry consists of one or two eggs, a few rashers of bacon, two or three slices of fried bread, a sausage or two, maybe three—perhaps even a chop, soda bread soaked in fat, and anything else that happens to be lying out in the kitchen and can find its way into the frying pan. This concoction is referred to locally as a 'heart attack on a plate'; there is a certain pride in the knowledge that Northern Ireland has the highest rate of death from heart disease in Europe. I persuaded myself that a huge breakfast was necessary for my day's flog to Limavady, some fifteen miles away, and worked my way through a vast plateful before getting ready for the off.

ABOVE *The author started his day with a traditional Ulster Fry—otherwise known as a 'heart attack on a plate'.*

It was one of those hazy mornings, but clearing by the minute, and Billy pointed out the local landmarks.

'That's the Mussenden Temple up there on the coast,' he said, pointing to a small domed structure. 'It's right on the edge of the cliff. Beyond that, across Lough Foyle, those hills are in Donegal, in the Republic... the Republic is actually north of Northern Ireland over there. We do it to confuse you.'

They succeed. Since I was two miles north of Coleraine and every step in the wrong direction was one wasted, Billy volunteered to drive me back to my route and drop me off on the 'Murder Hole Road'.

'Don't be anxious,' he said, catching the look on my face. 'It's not recent. Some highwayman used to hide there 200 years ago. Follow the Murder Hole Road and it will take you into Limavady.'

When we got to the Murder Hole Road, just south of Coleraine, Billy got out of the car and helped me on with the rucksack. Then he shook me by the hand. 'Remember now, Robbie, when you write that book, be sure to tell them we're not all murdering maniacs over here. Will you do that? And come and see us again?'

'I will, Billy. I will.'

I stood by the side of the road, waving until he drove out of sight. It was Sunday morning and people were driving past on their way to church, every driver lifting a hand to acknowledge me.

CHAPTER TWO

ON THE ROAD TO ENNISKILLEN

THE MURDER HOLE ROAD rolls out of Coleraine, west across the moors between vast fir-tree plantations, with the Keady Mountain to the south. Since my night stop lay to the south of Limavady I thought I would get off the road after a few miles and walk around or over the Keady Mountain, 1,093 feet high—and so to my destination.

It was another beautiful morning and the gardens of the neat houses and cottages beside the road were ablaze with flowers and shrubs, so it was no hardship just to plod along the main road, nodding at the church-bound locals for a few miles or so.

My track petered out by a chain-link fence, so I consulted the compass, fixed a bearing to Limavady, hopped over the fence—and sank knee-deep into a bog. I got out of the bog, splashed across a stream and sank into another bog. This went on for some time. The trouble is that most of Ireland, North or South, is just a great big sponge.

The best place to walk, and I use the word 'best' with reluctance, is along the sides of the hills, where the water may have drained down into the valley from the peat bogs on the tops. The snag is that walking on a slope is very hard on the ankles. I hobbled along a sheep track around the slopes of the Keady Mountain, which took me off track but also gave me a clear view of the numerous streams and ponds and other obstacles that lay between me and the whitewashed houses of Limavady. Eventually I squelched past a quarry and through various lanes and then down into the town. It was now well into Sunday afternoon and everyone but me was in their Sunday best. I felt very much out of it in my wet and muddy clothing, trudging through the streets under my heavy pack.

The cure for a state like this is tea, and I found a tea shop where I became the object of general interest. 'Good luck to you,' they said. They too would take a good walk—if only they had the time.

'Did you hear the story of the three cardinals discussing the meaning of time?' I was asked. 'No? Well, the Italian cardinal said that the word *domani* was a lovely word, meaning not just tomorrow, but sometime when they could get round to it. The Spanish cardinal said *mañana* was much the same, and when someone said "I'll do it *mañana*" you knew he wouldn't do it at all. Then they looked at the Irish cardinal and he said his country didn't have any words that had the same sense of urgency.'

Limavady is a nice little town. It has a monument to William Massey, Prime Minister of New Zealand from 1912 to 1925, who was born in Limavady. Ulster has had more than its share of famous men, many the sons of Presbyterian dissenters who left Ireland in the 18th century. Five men who signed the American Declaration of Independence had roots in Ulster and the Declaration was printed by John Dunlap, from Strabane. Eleven American Presidents had Ulster ancestry,

THE IRISH VOTE

LEFT *Derry's streets became a sea of red, white and blue—the colours of the American flag—when US President Bill Clinton came to the city in 1998.*

RIGHT *John F. Kennedy visited Ireland, the land his ancestors left in the 19th century, in 1963. He certainly looked happy to be home in this photograph, taken in Dublin.*

THROUGHOUT HISTORY the Irish have forsaken their native land in search of a better future elsewhere. The first emigrants to America left in the 1700s, but a mass exodus began in the middle of the following century, when famine forced many to flee poverty and starvation in Ireland for a better life in the New World.

As the population of America grew, so too did its infrastructure. Railways appeared across the country's vast expanses, carrying immigrants out west in search of soil of their own. But the Irish, mistrustful of the land after their experiences of failed crops and famine,

and too poor to buy their own patch anyway, largely stayed in the cities of the eastern seaboard. Those who did go west provided the labour that built the railways.

This 'Irish power' was not the only contribution that the immigrants made to a young and developing American society, however. Their talent for blarney and passion for democracy soon made the Irish a force to be reckoned with in politics. The first American President of Irish descent was Andrew Jackson, in office from 1829 to 1837. He was followed by no fewer than 14 men with Irish roots. The first of these

to visit Ireland, and the first Catholic, was John F. Kennedy, who, in 1963, stood at the quayside in County Wexford from which his great-grandfather had set sail for America in 1848.

In 1998 President Bill Clinton also visited his ancestral homeland. To many of the 40 million Irish-Americans back home, this trip may have represented a symbolic retracing of their own roots.

as did Sam Houston, founder of Texas, and the astronaut Neil Armstrong, the first man on the moon…and that is without such luminaries as John F. Kennedy and Ronald Reagan, whose ancestors came from other parts of Ireland.

More than that, though, there is culture here. It was in Limavady in 1851 that Jane Ross heard a blind Irish fiddler playing the tune that is now known as 'The Londonderry Air', or 'Danny Boy'. There is a plaque to this event on the wall of Miss Ross's house in Main Street.

My B & B hosts, the McCormicks, were Catholic. They had several pretty daughters and a lot of religious insignia around the walls, so I could work that out for myself. They were also instantly hospitable to the muddy heathen. My socks went to be washed, there was tea and scones in the parlour, and Robin McCormick had a suggestion for the evening.

'We are off to Mass,' he said, 'but we have fixed you a dinner at a restaurant in town. We'll pick you up after that and all go for a drive.'

After I had cleaned myself up we all piled into the car with the girls and they dropped me off at the restaurant. Things were to pick up later, but I have to say that so far Irish food had been terrible. The basic staple of the Irish diet is still the potato, and I was alarmed to learn that the Irish people each get through about 178 pounds of potatoes a year. In the Republic they get through all they can grow and import thousands of tons besides. Not for nothing are the members of Ireland's largest clan, the Murphys, usually nicknamed 'Spud'.

The potato tuber was brought to Ireland in the 16th century by Sir Walter Raleigh, who had estates here, and in this mild climate and fertile soil the potatoes flourished. These Irish potatoes are not neat Jersey potatoes the size of ping-pong balls, but great heavy King Edwards, huge menacing spuds that lie in wait at every meal, variously disguised. Irish potatoes come by the plateful—fried, boiled, mashed, roasted. With them comes overdone lamb or overdone pork with over-done vegetables, all cooked to a pulp. After two days crossing Northern Ireland I would have killed for a salad.

Having given offence, let me add that I understand all this. Many years ago, I worked in the Welsh valleys and Black Country of England. The tastes of the people there were just the same. They needed something that sticks to the ribs, something a man could go to work on. The solid, heavy Irish meals and the craving for sticky cakes and rich food are tastes nurtured by generations of deprivation.

I had a grand evening with the McCormicks. We went to the Roe Valley Country Park, a very pretty spot to the south of the town where the engine sheds that first brought electricity to Limavady have been converted into a museum. We took a stroll beside the rock-strewn River Roe and, as I also have daughters, we talked about bringing up girls. I went to bed sober but very content.

After the now-familiar massive breakfast I got away early. Maud McCormick and her four girls were all there to see me off, with my clothes washed and a packet of sandwiches ready to fend off starvation. Robin had already gone to work. I could see the Sperrins dead ahead now, barring the skyline on this warm and misty morning, and I pressed towards them at my best speed.

SUNK BY THE SPERRINS

Some romantic I had talked to in England told me about the Sperrins in the most lyrical terms. They were, he eulogised, the most splendid mountains: 'the most beautiful part of Ulster, long ridges, rolling hills, deep, open valleys, great for walking…you'll love it.'

His description of these mountains sounded idyllic, and up to a point the reality lived up to it. Only on closer inspection did I discover the snags: all the ridges lay east to west, while I was going north to south, and there were precious few footpaths leading in my direction.

Part of the reason for this shortage of footpaths goes back to the plantings, one effect of which was to deny the Irish any rights of way over their native land, but footpaths were anyway in short supply, for in Ireland the footpath as a means of getting about never came into the scheme of things at all. The 8th-century invaders, the Vikings, were not interested in footpaths. They started raiding the Irish coast in AD 795. Then, having harried the coast into ruin, they began to settle. Eventually whole armies of Norwegians and Danes arrived to set up proper colonies, and over the next two centuries they established the first real towns in Ireland—Dyflin (the Black Pool, or Dublin) was one; Waterford was another— but that was the extent of their settlement.

So for most of its history, Ireland had very few roads of any kind. Most Irish roads only date back to the famine of the last century when road work was offered as a means of providing starving people with money for food. These famine roads make Ireland a marvellous place for cycling, and were to provide most of my routes on the walk south to Valencia. They added to the distance and played havoc with my feet, but the end result was that I met more people.

I walked on happily enough out of Limavady through the hamlets of Ballymore and Moys, along lanes thick with yellow gorse and multi-hued rhododendrons,

ABOVE *A plank incised with the image of a Viking ship is one of few artefacts that remain from these early invaders' stay on the banks of the Liffey.*

BELOW *In the 19th century starving Irishmen earned much-needed money building the so-called famine roads, which were organised as relief aid.*

THE BOG LANDSCAPE

RELAND'S BOGGY LANDSCAPE is the butt of many a joke about the country, but Ireland has the last laugh, as bogs are a profitable commodity: they provide turf for household fires, and more recently for power stations; peat moss for compost; and archaeological treasures which the peat, with its unique preservative properties, keeps yielding—from pots of medieval butter to Bronze Age wooden walkways, and intact human corpses from centuries or even millennia ago.

BELOW *Mechanical peat cutters destroy in no time vast swaths of peat which have taken thousands of years to form.*

Some 14 per cent of Ireland's terrain consists of bogland. Bog formation began over 8,000 years ago in marshes or muddy lakes. As sedges and reeds died, the water became acidic, an environment in which sphagnum moss thrived. The bacteria- and oxygen-poor conditions that subsequently formed prevented the moss from decomposing when it died; instead it slowly built up into layers of peat 20 feet deep or more.

Irish bogs are of two main types: blanket bogs and raised bogs. The flatter, broader blanket bogs developed in high-rainfall or high-altitude regions, such as Connemara or the Wicklow Mountains. Raised bogs, relying more on ground water than on rain, developed in lake basins in the Midlands (notably in the Bog of Allen region), where dead moss would accumulate into dome-like hummocks often as high as 25 feet.

On these drier footholds grow lichens and rare heathers, and in the summer bright patches of pink bog pimpernel and yellow tormentil. On the waterlogged surface of either kind of bog are such varied plants as deergrass, beak-sedge, bogbean, and several 'carnivores'—including butterwort, bladderwort and sundew—which trap insects and then digest them. Dragonflies and damselflies haunt the wetlands, and the large marsh grasshopper flourishes in raised bogs. Bird life abounds: redshanks, snipe and skylarks are all common. In spring, golden plovers and curlews nest on hummocks in raised bogs; and in winter,

BELOW *Bog cotton manages to survive by recycling the nutrients from its own dying tissue.*

flocks of Greenland white-fronted geese feed on the roots of blanket-bog grasses.

This unique range of flora and fauna is now under threat. So much peat has been extracted by the spades of generations of cottage-dwellers and, more recently, by the huge mechanical cutters of the Bord na Mona (the Irish Peat Board) that the fragile ecology is suffering. Some stretches of surviving bogland are accordingly now protected as nature reserves.

BELOW *Raised bogs are the perfect habitat for the colourful large marsh grasshopper.*

past gardens still bright with azalea bushes, and along a track into the Loughermore Forest. This was the third day of sunshine, so hoping that the countryside had dried out I climbed over a fence—and promptly sank in a bog. I have to say I found it rather frightening. I kept going down, with no apparent bottom under my boots, and only stopped sinking when my rucksack splashed into the water. There followed some Houdini-like contortions to hook the handle of my stick back into the wire of the fence, and to wriggle out of the rucksack straps. Then, by lying on the rucksack and pulling on the stick, I could slowly haul myself from the sucking embrace of the bog. By the time I had climbed back over the fence I was exhausted and not a little shaken. After that I became a bit more careful crossing open country.

I sat on the track, pouring black water from my boots and changing my socks before I decided to try again. This time I took care to pick my way from tussock to tussock, carefully avoiding the bright green patches. There is a certain trick to bog-trotting. It is possible to sweep the feet sideways through the grass and put the weight on the mattress thus created. On open, flat, blanket bog, the going is easier. The sensation is very springy, rather like walking on a waterbed. It is also possible to follow sheep tracks through the bogs, for the sheep seem to have the knack of finding a way across.

What with climbing in and out of peat hags—the wide trenches cut by the peat gatherers—I was covered in mud before I reached the far southern slope of Altahullion Hill, from where I could look down on the Fore Glen and the River Foreglen. I could see the white walls of a chapel in the valley which, if that was indeed the chapel at Ballymoney, meant that I had come out dead on track.

I made my way directly down the hillside, bouncing lightly over the blanket bog, only falling in half a dozen times, and came out over some farmland and through the back of a garage yard just beside the Dungiven to Londonderry road. The garage proprietor, who was standing with his head half buried in an engine, was startled at my appearance and not very pleased to see me.

'Where the hell did you spring from? Are you with the soldiers?'

I suppose that in my wet Rohan clothes and humping a dark green rucksack, this mistake was understandable.

I shook my head. 'I'm just on a walk. I've come down from Limavady over the moor.'

The man still seemed perplexed, but he at once became more friendly. 'It's nothing against you, you understand, but the soldiers come crashing down through here in their bloody trucks, with guns and everything. Last week they damned near ran over one of my children. Anyway, you're very welcome…You'll be from the mainland, I take it…We don't see many of you over here.'

I borrowed his garage hose and his children had the time of their lives washing me down. This done, and steaming gently, I set off towards Londonderry and my next B & B, a mile or two up the road.

I have to say that Mrs Hayes took my arrival very well. Cecilia Hayes used to be a nurse in Belfast, so she is probably used to terrible sights.

THE ORANGE ORDER

The crack that night was interesting. There were five of us at the table: an accountant from Dublin, a carpenter who was working on a new shopping mall in Derry, Dr John from Belfast, Cecilia and myself. They talked and I listened, mostly to Dr John, who had done his training at the Royal Victoria Hospital in Belfast and seen more than his share of the sharp end of the Troubles.

'When a man comes in, say, hit in the head by a high-velocity bullet, it's a terrible thing, because there is not much you can do…his brains are on the stretcher. The kneecapping? Well, that depends on how it's done. They do it from the back, so if the victim struggles and the Provo bastards use a low-velocity pistol and miss the kneecap then the poor eejit might get away with an in-and-out in the thigh or calf. Otherwise he probably will need a stick or be on crutches for life. It's a terrible wound. We might only get two or three cappings a month these days.'

That seemed an awful lot to me but people here seem to take such matters almost in their stride—if that is the right term to employ about kneecapping. The Derry man had a kneecapping tale that was almost funny. Almost.

THE ORANGEMEN OF ULSTER

LEFT *The Loyal Orange Order parades through the streets of Belfast; Catholic houses fly the Irish flag in silent defiance.*

ORANGE SASHES, beating drums, and fluttering Union Jacks make for colourful and noisy processions in the streets of Northern Ireland each July and August. These religious and political demonstrations are rooted in the events of 1690 when the Protestant William of Orange defeated the Catholic James II at the Battle of the Boyne. But it was only after the sectarian Battle of Diamond in Armagh in 1795 that the victorious Peep O'Day Boys, a violent Protestant group, organised themselves into a secret society dedicated to both 'King Billy' and the British Crown: the Loyal Orange Order.

The Orange Order rapidly grew into one of Ireland's most powerful political organisations, rivalled only by its Catholic counterpart—originally the United Irishmen, later the Irish Republican Brotherhood, and today Sinn Fein.

The centuries-old conflict between Orangeism and Fenianism, loyalism and nationalism, Protestantism and Catholicism continues to be a dominant element of life in Ulster. Every year the province braces itself for the contentious 'marching season'. Orange marches are often routed through Catholic areas, and violent clashes are a regular feature. These days extensive negotiations over routes take place, but on some occasions the parties reach deadlock and the police ban the marches altogether.

'You know that they tell you you'll be done, so they do? Drug pushers or joy-riders or people that get too pally with the soldiers? Well, there was this fella… I don't know what he'd done, but they rang him and said, "Right, boyo, you're for a capping. Be at the corner of the street tomorrow morning and we'll see to you."'

'Well,' went on the Derry man, 'he was so worried he went and got drunk and when he woke up next day the time for his capping was long gone. Imagine! So he went rushing about the street looking for the hard men and hoping they'd not be too rough on him. He found someone to pass the word and they gave him another appointment. That afternoon he went off for his capping, quite relieved.'

It would be wrong to imply that the Troubles are the only topic of conversation around an Irish dinner table. You talk about everything, but as the lone Brit I found myself the focus of the need to explain, to get me to understand what it is like. I can only say I tried. A little history certainly helps, especially here in County Londonderry, a few miles from the city itself.

The siege of Londonderry in 1689 is one of the most heroic, or tragic, events in Irish history. It depends on your point of view, but the facts are as follows.

James II of England was a Catholic. But the English would not have a Catholic on the throne, and in 1688 replaced him with William of Orange. James had dealt kindly with the Irish people, and when he was deposed he went to Ireland. Ireland then split over the issue of whether to support the Protestant King William, or the Catholic King James.

Matters came to a head in Londonderry in the autumn of 1688 when news arrived that James was sending in

a Catholic regiment to replace the existing garrison. The mainly Protestant population was worried about letting in a large Catholic force, but even the Protestant bishop felt it would be difficult to keep them out. The regiment was within sight of the city on December 7, 1688, when thirteen apprentice boys seized the city keys and slammed the city gates in the faces of King James's soldiers.

A convoy of English troops from William's army soon arrived on the River Foyle, but their ships failed to break the boom and they withdrew. So the siege of Londonderry did not actually start until April 1689. The townspeople somehow held on, close to starvation, right through the spring and early summer, until relief supplies finally reached the city.

King William landed at Carrickfergus in 1690 and smashed the armies of King James at the Battle of the Boyne. In 1691 the remnants of the Catholic armies surrendered at Limerick, but that long, hard summer of 1689 has never been forgotten by the Protestants of Ulster. The slogan of 'No Surrender' is scrawled on their walls to this day, usually above a picture of King Billy on his prancing charger, and every December the Protestant Orange Orders assemble

ABOVE *Romeyn de Hooge's 17th-century hand-coloured engraving of the Battle of the Boyne recounts William of Orange's victory in 1690.*

TOP *In Londonderry's Guildhall, a stained-glass window depicts 13 apprentice boys closing the city's gates to lock out a large Catholic force in 1688.*

in Londonderry to celebrate the actions of the apprentice boys 300 years ago by parading through mainly Catholic Derry—as the Catholics call it—with fife and drum. 'No Surrender'—the defiant shout of the apprentice boys—echoes down the history of Ulster, a total rejection of Catholic or Republican rule.

The Orange Order was formed in 1791, to resist Home Rule. It took its name from King William of Orange, but arose out of a secret organisation, called the Peep O'Day Boys, who spent their spare time terrorising local Catholics. The Peep O'Day Boys were the first to introduce the practice of kneecapping, which has been used here most barbarously ever since.

This side of Orange Order activities then did no more to endear Orangemen to the Protestants than the activities of the IRA find approval with the majority of decent Catholics today.

I had already seen signs of Orange activity and these would multiply near the border. Ambling down one side road I had passed a bus shelter totally decorated inside with a mural depicting King Billy on his horse supported by the marching band of the local Orange Lodge. I had also heard the tapping of drums and the squealing of pipes, for all over Northern Ireland at the start of the summer the marching bands of the Orange Order tune up for their July and August parades. I had seen these parades often enough on television—gaudily clad bands led by baton-twirling youths in front of long columns of men in bowler hats, wearing Orange sashes and marching along with umbrellas. With luck I would be out of Ulster before they took place.

SHEEP STEALING

What with one thing and another, it was quite a heavy night. When I went in for the usual heart-stopping breakfast next morning, all the others were long gone and a stiff walk lay before me. My route led over the next range of the Sperrins, from the River Foreglen, a tributary of the River Faughan which flows into the Foyle north of Londonderry, and over to the Glenelly Valley which lay some twenty miles to the south in the heart of the Sperrin Mountains. The main range of the Sperrins now lay ahead, quite glorious to look upon.

I made good time along empty lanes, weaving round a series of steep little rounded hills, all at around the 900 feet mark. That done, I set off on the long, steep haul over the open moors to the Sawel Mountain, at 2,240 feet the highest peak of the Sperrins. On the way I had a curious encounter with a sheep.

There are a lot of sheep in these parts, blackface Scots sheep for the most part, hardy enough to survive on the wet moors. I had paid little attention to them, and they generally got up and trotted off when I came close. I was trudging along a lane, thinking of something else, when an insistent bleating drew my attention to the field beside the road.

There, just inside the fence, was a lamb. It was trotting along to match my pace and bleating loudly. I stopped for a closer look, at which the lamb tried to climb through the fence towards me. After scratching his woolly head, I had some trouble pushing him back.

ABOVE *A friendly and determined lamb joined the author for part of his walk. Scottish blackface sheep are the most popular breed of sheep in the British Isles, being hardy enough to survive the roughest terrain and weather.*

'You stay in there, little fellow,' I said firmly. 'Come out here and you'll get run over.'

'Baah!' said the lamb. 'BAAAAH!' It was a remarkably noisy lamb. His last bleat was like a trumpet call. There came a drumming of hoofs and a score of sheep, a mixture of big ewes and small lambs, appeared behind him, lining the grassy bank above the lane. I stood there over the lamb while the assembled sheep went demented. I legged it as if to escape a lynching, but fifty yards up the road there was a gate. The lamb sprawled itself under the gate and came clattering up the road after me on his little black hoofs, still bleating piteously.

'Now look,' I said to the lamb. 'This can't go on. Go back.'

'Baaah!' said the lamb.

I picked him up, carried him back to the line of sheep and tipped him into the field.

Two minutes later he was under the gate, back in the road and clattering after me again. I put him back in the field. Quick as a flash he shot back out again. This went on for some time.

'Sod you then,' I said at last, quite worn out. 'I've got other things to do with my time than mess about with you. If you get run over it's your own bloody fault.'

'Baa…ah!' said the lamb, happily.

So off we went, the lamb and me, striding along together for half a mile or so. We might have been together now had not a farm tractor appeared ahead, filling the lane from side to side and trundling fast towards me. Here was an opportunity. I picked the lamb up and stood in the tractor's path until it stopped.

'Is this your lamb?' I asked the driver. 'He comes from a field about a mile back and he won't leave me alone.'

The driver switched off the engine, pushed his cap back and studied us both for a moment, nodding. 'He thinks you're his daddy, so he does,' he said at last.

'Well, I'm not his daddy,' I said. 'Can you take him back where he came from?'

'I'll sell him to you,' said the farmer. 'Since you've taken to each other. Call it £25…cash, mind.'

Are these people mad? For a second I wondered how a book called *Travels with my Sheep* would sell, but then I came to my senses. I declined the offer, handed up the lamb and fled. When I reached a turn in the road and looked back, I could see that anxious little face peering over the farmer's shoulder, bleating after me above the noise of the engine, as if its little heart would break. I pressed on up the road feeling like a real swine.

Getting to the top of the Sawel Pass over the main ridge of the Sperrins was a hard walk, on one of those narrow mountain roads that never seems to end. The road was quite empty and the moors quiet except for the sound of skylarks and water tinkling in the streams. I took a breather at the col, then plunged down the hill for the Glenelly Valley and the village of Cranagh. Give or take a sheep or two, I had not met more than a handful of people all day. The pub at Cranagh was shut, which is most unlike an Irish pub, so I sat on a pile of gravel. I had a good

ABOVE *Scattered farms dot the peaceful Glenelly Valley, where low-lying lush green fields merge with purple heather on the moorland above.*

chance to look around me. Like a lot of these Sperrin valleys, the Glenelly Valley falls into two parts, with rich bottom lands along the banks of the river, split into neat fields and farms, and then halfway up the hillside the open moors begin. The sun was just starting down to the west, sending big shadows over the fields. I could have sat there quietly for hours, just enjoying it, but I had a long day on the morrow, and just down the road was Billy Conway's B & B.

Billy Conway kept sheep on his smallholding next door, a task to go with his job in the nearby town. I suspect that Billy kept sheep because he was a farmer at heart and he soon put me right about the lamb I had met on the road.

'That would be a house lamb,' he said. 'His mother wouldn't feed him so they'll have taken him into the house and given him the bottle. Now he doesn't think he is a sheep at all, and when he sees you... you're it. Now, if your feet will stand it, why don't we take a little walk down the road after tea and try a little panning for gold?'

PIG SMUGGLING

I was surprised to find goldfields in Ireland, let alone on the green slopes of the Sperrins, but sure enough, gold panning was one of the options at the Sperrin Heritage Centre, halfway down the Glenelly Valley. The centre has the usual folklore displays including one concerning the distilling of poteen, the raw Irish

BELOW *A group of schoolchildren, looking to find their fortune, try their hand at gold panning at the Sperrin Heritage Centre. The Sperrin Mountains have an estimated 80 sites containing gold, and consequently have seen the occasional gold rush.*

whiskey, but they also provide a pan with which you can sift sand for gold in the nearby stream.

There has always been gold mining in the Sperrins. Prospectors can find it in small amounts, but recent estimates have it that there are some 300,000 ounces hereabouts, ready for extraction, which at £250 an ounce is serious money. The thought that some Anglo-American company will tear these green hills apart for profit has brought the conservationists into the fray. Mind you, I found nothing, not a glint or glimmer.

When I got back from the gold fields, I took off my boots in the bedroom and made an alarming discovery. In the last twelve hours I had collected an impressive array of blisters. Thus does constant road walking, interspersed with wetting the feet in bogs, take its toll of the lower extremities.

The snag was that I had a lot more road walking ahead unless I could find a footpath. Here I was lucky, for my map revealed that the Ulster Way footpath ran across the top of the long east-to-west ridge across the valley that I could see from my bedroom window. By following it to Gortin I would have twelve miles or so of soft hill path, half a day at least of gentle walking on the following day.

The Ulster Way is the longest trail in Ireland, circling the entire province and broken into five main sections, each a footpath in its own right. The trail ran before me and led west to Gortin. That was followed by a ten-mile trail to the Ulster-American Folk Park and Omagh. It then led on to the border with County Fermanagh, which I must cross on my way west to Enniskillen. All I had to do tomorrow was cross the river and turn right, then follow the Ulster Way all the way to Gortin and beyond—perfect.

My second bit of luck came that evening over dinner, when Billy mentioned he was going into Omagh next day and would take my rucksack in for me. I went to bed that night anticipating a long, light, easy day tomorrow.

I began the day with an early start, and set off across the River Glenelly for the 1,257-foot top of Corratary Hill. Halfway up the hill all my fine ideas ran onto tarmac. The Ulster Way no longer ran along the top of the ridge—path erosion had forced a diversion down to the road through Corramore. I was back on the hard stuff.

ABOVE *The 500 miles of waymarked trails that make up the circular Ulster Way traverse forests, parkland, cliff tops and mountains.*

RIGHT *Exhilarating walks along the Ulster Way can lead to outstanding views— making all the hard work worth while.*

Well, at least I didn't have a fifty-pound pack crushing my feet flat. It was also another beautiful sunny day, so I strolled along happily enough, cutting through the Sperrins at the road fork by the Eagle's Nest to the Barnes Gap. Here the Ulster Way ran off the road and I was able to divert onto it for the last mile or so into Gortin. I came into Gortin just after midday, crossing over the beautiful River Owenkillew and past the grounds of Beltrim Castle, once the residence of the Houston family whose son Sam founded the state of Texas.

Gortin is one of those pretty Irish towns with a main street wide enough for a cattle market, and three small pubs. It is an old town, dating back to the time of St Patrick, and it must once have been bigger and more important than it is today, when it lives by the river fishing and as a forestry centre. Since it was now very hot and the middle of the day, I found my way into a cool, shady pub and a curious conversation.

It can sometimes take up to a minute for a total stranger to meet an old friend in any Irish bar, but here it took rather less. Irish pubs are endowed with tall bar stools and I had hardly climbed onto one for my pint of Smithwicks before the man on a nearby barstool had discovered my name, occupation, place of residence and current activity. Well, two can play at that game.

'And yourself, sir,' I said. 'What do you do?'

'I, sir,' he said proudly, 'am the finest pig smuggler in Monaghan.'

In the next half-hour or so, I learned more about pig smuggling than any law-abiding Englishman should know. It appeared that the European Economic Community tried to level commodity prices by paying a subsidy to Irish farmers who shipped pigs into the North. (It might have been the other way round but that's the gist of it.) You heaved a few porkers into the transit van, got your import form stamped at the border and in due course got a fat cheque from the EEC, making up the difference between the Northern Irish price and the one available in the Republic…What you didn't do was sell the pigs.

'Oh no,' said the Finest Pig Smuggler in Monaghan. 'You never sell the pigs. You'd have to buy more and then where's the profit?'

'But…?' I said. 'What…?'

'What you do,' said the Finest Pig Smuggler (as to an eejit), 'is you drive back across the border, down one of the unpatrolled roads, and you repeat the process a day or two later.'

BELOW *Gorse-clad hills greeted the author as he walked towards the pretty village of Gortin.*

So it went on, the pigs circling through the customs posts, picking up money all the time. As to the 'eejit', that's the Irish for 'idiot', I soon got used to people nodding in my direction and pointing out the big eejit with the rucksack.

'It's a fine business, so it is,' said the Finest Pig Smuggler in Monaghan, '…and your glass is empty.'

LIMPING TO LOUGH ERNE

I fell out onto the bright streets of Gortin at about half past two and soon found a trail out, a real footpath this time, that led up to the top of the next ridge. I was drawn on by sounds of gunfire. When I emerged at the top I saw a rifle range to my left, with lines of soldiers sprinting down from point to point. I was taking all this in when a soldier of the Ulster Defence Regiment (UDR) suddenly appeared at my side and asked me a few questions.

ABOVE *Soldiers from the UDR patrol a country lane. In 1992 the UDR merged with the Royal Irish Rangers to form the Royal Irish Regiment.*

There were other soldiers dotted here and there among the undergrowth, acting as pickets for their comrades on the range. This one was in full camouflage gear, complete with helmet and rifle. He was polite enough and asked the usual questions: where was I from and where was I going? Since I had never met a UDR soldier before I wanted to talk to him, and once he discovered I was harmless he was happy to talk. He was a part-time soldier, working sixty to seventy hours a week.

'That's a hell of a lot of hours,' I said, 'even in my day. How do you manage that and a job?'

'Well, I'm unemployed at the moment,' he explained. 'Were you ever a soldier over here yourself, sir?'

I shook my head. 'I was a soldier, but not over here, thank God.'

'What were you in, sir?'

'45 Commando…Royal Marines.'

This was clearly a recommendation. Other soldiers were summoned from the undergrowth to say hello and sing the praises of my old commando, which clearly had earned golden opinions in the Province.

'45 Commando, eh? That's a hard unit…take no bloody nonsense at all, so they don't.'

I stood there in the sunshine chatting with the soldiers, while a few cars roared south for Omagh. Then range practice was over and everyone was climbing back into their civvies for the drive home. I was almost sorry to leave this bunch of lads and flog on south through the woods of the Gortin Glen, but it was better in there under the trees, hilly enough but cool and shady, the path soft under my sensitive feet. There are said to be deer here, for sika deer have escaped from the reserve at Baronscourt, but I saw nothing as I plodded on. Then, at about five o'clock, I emerged onto the road at the Ulster-American Folk Park.

The Ulster-American Folk Park is a little bit of Americana imported back to the Auld Sod, set around the cottage where Thomas Mellon was born in 1813. It's also a good museum that helps to explain the strong links that still exist between Ireland and the USA.

Mellon went to America and made his fortune as a steel magnate. His family virtually created the town of Pittsburgh, and both the Golden Gate Bridge of San Francisco and the lock gates of the Panama Canal were made of Mellon steel. Like a lot of Irishmen, the Mellons prospered greatly but never forgot their roots.

The Folk Park tells the story of how the Irish people were forced to migrate to the New World. It shows the state of poverty and deprivation they fled from and the hard times they met across the ocean. There is even a Conestoga wagon—

LEFT *Brightly coloured handmade quilts hang outside a traditional log cabin at the Ulster-American Folk Park, near Omagh. The Park recreates the lives of Irish emigrants from the 18th and 19th centuries, before and after their arrival in America.*

a 'prairie schooner'—dating from the end of the 18th century, as well as log cabins and schoolhouses. I bought an ice cream and enjoyed the visit. Then I had to get on south again, for Omagh.

Fortunately, the distance from the Folk Park to the town of Omagh is not very far, and beyond the Folk Park the land flattened out. I tottered on, finally limping across the River Strule into Omagh where, as Billy had promised, my rucksack was waiting at the Royal Arms Hotel. They even took pity on me and carried it up to my room.

I must have been getting fitter because after half an hour groaning on my bed I was able to limp around the town, which is rather pretty. It is set along the hill

ABOVE *The River Strule flows past Omagh's neo-Gothic Sacred Heart Church, whose spires are impressive, but strangely asymmetrical. In 1998 Omagh suffered a dreadful blow when 29 people died in a bomb explosion in the town centre.*

above the River Strule and although quite small it has a couple of impressive churches. It is the birthplace of Jimmy Kennedy, who wrote 'The Teddy Bears' Picnic'.

Stretched out on my bed that night, I took a good look at my feet. They were now endowed with open blisters, the result of a week of walking on hot roads under a heavy pack. Well, all you have to do is identify the problem and work out how to solve it, and then see if that solution is available. So I whimpered my way into my trainers and limped round to the bus station. Here there was good and bad news—yes, they would take my rucksack to Irvinestown, but I would have to go with it. It was the bombs, y'see. Accepting a parcel or carrying a piece of luggage without a passenger was just not on. I hauled out my map and explained my predicament. The man relented. If I would come a bit of the way and they could have a good peek inside the rucksack, then the driver might take it on a bit for me. We settled for a ride to Dromore and I limped off back to bed.

When I woke up next day it was pouring down with rain. I put on the Rohans but by the time I got to the bus station I was drenched. I stood in a widening pool of water while the driver took a cursory poke about inside my rucksack and carried it on board the bus for me.

'You don't look like a tearaway to me,' he said, 'and that's a fine limp you have there. How are the feet?'

Just pulling on the boots that morning had made my eyes water. 'Don't ask,' I told him.

There is an advantage in hopping on a bus now and then. Even when the rain isn't streaming down the windows you get to meet the local people who come climbing aboard to commute to their jobs. With my rucksack as a conversation piece the crack was soon going strong.

Most of the people here, like most of the other people I had met so far on this journey, had long since learned to live with the Troubles. Unemployment, the current curse of Ireland, was also dismissed in a very Irish fashion.

'I know plenty of fellows who are drawing the dole on this side of the border and then nipping off to jobs in the Republic,' said one man. At this there were vigorous nods from those who agreed, but none from those who were probably heading across the border. So, chatting the time away, we came to Dromore, where I heaved myself out of the bus and into the rain.

While conscience made me get off, honesty compels me to add that I would have done just as well to stay on the bus. The day was just another road walk south and west. The rain was tipping down, the visibility almost zero and all the sensible people were in the pub. I picked up my rucksack at Irvinestown and by about four in the afternoon I was near Killadeas, on Lough Erne, where I had a provisional booking at Mrs Flood's B & B.

Bed and breakfast accommodation is widely available in Ireland, not just in rooms left empty after the children leave home but in proper small hotels. I came to think of them as 'half-hotels', for you have your own room and bath, often in an extension, and are welcome to join the family in the kitchen or sitting room for dinner or tea or a drink. They are marvellous, well kept and very hospitable.

Next morning I made my way south beside the northern arm of Lough Erne, down the road into Enniskillen. The road comes into town just by the war memorial, where the IRA exploded a bomb during the November Armistice Service of 1987, killing eleven people. A long brass strip on the memorial records this atrocity with the names of the victims.

Here for the first time I ran into a mixed patrol of the Royal Ulster Constabulary (RUC) and the British army, who were manning a checkpoint at the entrance to the town. The RUC were friendly enough, telling me where to find a hotel, but the soldiers were sullen and wary, the infantry deployed on either side of the road, a chatter of contact coming from the radio in the back of their armoured personnel carrier. I nodded my way past and went to find a pub.

By now I had a routine going for my arrival at any town: I would limp along to the first bar and turn in at the door. So it was here, but I had been at the counter perhaps thirty seconds and barely dropped the rucksack on the floor when a man was at my elbow with a question.

'What are you doing here?'

It was not a friendly question. Nor was it an easy one to answer. Irish bars are not often small, but this one was very small, very quiet and very full of people. All of them were looking at me.

When I said I was getting a drink, if he had no objection, that didn't deflect him at all. Maybe it was my accent. I got a grilling about where I had come from that day and where I was going. Only when he had hefted the rucksack off the floor did he nod, shrug, and vanish out the back. I had walked into a Republican bar where strangers, and especially English strangers with rucksacks, are not made very welcome…at least to begin with.

'When are you Brits going to hand back the Six Counties?' asked the barman, passing over my pint. A dozen faces turned to await the answer.

'Well, if it was up to me, you could have them back tomorrow,' I said. 'As it is, it's up to you. I think you'd better sort that out among yourselves.'

Frankly, Enniskillen isn't the place where Republicans have much to boast or complain about, not with that memorial down the road. There was a bit of a silence and I tried not to drink my beer too fast. Then someone offered to refill the glass and things were suddenly back to normal. We spread the map on the counter and discussed the route and the bogs and the 'Finest Pig Smuggler in Monaghan'.

Then it was my turn to buy a round and one thing led to another. I had walked across Northern Ireland and knocked a hole in this journey. As the beer got to work, my feet stopped hurting and the upshot was that I stayed in there for hours. I think there was singing.

ABOVE *The war memorial at Enniskillen records not only the names of local servicemen who lost their lives in two world wars, but also those civilians who died in an IRA bomb attack here in 1987.*

FAREWELL TO THE NORTH

I took two days off at Enniskillen. This was partly because there is a lot to see there, all of it within easy reach, but there was also another reason. I had been very taken with Northern Ireland and I didn't really want to leave.

I had begun to feel some empathy with these good people, caught as they are in some terrible time warp, unable to escape from their past. One might not see or sense danger in this province but it was there all the same. Even so, I liked the place and the people and I liked Enniskillen.

Enniskillen is the capital of County Fermanagh, the lakeland country of Ulster. The county is divided by the River Erne, which flows so slowly through relatively flat country that it has widened north and south of the town into two great loughs. There is the Irish touch in that Lower Lough Erne lies to the north, which is downstream. Enniskillen stands like a sentry in the narrow throat of land between the two loughs, astride the road out to Sligo and the west of Ireland.

Before the English got this far west, Fermanagh was a stronghold for the powerful Maguire clan, who held on until the Jacobean planting in the 17th century. The Maguires took a leading role in the rebellion of 1641. By 1689, however, Enniskillen was a strongly Protestant town and the Protestants held the town for King William against Jacobite forces serving King James.

I took myself off along the river to see the historic Watergate, which is part of the former Enniskillen Castle, and the only fortress in Fermanagh to escape

BELOW *In times past the twin-turreted Watergate protected Enniskillen Castle from invaders approaching the town from Upper Lough Erne.*

destruction during the wars of the 17th century. As castles go, this one is quite small. It was begun in the 15th century by Hugh Maguire, whose marvellous nickname was Hugh the Hospitable. It was rebuilt after the 1641 rebellion, when the Watergate was added to the medieval keep. The Cole family lived in the castle for 100 years until they moved to Florence Court, a splendid country house outside Enniskillen, now owned by the National Trust.

The castle complex contains a heritage centre which displays local archaeology, natural history and folk life, and a military museum celebrating the history of the local regiment, the Royal Inniskilling Fusiliers. All their regalia is there, from Waterloo guidons to Great War VCs. One of the most famous Inniskilling officers was Captain Oates, who in Scott's doomed Antarctic expedition walked to his death in the blizzard with the words, 'I'm just going outside. I may be some time.' There is a memorial to Oates in the town hall.

Other famous sons of Enniskillen include Oscar Wilde and Samuel Beckett, who both went to school here. This must still be a pleasant place for schoolboys, with a wealth of lakes and woodlands to roam about in. When the rain slackened that is what I did, taking a boat excursion up the Lower Lough to Devenish island. This used to contain a monastery founded in the 6th century by St Molaise, one of those Celtic saints who abounded hereabouts at the time. The buildings are in ruins except for the tall round tower, about eighty-two feet high, which looks like a lighthouse but was built as a bell tower to call people to prayer as well as to protect the community from marauding Danes.

Many Irish monasteries contain round towers, and they are a fine example of passive resistance set in stone. The monks simply climbed up a ladder into the tower, which had a door high up the wall, hauled up the ladder and made faces at the Danes until they went away. Most of the islands on Lough Erne support a church or a priory, while the lake itself pokes up towards the border of Donegal like a boomerang, and supports a fleet of cabin cruisers.

I left Enniskillen and Northern Ireland with considerable regret. Nine days on foot had changed my preconceptions of the place and the people, altering views distorted by twenty years of seeing the province only through the eye of the television news.

Try as I might to arrive with an open mind, I had imagined a country crammed with whey-faced, ranting bigots where, under a steady downpour, men in black balaclavas shot it out with the military, while priests and women in pinafores raised their hands for God's justice, or wept.

Yes, that sort of thing certainly happens in Northern Ireland, but that is not all of it. Northern Ireland is my kind of place, beautiful and historic, while the people are marvellous. What I took with me as I walked west past the Watergate was the memory of the open-hearted folk I had met along the way.

ABOVE *The sturdy 82-foot round tower on Devenish island is remarkably intact after 800 years.*

WAY OUT WEST

HE WATERGATE WAS CROWNED with a flagpole from which fluttered the defiant cross of St George. Once that had faded from view there was nothing for it but to march for the border of the Republic at Belcoo. There was no footpath, so this was simply a bash down the main road on a verge wide enough to avoid most of the traffic. It was a dreary day. Clouds sat on the tops of the hills, my head was tucked into the hood of my anorak and the rain swept relentlessly down.

ABOVE *The quiet border village of Belcoo, with the fortified British army and RUC guard post visible at the end of the street.*

At Belcoo the road did a left and then a right dogleg, first past the fortified British army–RUC guard post and then past a lone Garda constable. Suddenly, there I was in the Republic, with the first stage of my journey finally completed and only about 300 miles to go. No one asked to look at my passport, and the traffic at the frontier hardly slowed down. If this was the border, it all seemed far too easy.

I stopped just across the border that night in the village of Blacklion, fairly wet on arrival but otherwise content. My feet seemed to be on the mend and the rain could not last for ever.

Some feel that Sligo is overshadowed by Mayo and Connemara. If so, that was a cheerful prospect because, even in the rain, Sligo looked good. Ulster is beautiful but the scale of the country increases in the west. The hills are higher and steeper, the valleys deeper, the lakes more frequent. Sligo is a region of lakes and mountains, and most of the mountains have delightful names, like the Ox Mountains and the Curlew Mountains, and Benbulbin, which hangs above the village church at Drumcliff, resting place of the poet William Butler Yeats.

This was a target on my walk next day. To get there I had only to walk due west, along the deep glacial valley of Glencar. It would be a long walk, twenty-five miles at least, but the country was beautiful and the road flat.

I was out early next day, forging west down a valley road lined with tall trees and clumps of purple fuchsia. I could have swerved south after Manorhamilton and taken the track over Benbo Mountain to Lough Gill and Yeats's 'Lake Isle of Innisfree', but I was finding it difficult enough reading the map.

On crossing the border I had changed from the bearable British 1:50 000 scale to the Irish ½:1 mile or 1:126 720 scale, which is barely adequate for walking. The names of places were in tiny script, and gauging where I was from the map would become one of my main preoccupations in the weeks ahead. I also seemed to be moving much more slowly because the scale had changed.

The Irish maps have not been fully revised for decades. As any walker knows, up-to-date, large-scale maps are a prerequisite for accurate cross-country navigation. This is especially true when a country has no footpaths. Well, all I had to do was turn south at the west coast and I would eventually get to Valencia. Anyway, there was no need to fret at the moment.

The Glencar valley fell away steeply to my right, then rose on the far side in a steep escarpment threaded with ribbon-like silver waterfalls cascading down the emerald-green face of the cliff. When the valley widened before the jut of the

ABOVE *At 1,730 feet, with its dramatic profile and emerald-green slopes, Benbulbin is one of Ireland's most picturesque mountains.*

ABOVE *Nobel prize-winning poet W. B. Yeats championed Ireland through his writing, and sought to preserve the country's Celtic legends and myths.*

ABOVE *W. B. Yeats met Maude Gonne in 1889, and promptly fell in love with her. A revolutionary herself, she drew Yeats into nationalist politics.*

King's Mountain, I came down off the main road and crossed the River Drumcliff. From there I made my way on a minor road towards Drumcliff Bay and the church at Drumcliff. I saw the church tower from a mile away and diverted towards it, and there, inside the gate and just to the left of the church door, stood a plain, grey slab. The grave of William Butler Yeats, last of the Romantic poets.

The Irish are wonderful with words. They are fluent in poetry, song and drama, and this seems to be their cultural gift. Few countries in the world have produced so many writers, playwrights or poets. I can think of a dozen without much effort, from Shaw to Behan, but my favourite is Yeats.

William Butler Yeats was born into a Protestant family at Sandymount, outside Dublin, in 1865. He died in the South of France in 1939, so his life spanned the most turbulent years of modern Irish history, from before Charles Parnell's death in 1891, through the First World War and the Easter Rising to the setting up of the Republic.

Yeats belonged to that class of Protestant gentry known as the Anglo-Irish ascendancy, and spent his youth shuttling between London and Dublin. The great love of his life was Maude Gonne who, though the daughter of a colonel in the British army, was an active Republican. Yeats pursued Maude for many years, but in 1903 she married the patriot Republican, John MacBride, and Yeats was desolate. He abandoned revolutionary politics for a while and took up the theatre. He was general manager of the Abbey Theatre in Dublin from 1904 to 1910, though he continued to write poetry and pine for Mrs MacBride. Then came the Easter Rising of 1916, after which John MacBride, who was one of the leaders of the Rising, was tried and shot by the British.

Yeats then proposed marriage to the widow who had, anyway, separated from MacBride some time before his death, but he was again rejected. Then, at the age of fifty-two, he finally married Georgie Hyde-Lees and was, somewhat to his surprise, very happy. This was in 1917, a year after the Easter Rising, an event which affected him far more than the slaughter then taking place on the Western Front. He made it very clear where his sympathies lay in 'An Irish Airman Foresees His Death':

> *Those that I fight I do not hate,*
> *Those that I guard I do not love;*
> *My country is Kiltartan Cross,*
> *My countrymen Kiltartan's poor…*

In 'Easter 1916', written when the Irish people were tearing themselves apart, he wrote about the effects of the Rising that, 'A terrible beauty is born.' Yeats became a Free State senator, and was active in the Dail for some years, though he continued to write and was awarded the Nobel prize for literature in 1923.

Yeats's grandfather had been the rector of Drumcliff, and Yeats expressed a wish to be buried here, 'Under bare Ben Bulben's head.' William's brother Jack was a fine landscape painter, and his works are displayed in the

County Museum in Sligo along with a lot of W. B. Yeats memorabilia, including first editions and early manuscripts.

The local people are proud of the Yeats connection, so much so that the Tourist Board often refers to Sligo as 'Yeats Country', clearly with considerable success. People were pouring into this quiet churchyard throughout my visit, photographing the headstone and touring the church. It is certainly a pretty spot, tranquil but for the roar of passing traffic, and I sat on the wall at the back of the churchyard, looking out across the valley to Benbulbin, which is only 1,730 feet high but still impressive and set in breathtaking scenery.

ABOVE *Yeats's grave lies within sight of Benbulbin. He had written that he wanted to be buried here in a poem composed just months before his death in 1939.*

Another haunt of the literati hereabouts is Cuidreven, scene of the Battle of the Books in 561, between St Columba and St Finian. St Finian had loaned St Columba a psalter and St Columba copied it without his permission. St Finian then demanded the copy back, St Columba refused and the dispute ended up before the High King of Tara, who gave judgment in favour of St Finian. 'To every cow its calf,' he said. 'To every book its copy.' St Columba was furious and took himself off to Iona in a huff.

I was considering walking north for a while, past Streedagh Point, where three Armada galleons came to grief in 1588, for a look at Mullaghmore Bay, where Lord Louis Mountbatten and members of his family were blown to pieces by the IRA in 1979, but I had had more than enough of the IRA by now. Instead I would turn west for my first real climb of the trip, up Knocknarea, a most distinctive hill with what looked like a nipple on top, and I would keep that for tomorrow, for the evening was drawing on and I had walked a long way that day.

WEDDING SLIGO STYLE

I took a drink out onto the hotel terrace before dinner and sat there sniffing the evening air, which was mild and moist and tinged with the smell of the sea. I stayed there, looking around at the surrounding hills, the map across my knees, thinking of the way I must go tomorrow.

Like most visitors, I was overwhelmed by the beauty of the Sligo landscape. This is a mixture of coast and lake and mountain, of rushing river and tumbling waterfall. It rained a fair bit for the rest of my trip, but in the west of Ireland the rain hardly matters. You can see the rain sweeping in from far out in the Atlantic, masking the offshore islands as it comes, picked out with great rainbows which trail a path across the clouds.

The mountains of Sligo are not very high but they are very old. The Ox Mountains, or Slieve Gamph, which I must cross tomorrow or the next day, are said to be the oldest mountains in Ireland, 500 million years old, or more. Time has worn them down into long, rolling ridges, green and beguiling to look on but carpeted from top to bottom with blanket bog. When you get onto them the ground is quite rough and seamed with streams and eroded gullies. All this I had yet to discover.

Future problems hardly matter when you are sitting in the soft Irish light, looking at a rainbow arcing over the dark hills across the bay. Tomorrow I would take a quick look at Sligo town and shin up Knocknarea. Then I would march for the town of Ballina.

That decided, I limped back to the bar. It was being propped up by a bride, clad in flowing white wedding dress and veil, her bouquet resting on the bar top. She had at her elbow, instead of a flute of champagne, a pint of Guinness. There was no sign of the bridegroom, and the bride and the barman were deep in conversation. I ordered a large Blackbush, toasted the bride by raising my glass and was rewarded with a big smile.

More and more people drifted in, clearly the wedding party, some with button-holes and slicked-down hair, and the atmosphere became steadily more convivial.

SLAINTE!

RIGHT AND BELOW
An Irish pub is a beacon of light and warmth, drawing in visitors for a pint or two of Guinness and good 'crack'. Unusually at Morrissey's, in Abbeyleix, patrons can do a spot of grocery shopping as well as slaking their thirst at the bar.

TRAVELLERS THROUGH Ireland will find it hard to go far without stumbling across a tavern or two. Up and down the island, cries of '*Sláinte!*'—the Gaelic drinking toast, pronounced 'slahn-che'— ring out everywhere. Pints of lovingly pulled Guinness line the counters, interspersed with the subtle amber glow of whiskey chasers.

Pubs are the vibrant focus of Irish local life, as they have been since the Middle Ages. Births, marriages and deaths are marked there, old scores are settled, and many fables told; friends meet in the 'snug' to gossip and share woes. Partitioned off from the rest of the bar for privacy, snugs were historically used by women who wanted to take a drink without causing a scandal—for, until the 1960s, a woman was a rare sight in a pub.

An Irish pub's interior is often simple and unadorned. The atmosphere is created by the passion for crack, or convivial conversation, and by a strong infusion of music and song, often performed impromptu. The rousing notes of fiddlers and pipers recall heroic tales of victory and loss, but the music on offer can range from jazz, rock and blues to country.

Its heady mixture of grit and romance has made the Irish pub popular the world over. 'Traditional' Irish pubs have sprung up everywhere from Amsterdam to Korea, though experts agree that a pint of Guinness brewed and pulled in Ireland cannot be faithfully imitated anywhere outside the Emerald Isle.

This was the main bar, not a private function room, and I was soon drawn into the party. I found my glass being refilled and was soon in conversation with the best man.

'What day is it?' I asked.

'Lemme see…sure, it's Sunday. No…it's Tuesday.'

I nodded. 'I only asked, because in England people usually get married on a Saturday.'

He seemed surprised. 'If we tried that here, the priest could never pack them all in. Eileen here got the afternoon off from the tourist shop, and we hired the band, and away we go.'

Away we went indeed. Later that night the guests danced in the ballroom. I have never seen a priest doing the Twist before, but he did it very well. The whole hotel vibrated slightly for most of the night and there seemed no point in going to bed.

I remembered that evening in fragments next morning as I flogged round to Sligo town in the rain. Sligo town sits snugly astride the Garavogue estuary, the River Garavogue draining Lough Gill. By local standards Sligo is quite a large town with a population of some 16,000 who inhabit the usual mixture of narrow streets lined with terraced houses, pubs and small shops. There is a harbour, now only half full of fishing boats, but this was once a great port.

Long before that Sligo was the capital for the Fitzgerald family, a Norman brood who came across with Strongbow at the end of the 12th century. Sir Maurice Fitzgerald founded Sligo Abbey in 1252, but this was destroyed by a Puritan general during the rebellion of 1641. The ruins by the river are impressive, and I spent a little time there before setting out for the hill of Knocknarea.

Knocknarea is a small hill, only 1,076 feet high, but most people who visit Sligo make the time to climb it. I found that out when I couldn't find the path from the road to the summit and banged on the door of a small cottage. Before I could open my mouth, the lady who opened the door said, 'It's half a mile up on the left.' Sure enough, half a mile up the road a track led to Knocknarea.

The top of Knocknarea is flat and open but crowned with that massive nipple-shaped cairn I had seen from Drumcliff the day before. This is actually one of the biggest burial mounds in Ireland, has yet to be fully excavated, and like most such things in Ireland, is a source of legend. I met a man huddled on the leeward side who told me the cairn was the burial place of Queen

ABOVE *Sligo's long and eventful history began in the 9th century, when the site was first settled. During medieval times the town was strategically important, the estuary serving as a gateway between Connaught and Ulster; today Sligo is a bustling market town.*

Maeve, ruler of Connaught in the 1st century AD, and that she had been buried upright, ready to spring to life at the last trump. I hate to spoil a good story but it is more probably a passage grave, a good deal earlier than the 1st century AD.

Out in Sligo Bay I could see the green hump of Coney Island. This takes its name from the fact that it was once infested with rabbits, or coneys, and gave its name across the Atlantic to Coney Island near New York City; so, carried in the cramped holds of the immigrant ships, did memories of Ireland slip across to the New World. I turned west and took a good look at the Ox Mountains, which lay across my route to Ballina and Mayo. Coming off the hill I was advised by another walker not to leave Knocknarea without visiting 'the Glen'.

I found 'the Glen' tucked away at the end of a muddy path, halfway down the mountain. It is a ravine slashed into the rock, only thirty feet wide but nearly a mile long and somewhat eerie. There was no sound there but the patter of the rain, and lush green vegetation sprouted from every nook and cranny of the rock. This was worth seeing, but it took time so I struck out fast for the point where the main road across the Ox Mountains heads south over the moor towards Easky Lough.

A TREASURE HOUSE OF LEGENDS

THE IRISH ARE BLESSED with one of the world's richest treasuries of myths and legends, which were passed down orally for centuries until the Christian era, when monastic scribes wrote them down. Scholars have now classed them into four major groups or cycles.

The Mythological Cycle centres around the Tuatha de Danaan, a supernatural people who are said to have ruled Ireland until they were defeated by invaders called the Milesians and disappeared into 'fairy mounds'. They then became identified with the fairies, or 'little people', of whom the leprechaun—the crotchety shoemaker who owns a crock of gold—is the best known.

One of the cycle's most poignant stories is the 'Children of Lir', which tells how the four children of King Lir were turned into swans by their jealous stepmother, Aoife. After 900 years, the children were released from their enchantment—but found that their

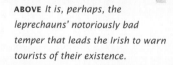

ABOVE *It is, perhaps, the leprechauns' notoriously bad temper that leads the Irish to warn tourists of their existence.*

LEFT *Finn MacCool is one of the most celebrated of Irish heroes. Leader of the Fianna warriors, he was famous for his fighting skills.*

RIGHT *The Danish Gundestrup cauldron is believed to depict the 'Cattle Raid of Cooley', a legend about Cuchulain and Queen Maeve.*

The Ox Mountains are not very high, running up to some 1,600 feet, but they are very open and wet and quite without shelter. Their main spine straddled the road, but lay to my right for the first few miles. After that I came over a low rise and skirted the eastern shore of Easky Lough, a great expanse of empty, wind-ruffled water. I trudged across this empty moonscape, ducking into my hood when the storms swept past, quite content to be out here on my own.

A mile or so past Easky Lough I turned off across the moor and began to climb a little. Apart from shinning up Knocknarea, I had now been on the go all day and was starting to flag. I came onto the main road to Ballina, still six miles away. Enough was enough. I found a wayside B & B, took off my boots on the doormat and hopped my way in towards the tea and scones.

RUNNING TO PARADISE

There is a wonderful sense of space out here on the west coast of Ireland. Few countries in the world can offer such varied scenery or such gloriously empty country—I often hardly met a soul all day. The valleys are wide and the hills not

bodies had become weak and shrivelled by time.

Of the remaining cycles, that of Ulster revolves around Cuchulain, Ireland's greatest hero; the Kings' Cycle is based on legends of Ireland's ancient kings; and the Fenian Cycle features the hero Finn MacCool and his warriors, the Fianna. One famous Fenian tale describes how Ossian, Finn's son, returned to Ireland from the Land of Youth, not realising that 300 years had elapsed. When he touched Irish soil again, the years that had not aged him in the Land of Youth suddenly turned him into a withered old man.

But Ireland's most famous legend is the 'Cattle Raid of Cooley' from the Ulster Cycle, which pits the powerful Queen Maeve of Connaught against Cuchulain of Ulster. Jealous of her husband Ailill's magnificent white bull, Maeve decided to steal a rival animal for herself, the famed brown bull of Cooley, in Ulster. Although Ulster's warriors had

been struck ill by an evil spell, Maeve's armies were initially baulked by Cuchulain, who could alone kill 100 men with his sling. But eventually Cuchulain was fatally wounded, and Maeve took the bull. Her triumph was short-lived, however: the brown bull soon killed Ailill's white bull, then, itself mortally wounded, returned to Cooley to die.

LEFT The alluring Queen Maeve, who went to war with her husband Ailill because of a bull. Maeve is said to have been wedded to nine kings in her lifetime, who reigned by virtue of their marriage to her.

RIGHT This statue in the Garden of Remembrance in Dublin depicts the Children of Lir, who were turned into swans for 900 years by their jealous stepmother.

too high. I am not a great lover of mountain ranges, because they make me feel hemmed in. Ireland is just about right, with enough hills to make the scenery interesting but plenty of glorious views.

Once across the Ox Mountains I descended gently, on a bright, fresh morning, to the green limestone plain that surrounds Ballina. The town, the largest in County Mayo, straddles the narrow estuary of the River Moy which runs for six miles to the sea on Killala Bay. Sleepy Ballina is a pleasant place, with a population of about 6,000. The main street is the usual mixture of small shops, cafés and pubs. I had a lunchtime drink and a look at the map in a pub in the High Street,

and set off south again towards Castlebar. Before I got there, though, I made a stop at the Mount Falcon.

The Mount Falcon Hotel is a few miles south of Ballina. Here, so rumour had it, the owner was a real character. If I was stopping anywhere in Mayo, they all said, then I had to stop at the Mount Falcon and meet Mrs Constance Aldridge, but I had better hurry because Mrs Aldridge had been eighty-six for as long as anyone could remember, and you never knew, did you? I therefore hurried down beside the Moy and was soon crunching up the gravel drive to the door.

I could see at a glance that this hotel was not as other hotels. The car park was full of cows placidly licking the raindrops off the assembled vehicles. I skirted the cows, opened the front door and was instantly submerged in a flood of spaniel puppies.

Mrs Aldridge, who was within, told me later that she was 'very good at puppies', and this indeed seemed to be the case.

ABOVE *Constance Aldridge welcomed the author to the Mount Falcon Hotel* (top) *in her own inimitable style.*

Mrs Aldridge had lived in Mayo since her husband left the army and they decided to open a hotel. They bought the Mount Falcon estate, fields and herd, river fishing and large house in 1932.

'We set up as a fishing hotel,' she said, 'and we only wanted fishermen. Their wives could come if they could fish, but no children. Of course we have children now, if they behave, and we get a lot of foreigners: Italians, French, German, some Americans, but not so much to fish because some idiot dredged the Moy and the fishing is not what it was.'

The Mount Falcon still had the feel of a fishing hotel. Behind the heavy front door lay a vast hall off which led various rooms full of comfortable furniture, though every chair was occupied by a spaniel. The bedrooms had unusual names: there was 'The Brigadier's', the 'Over the Kitchen', the 'Yellow Carpet', and the 'Far Corridor'. The honeymoon suite was 'Above the Dining Room'.

The hall was a litter of green wellies, Barbour jackets and wet puppies, while antlered heads of long-shot stags gloomed down from the rafters. The

'Help-Yourself-on-Honour-System' bar was in the larder, and all the guests dined together around a long refectory table with Mrs Aldridge as the matriarch sitting at the top. We dined very well that night on roast beef, which Mrs Aldridge carved at the sideboard, knives flashing. Everyone was very careful to keep their elbows off the table and clear their plates.

Halfway through dinner there came a tremendous crash from above, and a thud that shook the ceiling. Apart from muttering 'Honeymooners!' Mrs Aldridge made no comment.

I spent a very cosy evening at the Mount Falcon, dipping into books and talking to the other guests. Most of them were there for the fishing and had come back for the umpteenth time. When I went to bed, well after midnight, Mrs Aldridge was still going strong and rounding up the guests for a game of cards. Just before I dropped off there came another crash as the honeymooners' bed fell apart again.

Next morning all was bustle. The cows were chased out of the porch and a litter of puppies raced out of the door and fled yelping across the lawns. The hall was full of people gearing up for a hard day's touring or going fishing, packing up their picnics and Thermos flasks, selecting flies, debating on the certainty of rain. Mrs Aldridge stood in the middle of all this, sturdy as a tree, giving orders and advice, sweeping down upon me like a ship in full sail.

'You must go there. I insist. You cannot miss it … Not there, you silly girl—there, in his lunch. I've put in some hard-boiled eggs. Catch that dog … too late! Are you off? Well, you should stay two nights. It takes two nights to get used to this place. Well, if you must … Come again, but do try to book in advance … I'll always fit you in but you must be more responsible.'

Duly chastened, I slunk off into the rain.

By staying at the Mount Falcon I had already gained some distance on that day's walk towards Castlebar and it was easy walking to the south, down first to the breezy shores of Lough Conn, and then south across the bridge and islands that run like a causeway between long Lough Conn and the small, pretty Lough Cullin. Once across the causeway, I could go south, along the road to Castlebar, or northwest, round the shore of Lough Conn and up Glen Nephin for the narrow track that climbs towards Castlebar through Windy Gap. This last was a bit longer but more picturesque, and since Windy Gap is mentioned in a poem by Yeats, 'Running to Paradise', there was really no contest.

> *As I came over Windy Gap*
> *They threw a halfpenny into my cap,*
> *For I am running to Paradise.*

So west it was, running to Paradise. I slogged up the empty winding road to Windy Gap, which the wind came roaring through to buffet me about. I made my way up the hill and round the stone cross on the col. A river cascaded along to my left, and not a car passed as I made my way down the far side of the hill, over the pond- and stream-littered plain towards Castlebar.

THE GREAT HUNGER

Castlebar is the county town of Mayo and about the same size as Ballina, which is to say it is really a rather large village. Even so, there is a fine big church at the top end of the High Street and a great open park in the centre, the celebrated Castlebar Mall.

This Mall contains the grave of John Moore, who was the Provisional President of the Republic of Connaught in 1798. This was at the time when a force of 1,000 troops from Revolutionary France, under General Humbert, landed at Killala Bay and defeated the troops of the English General Lake—a rout that has gone down in Irish history as the Races of Castlebar.

Although General Humbert was soon defeated, this invasion proved the decisive factor in prompting the Act of Union between Ireland and Great Britain in 1800, which set independence back 100 years. It also saw the end of one of the great heroes of the Irish independence struggle, Wolfe Tone.

Wolfe Tone was a Dublin Protestant who helped to found the United Irishmen in 1791. This was a secret organisation, dedicated to making Britain grant Irish independence, but also, as the name implied, to uniting all the Irish people, Catholic or Protestant, into this common cause. Thousands of United Irishmen went to join Humbert's small army, but the result was disaster. After Humbert's defeat, the French survivors were shipped back to France, but the captured Irishmen were hanged as traitors. A British squadron also captured a French frigate with Wolfe Tone aboard and he cut his throat in prison rather than die on the gallows. He remains one of the great Irish patriots, and his aim of replacing Catholic and Protestant with the single name of 'Irishman' is one that should be revived.

Castlebar was a place I wanted to see because it has associations with the Bingham family, better known as the Earls of Lucan. One Lord Lucan, the third earl, was involved in the disaster that befell the British cavalry when the Light Brigade charged the Russian guns at the Battle of Balaclava during the Crimean War. Lord Lucan was commanding the Cavalry Division with an incompetence matched only by that of his detested brother-in-law, Lord Cardigan, who commanded the Light Brigade. Lord Cardigan actually led the fatal charge down the 'Valley of Death', but his antipathy towards his superior officer and brother-in-law played a part in the disaster.

There was also another reason for putting Castlebar on my itinerary, a more serious one: Castlebar was one of the many places stricken by the Irish Potato Famine—the Great Hunger—of 1845-9.

The British visitor today, learning about the Hunger in the place where it actually happened, discovers the full extent of the tragedy with a terrible and shameful impact. The tumbledown, roofless cottages, the shuttered, abandoned hamlets, the sheer loneliness of the countryside through which I had passed

ABOVE *The Irish patriot Wolfe Tone was captured by British forces in 1798, an event illustrated in this late 19th-century engraving. Tone was later tried in Dublin for treason, but committed suicide before he could be hanged.*

recently and was to pass through in the weeks ahead, can all be traced directly back to the Hunger. In Castlebar it can be traced to the actions of the third Earl of Lucan.

Lord Lucan—George Charles Bingham—was born in 1800, the year of the Act of Union. He was a professional soldier, or as professional as any soldier needed to be in the decades after the Napoleonic Wars, which is to say he knew and cared more about pretty uniforms than the management of men. By a series of purchases he became lieutenant-colonel commanding one of the smartest cavalry regiments in the British army, the 17th Lancers—'Bingham's Dandies'—by the age of twenty-six.

Lord Lucan's family had made their mark as soldiers in Ireland, in the days of Queen Elizabeth I. They had since acquired the baronetcy at Castlebar but, like many others, the Lucans were absentee landlords. They kept an agent whose task was to wring as much money as possible out of the tenants and send it to England. They themselves rarely ventured across the Irish Sea.

In the same year that he purchased the command of the 17th Lancers, Lord Lucan was returned as Member of Parliament for Mayo. Lucan's election was gained with the aid of votes in the gift of another landowner, a Major Fitzgerald. The major had been offered a 'comfortable appointment in a good climate' as his reward for polling his tenants' votes in Lucan's favour.

The Irish have always had a somewhat cavalier attitude to the exercise of democracy. To this day, it is necessary to issue warnings before polling day against 'personation'—the practice of appearing at a polling booth under various names to cast several votes for one's favourite candidate. One of the sayings in Ireland as polling day approaches is a reminder to 'Vote Early and Vote Often'.

Ten years later, in 1837, Lucan relinquished his command of the 17th Lancers and retired on half pay to his estates in Ireland. The move was necessary. Revenues from rents had fallen steeply in the last ten years and something had to be done. Since the turn of the century the Lucans' agents had been the O'Malley family, but Lucan was not satisfied that the O'Malleys were paying over all they collected.

THE HUMBLE POTATO

BELOW *All hope of sustenance gone, an Irish peasant family survey their blighted potato crop in despair in this painting by Daniel McDonald from c.1847.*

RIGHT *Potato blight, or Phytophthora infestans, which caused the Great Famine of Ireland, can be seen here as dark brown marks on the skin and flesh of the potato.*

ABOVE *Sir Walter Raleigh oversees the planting of the first potato crop in Ireland on his Myrtle Grove estate at Youghal.*

ACCORDING TO LEGEND, the 16th-century explorer Sir Walter Raleigh planted the first potatoes in Ireland at his estate in Youghal. At first, Raleigh made the mistake of eating the berries; not surprisingly, he found them unpalatable, and ordered his gardener to root out the plant and throw it away. As he pulled it from the ground, the gardener discovered the tuber—which went on to become Ireland's national dish.

Within 100 years, potatoes were a staple in the Irish diet, and by the mid-1800s the peasantry were dependent on the vegetable to an astonishing degree. They did eat small amounts of fish and vegetables, but consumption of potatoes was huge—male labourers could tuck in to 14 pounds of potatoes a day (today's

ABOVE *The Irish produce potatoes by the sackload, and they appear in one form or another at most meals.*

RIGHT *If you try the crude, illicit spirit known as poteen, expect to be punished...by a crushing hangover.*

average consumption is about half a pound). Despite the monotony of their diet, the Irish were better fed than many in Europe, and no one foresaw the disaster that was about to hit the country. In 1843 a new disease—*Phytophthora infestans,* or potato blight—was noticed in the United States. Two years later the blight reached Ireland. A fungal disease, blight rots the potato's flesh, transforming a nutritious food into a mass of brown mould. Requiring damp conditions for germination, the blight spread rapidly

in the cool, wet Irish summer of 1845 and by October a third of the nation's crop had failed. The following year saw total crop failure, and people began to starve. Even an abundant crop in 1847 wasn't the end of the famine: blight struck again in 1848, leaving perhaps a million people dead by the end of 1849.

Despite the fact that failed potato crops were responsible for a famine that still haunts the Irish memory, potatoes remain a popular dish in Ireland today. Potato cakes, soup and colcannon—a creamy concoction of potatoes, milk, butter and onions—are typical. Renowned more for its effect than its taste, however, is poteen, an Irish spirit distilled illegally in hidden stills. Once a keen competitor with licensed whiskey, poteen has the rare distinction of being one Irish potato product for which demand is now drying up.

In all this Lord Lucan was quite correct. The estate was a visible shambles and heavily in debt. The accounts reluctantly provided by the O'Malleys were both confused and inaccurate, so the O'Malleys were sacked.

None of this might have mattered much. It could have provided an amusing incident in rural Irish life, but the situation on Lord Lucan's estate was anything but amusing, for the state of Ireland in the 1840s was that of a disaster sliding inexorably into a catastrophe. There were no major industries to provide regular employment, and few trades outside the linen mills of Ulster. The destitution of the ordinary people was absolute and yet the population was soaring. It exceeded 8 million, nearly 40 per cent more than Ireland supports today.

The bulk of these people were tenant farmers, living on a few acres of field and bog, and their poverty and ignorance beggar description. In the Bingham fief of Castlebar in 1845 only seven people could read. Hardly anyone could afford shoes. Barefoot men and women stood ankle-deep in mud on the Mall when Lord Lucan rode by with his hounds. There were few schools outside the main towns, a lack of good roads, no system of trade or distribution, hardly any shops. Work for wages was rare, subsistence farming the common lot, and very poor subsistence at that. If he could not pay his rent, the tenant and his family were thrown out to starve. Even paying the rent was no security. If a tenant improved his farm, the landlord might evict him without compensation in favour of another farmer who could pay a higher rent. Only in Ulster did the—mainly Protestant— tenants have any rights at all.

The peasants lived by their fields, in cabins or mud huts or even in holes dug out of the bogs. Their ramshackle homes contained a peat fire, but they had rarely more furniture than a stool and a bed on the mud floor. In this squalid habitation large families lived with their animals, sleeping side by side with the pigs.

As the population increased in the 1830s and 1840s, the landlords' answer to the pressure on the land was that employed in other agricultural nations: to consolidate the small subsistence farms into larger, more economic units which would produce crops for money while providing work for wages. At Castlebar, the earl simply evicted his tenants, men and women, children, babes-in-arms, old folk; he threw them onto the streets to starve. Distrustful of the Irish peasants, he brought in Scots farmers to take over the unoccupied land and sent hired gangs of men called 'crowbar gangs' about the country to pull down any hovels his late tenants might have managed to put up for shelter. No one interfered with this action. Indeed, honours were heaped on Lucan's head. In 1840 he became a Representative Peer for Ireland. In 1845 he even became the Lord Lieutenant of Mayo, the county he was tearing to pieces.

The peasantry lived where they could and how they could and for a time they kept themselves alive on the potato. Then, in the summer of 1845, the potato crop failed.

The potato blight was first reported in America in 1843. In Ireland in 1845 the first indications for the potato harvest promised an abundant crop, but when the first potatoes were dug in September it was evident that the blight had arrived there, too. Potatoes rotted away swiftly. One-third of the crop was lost. By the winter of 1846 half the population of Ireland was starving.

Accounts written at the time make horrifying reading. Mr Cummings, a Cork magistrate, wrote to *The Times* in December 1846:

> On entering a deserted hamlet I went into some hovels to discover the cause…In the first, six famished ghastly skeletons were huddled in a corner, four children, a woman, and what had been a man. All had fever. Within minutes in that village I was surrounded by at least 200 such phantoms. My clothes were nearly torn off by this throng and in a nearby house the police found two frozen corpses, half devoured by rats. In a field lay the body of a girl of 12, dead of starvation, half covered by stones.

When the facts began to emerge in Britain there was a wave of public sympathy and large sums of money were swiftly raised for relief. Queen Victoria gave the

FAR AND AWAY

MILLIONS OF PEOPLE around the world claim Irish descent, and for the past three centuries emigration has been a characteristic of Irish life. It is only in the last 40 years, as Ireland has achieved economic stability, that the past torrents of departures have dwindled to a mere trickle.

From the 18th century people began to leave Ireland to find their fortune in young lands of opportunity, such as America, Canada and Australia. It was these first emigrants and their descendants who later provided refuge for their Irish relatives at the time of the Great Famine. When potato blight struck in 1845, emigration became a matter of survival rather than a search for prosperity.

Financing a passage out of a starving country was only the first of many problems the emigrants encountered. The journey itself was often life-threatening as overcrowding and unsanitary conditions propagated disease among the already weak passengers. On arrival, masses of unskilled and poorly educated men and women flooded into the cities to search for work which was often scarce. Thanks to the support of the Irish community abroad, however, many of the newcomers went on to find success.

It is a happy reversal of fortune that, 150 years on, many people of Irish descent are choosing to return to the land of their ancestors. Ireland is now a dynamic and flourishing country, bursting with home-grown talent, and those who choose to try their luck abroad today often do so with every intention of coming back some day.

ABOVE AND RIGHT *During the Great Famine Irish ballads (right) recorded the tragedy and despair of hundreds of families forced by hunger to leave their homeland on overcrowded emigrant ships.*

then-huge sum of £2,000, and her gift was followed by large sums from philanthropists and the Society of Friends (Quakers). Shiploads of Indian corn were sent across to replace the potato, soup kitchens set up, work on the roads for wages was offered, accommodation in workhouses was provided for the destitute. Yet none of this did more than scratch the surface of the problem, for the roads, the railways, the methods of distribution to get food out to where it was needed, simply did not exist.

While the Irish starved the evictions continued. In March 1846, 300 people were evicted from their homes at Ballinglass in Galway. In April an eviction in Tipperary was carried out by the police and the army, though it is reported that soldiers from the 49th Infantry were disgusted and gave the people money.

Those who could emigrated in search of work, but in 1846 another scourge had appeared: typhus. The emaciated men and women arriving at English ports brought with them a deadly fever which thrived in the crowded tenements where they were forced to live, and the Irish were now on the move in considerable numbers. Over 300,000 arrived at Liverpool in the first five months of 1847, more than double the resident population of the city.

Before long, Irish immigrant ships were being turned away from British ports. Tens of thousands took flight across the Atlantic to Canada and the USA, sometimes in ships so badly built that they became known as coffin ships. Shiploads of emaciated and destitute people crawled into ports along the eastern seaboard to horrify the American and Canadian people. Here, too, many immigrants were already stricken with typhus, so quarantine stations were set up. In the spring of 1847 at Grosse Island, the quarantine station near Quebec, there was talk of 'an avalanche of diseased and dying people' in numbers far beyond the capability of the doctors sent to help. By the time the quarantine station closed six months later, over 5,000 people had died.

It was not just the famine and disease that ravaged the Irish people. It was the total lack of care or kindness. People who should have helped, who had the duty of helping, did nothing, or as little as possible. What little they did, they did with great reluctance. That many hundreds of people—officials, charity workers, landlords, people of goodwill in many lands—did help cannot be disputed, but the government of Britain, to which Ireland was joined by the 1800 Act of Union, was either indifferent or reluctant to face the multiplying problems in Ireland.

When the figures were added together later it was estimated that at least a million Irish people died of disease or starvation during the years 1845–9. This must be an underestimate because thousands of deaths were never recorded. People died on the roads or in the fields and rotted away in the bogs or ditches. On the far west coast whole communities simply disappeared.

Another million people too had fled abroad, taking with them hard thoughts about the British government and people who had let their families and neighbours perish. The deep hostility towards Britain still found today in the Irish communities of America and Australia can be traced in large part to the hungry years of the 1840s.

ABOVE *Ration cards were distributed to the starving poor during the Great Famine, but they were an inadequate solution to such a protracted and widespread disaster.*

CHAPTER FOUR

IN THE
STEPS OF
ST PATRICK

I LEFT CASTLEBAR, on a bright and blustery morning, for the twelve-mile walk down the main road to Westport, a fine little town set in splendid country on the shores of Clew Bay. The bay is a litter of small, green islands, a picturesque natural harbour, one of the largest on the west coast. The entrance to the inner bay is protected by Clare Island, while the whole bay is overlooked to the south by Croagh Patrick, the Holy Mountain.

I was in Westport by noon, and by two I was out on the Louisburgh road, looking up at the peak of the mountain. There were people up there on the path, creeping up the steep rocky slope to the summit. Everyone who can climbs the Holy Mountain, at least if they are Irish.

There are a lot of pilgrim sites in Ireland of which the pilgrimage to Knock is the most recent, and the pilgrimage to Station Island on Lough Derg in Donegal is the most rigorous. This is the St Patrick's Purgatory Pilgrimage, on which the pilgrims have to spend three days barefoot, fasting on the island, and take part in an all-night vigil. This is to reproduce a measure of St Patrick's sufferings, for he fasted on the island for forty days. He did the same on Croagh Patrick, but modern pilgrims get up and down in hours.

At the top of the mountain are a small chapel and a pilgrim summit cross all hung about with rosaries. As for the reason behind this pilgrimage, it is said that, having climbed up here, St Patrick prayed and fasted for forty days. Then, at his command, when he rang his bell, all the snakes and venomous creatures in Ireland flung themselves off the southern precipice. It may be so. There are no snakes in Ireland. True or false, this story attracts some 30,000 Irish pilgrims to climb the mountain on Garland Day, the last Sunday in July. Many people climb barefoot,

LEFT *St Patrick looks down on picturesque Clew Bay from Croagh Patrick, where the saint once fasted for the 40 days and nights of Lent.*

ABOVE *Over the years thousands of pilgrims have climbed the rocky path up the Holy Mountain to attend Mass on the summit.*

ABOVE *This ornate shrine holds the bell St Patrick is said to have used to drive all snakes out of Ireland.*

though the path is rough and, for the last 100 yards or so up the scree to the summit, positively dangerous.

At 2,510 feet, Croagh Patrick rises directly from the seashore. There are three Pilgrim Stations on the way up, where pilgrims must stop and circle the Station several times, reciting the Creed or 'Hail Marys'. On this day there were only about fifty people on the mountain, most of them—thank God and St Patrick—more than willing to stop for a chat while I leaned over my stick and fought for breath.

For a while the path up Croagh Patrick follows a rushing brook. Then it gets steep and rocky, climbing up a well-eroded track about ten feet wide which leads to the centre col. Here the southeast face of the summit comes suddenly into focus, soaring up to a rounded shark-fin tip, the rocks glittering white against the sky. Silver granite scree rises steeply to the summit with no visible path up and nothing to stop you falling all the way to the valley far below if you should slip.

I trudged across the flat part of the col, and exchanged words with the priest, who climbs this mountain several mornings a week. I was soon on the lower edges of the final slope, trying to find some path. Since I could not even see the summit and there was this yawning void to my left, I made my way up by climbing gingerly across the jumbled scree towards anyone I could see on the slope above. One of these was a lady in a yellow anorak, who was sitting on a rock smoking.

'How far is it?' I panted, trying not to look down to my left.

She waved her hand vaguely over her head. 'Just keep going…it's there, it's there. This is my third time up and my last, you know. Enough's enough, you know, isn't it?'

THE CHURCH IN IRELAND

FROM THE 5TH CENTURY AD until the 16th century, when Henry VIII founded the Church of England, there was only one religion in Ireland: Roman Catholicism. But with Henry's break from Rome, the ruling English elite in Ireland followed suit, creating the Protestant Church of Ireland. The repressed Irish peasantry, however, remained Catholic.

In the early 1600s, to strengthen their hold on the rebellious province of Ulster, the English 'planted' there large numbers of Protestant English and Scots settlers, on land confiscated from Catholics. In 1695 new Penal Laws repressed the Catholics further. Although their lot improved in the late 18th century, it was not until the formation of the Irish Free State in 1921 that Catholics became the ruling order.

In today's Republic, Catholics—who comprise over 90 per cent of the population—now live harmoniously with their Protestant neighbours, and the Catholic Church is still a major influence in society. Yet its

standing has been increasingly buffeted by the secular winds of the modern world. Although the visit of Pope John Paul II to Ireland in 1979 drew thousands to open-air Masses, it could not mask the fact that church attendance was in decline. At the same time, the Church has had to face up to a number of contentious ethical issues: in the 1990s it could no longer stop the legalisation of divorce or restrict the right of a woman to have an abortion abroad.

In Northern Ireland the religious picture is very different. There, with Catholics making up just over one-third of the population, religion has fused with cultural and political history to fuel the long-standing confrontation between the Protestant Unionist and Catholic Nationalist communities.

ABOVE *Children play in the shadow of an impregnable wall in Belfast: Catholics on one side, and Protestants on the other.*

In Belfast and other cities the two sides often live in their own areas, rigorously maintaining their separate traditions. For many Catholics, religion acts as a powerful reminder of their minority status and their separation from their co-religionists in the Republic. Conversely, for many Protestants—the majority of whom are descended from Presbyterian Scots—religion helps to stiffen their resolve to remain part of the United Kingdom.

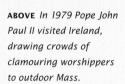
LEFT *The 9th-century cross at Clonmacnoise dates from a time when Catholicism was Ireland's only religion.*

ABOVE *In 1979 Pope John Paul II visited Ireland, drawing crowds of clamouring worshippers to outdoor Mass.*

LEFT *Young Catholic girls, dressed in white to symbolise their 'marriage' to Christ, walk to their first Holy Communion.*

RIGHT *The Protestant Cathedral of St Patrick's in Dublin, dating from the 12th century, is Ireland's largest church.*

I didn't know at all but this question clearly required some comment. 'This is my first time, and my last,' I said. 'I'm getting too old for this sort of thing.'

'Ah well, you see, I have my reasons,' she said, pausing significantly. 'I wouldn't be here otherwise.'

The Irish are like that. Give them half a chance and they settle down for a crack, even on the side of a sheer slope and in the teeth of a howling wind. Did I mention the wind? Sparks were pouring from the lady's cigarette and the wind was trying to tug me off the rock. Irish winds are strong, but when they stop blowing the clouds rush in and the rain comes down. You can't have it both ways.

'Why is that?' I asked. 'What reason can it be?'

'Well, you see, himself always wanted a boy. We had the girls but we wanted a boy and, I thought, I'll try anything. I was that desperate, so we made the pilgrimage to St Patrick last year and sure enough we had a boy… he's nearly ten months old now.'

'Well done,' I said.

'Then himself said we should come up again for Mass, to thank St Patrick… So we did—the whole family.'

'How many children have you?' I asked.

'Five. Four girls and now a boy.' She got up off the rock and began to look for a safe way past me.

She had gone a few steps when a thought struck me and I had to shout after her. 'You said this is the *third* time… are you wanting another boy?'

She stopped with a rattle of scree and edged round to look back up at me. 'God, no! This is to tire the man out… five children is enough for anyone. He's up there, lying in a heap. You can't miss him. Tell him to hurry along.'

'I see.' Another thought occurred to me. 'And what did you call the boy?'

She gave me one of those great, wide Irish grins. 'Patrick, of course,' she said. 'What else?'

ON THE HEIGHTS OF THE HOLY MOUNTAIN

Patrick of course; what else? St Patrick is as much a symbol as he is the patron saint of Ireland, for Ireland is a place where a name can be a statement. In the North, for example, if you meet a man named Pat and another named Billy, you don't need to ask which is the Catholic and which the Protestant.

St Patrick was born in Britain when it was still under the rule of the Roman Empire, some time around 400. When he was about sixteen he was captured by Irish pirates and remained a slave for ten years before he managed to escape to France. Some time during his captivity he got the idea of bringing Christianity to the pagan Irish so, after studying theology, he returned to Ireland in 432 as a missionary. The Irish were then devoted to the Druidic religion, but the Druids seem to have put up no great resistance to Christianity, and the Irish kings were interested.

The new religion spread, and by 444 St Patrick had built the first cathedral at Armagh, a town that is still the centre for the Catholic Church in Ireland. By the

RIGHT *Crowds gather outside Dublin's General Post Office—the rebel headquarters during the uprising—to view the damage caused by gunfire.*

BELOW *Irish nationalists fighting for a republic defiantly flew this banner from the roof of the General Post Office.*

time he died in 461 the entire country was Christian. The Christian religion was so strongly established in Ireland that it was here, on the western fringe of Europe, that Christianity survived the various pagan invasions that swept away the Roman Empire during the 5th and 6th centuries. Thanks to St Patrick and the Irish monks and saints, clinging on in remote abbeys and on lonely rocks, Christianity survived. Even civilisation survived, and from Ireland it eventually spread back across the barbarous lands to the east.

The Irish (or Celtic) Church, which had by now spread to Scotland and Northumbria, found itself in dispute with the Church of Rome, notably over the date of Easter, but after that matter was settled by the Synod of Whitby in 664, it slipped under Roman rule and has remained there to this day, the longest-serving member of the Christian faith. No wonder the Reformation failed to take root here, and no wonder the Protestants fear the enduring power and influence of the Irish Catholic Church, however unreasonable those fears may be in practice.

Just thinking about St Patrick brought me gasping and panting on a final rush to the summit, though I was overhauled on the last few yards by four young men who came swarming up the scree slope like fell runners. They had, they told me, done it for a bet. They were students from Dublin, up here for the weekend. They had decided to climb Croagh Patrick after a few jars in the pub at Westport Quay, and but for running into me they would probably have nipped up and down Croagh Patrick in about ninety minutes.

The views from the summit were glorious, though in that wind it seemed wise to stay away from the edge of the drop. I could see the green mass of the Partry Mountains to the southeast, Clew Bay and the beckoning bulk of the sharp little hill on Clare Island. The five of us sat out of the wind in the lee of the chapel and had a good chat before starting down.

BELOW *This poster, a contemporary example of Republican propaganda, depicts 14 leaders of the 1916 Easter Rising—plus two more shown in portraits behind the group—at an imaginary signing of the Proclamation of Irish Independence. All the men were executed by the British government.*

There was some talk of going to the pub, but they had a long drive back across Ireland to Dublin, and Irish roads are not the sort you can hurry on. They came roaring past as I was walking back into Westport, and a great blast on their car horn ushered me into town.

HEROES OF WESTPORT

Westport has many Georgian buildings and, unlike most Irish towns, is quite pretty. The River Carrowbeg flows through the town centre and under a couple of bridges along a tree-lined promenade known as the Mall. The Mall is endowed with a bronze bust of Major John MacBride of the IRA, who was shot for his part in the Easter Rising of 1916.

It will be recalled that when the Home Rule Bill was finally passed in 1914, the implementation of the Act was deferred until the First World War ended. This deferment found no favour with a number of Irish politicians, and by 1916, with no end to the war in sight, some leaders of the paramilitary Irish Volunteers, including John MacBride, decided to implement the Act immediately and declare the Irish Republic, on Easter Monday 1916.

It all went terribly wrong. Eoin MacNeill, the actual commander of the Irish—or Southern—Volunteers, was not informed but got wind of the Rising and put notices in the paper cancelling any 'manoeuvre' planned for the Easter weekend. Even so, the Rising went ahead. By Monday morning the Volunteers had captured all the important buildings in Dublin and set up their HQ in the General Post Office. They then fired on a cavalry patrol, and fighting gradually spread across the city. The British army promptly moved in and during five days of fighting the heart of Dublin was severely damaged. Artillery was deployed in the streets and a Royal Navy gunboat sailed up the Liffey to bombard the General Post Office. On the Friday, the General Post Office was surrendered and the other strongpoints fell shortly afterwards.

Most of the Irish people saw the Rising as a betrayal of those tens of thousands of Irishmen then fighting Germany on the Western Front. This disapproval disappeared when the British military gave the leaders a rapid court-martial and had them all shot. John MacBride, the husband of Yeats's unrequited love, Maude Gonne, was rather unlucky to be shot. He had only taken a minor part in the Easter Rising, but he had fought on the side of the Boers against the British during the South African War and that was enough to tilt the balance against him. MacBride's bronze bust glares defiantly at passers-by along the Westport Mall.

That evening I had to hurry past it, because I had an appointment with another local hero, Matt Molloy.

Matt is famous in Westport, partly because he owns 'Matt Molloy's' pub in the main street, but mostly because he is a member of Ireland's leading folk group, the Chieftains. At Matt Molloy's, food and music and a good crack are always available, and mercifully without such modern gimmicks as slot machines and piped music.

IRISH MUSIC

DISTINCT FROM mainstream folk, pop, rock and jazz but an increasing influence on each, Irish traditional music has its own unique sound. Core instruments include the fiddle; the accordion; the uillean pipes (akin to bagpipes); the flute; the tin whistle; and the *bodhrán*, a goatskin drum beaten with the knuckles or a short stick. There are also the guitar and banjo and, more rarely, the harp— an instrument commonly found in Ireland from medieval times until the 17th century and which is currently enjoying a revival.

Although traditional music can be heard live all over the world, at Irish *fleadhs* (festivals), and

ABOVE *The harp is one of the symbols of Ireland; this 14th-century example in Trinity College, Dublin, is the oldest in the country.*

in concert halls, it is in local smoke-filled Irish pubs that it seems to find its natural milieu. Gigs, or 'sessions', are informal, semi-improvised affairs, when musicians launch into a repertoire of toe-tapping jigs, reels, slip jigs and hornpipes that sound as intricate as ancient Celtic knotwork. There may also be a solo singer, whose unaccompanied laments for doomed love affairs, long-departed heroes and the travails of emigration add an emotional tinge to the evening. The tunes and songs are all part of a tradition stretching back hundreds of years and passed down orally until the late 18th century, when the words and music began to be written down for posterity.

The modern revival of traditional music started properly after the Second World War, particularly through the work of

BELOW *Traditional Irish music is often played informally in pubs; typical instruments include the accordion, banjo and fiddle.*

Sean O'Riada (1931–71), whose group Ceoltóirí Chualann gave birth to the Chieftains, the best-known exponents of Irish music. Formed in 1963, the Chieftains have performed all over the

'What would we want a slot machine for?' he said. 'It would only cost money better spent on Guinness, and if they want music we have that from about nine or ten every evening. We have some good local musicians and anyone can sit in and play—if they're not actually quite awful that is.'

Irish music is a feature of most Irish pubs, certainly in the countryside. The Irish are a very musical people and produce a great many skilful musicians, enough to provide most of the country pubs with a resident group. The basic instruments are the fiddle and the flute and the accordion and concertina, backed up by the *bodhrán*, which is a shallow drum not unlike a tambourine, with goatskin on one side. The harp which, with the shamrock, is the most famous symbol of Ireland, is apparently quite popular too, but I never saw one. Folk groups, on the other hand, can be heard everywhere, playing away for hours every evening if provided periodically with glasses of Guinness. The music tends to be of the lilting repetitive kind that jogs along in a heart-warming way, and it adds a great touch of gaiety to any evening in the Irish countryside, broken up with singing.

LEFT *A medieval lady plays the tympan, an ancient Irish stringed instrument played with a bow. The illustration is taken from the 12th-century manuscript* The Topography of Ireland *by Gerald of Wales.*

LEFT *The Chieftains are perhaps the best-known exponents of Irish music. Formed in 1963, the band play traditional instruments, but their musical arrangement and interpretation are modern and innovative.*

world, winning prestigious awards for their work. They have also collaborated with artists from other genres, including Van Morrison and Marianne Faithfull, showing that traditional music can fuse with rock and pop to produce successful hybrids. This was certainly the case with Clannad, whose dreamy, lyrical style transcended musical boundaries, as well as with the ex-Clannad singer Enya. But many other Irish groups have blended their traditional heritage with rock and pop, from Thin Lizzy in the 1970s, to U2 a decade later and the Corrs in the 1990s.

RIGHT *The Green Note music shop in Kinmare, County Kerry, stocks all manner of musical instruments, CDs and books.*

The singing, on the other hand, tends to be doleful. Most of the songs concern people who are dead or drowned or gone away, and there is always the danger that any stranger will be asked to join in a chorus or even get up and entertain the company with a song of his own.

One of the nicest things, though, about an evening in an Irish pub is that there never seems to be any trouble. Whenever I go into pubs in England there always seems to be a hint of menace from some crop-haired yobbo in the corner who goes to a pub in search of trouble. In contrast, Irish drunks are Irishmen writ very large and very friendly.

If the Irish need lubrication, Guinness fits the bill. I suspect that half the attraction of a pint of Guinness is the ritual that goes with it. To begin with, you don't pour a pint of Guinness, you 'build it', pouring in more of the black nectar as the white foam collar creeps slowly up the glass. This can take ages, so committed Guinness drinkers will order their 'pints of plain' well ahead, like a special dish on a fancy menu. Then everyone sits around with foam on their upper lips, telling each other how Seamus or Eamon pulls the best pint of plain in town.

IRELAND'S BLACK NECTAR

THERE IS IN DUBLIN a secular shrine at which all Ireland worships: The Brewery. From its hallowed portals emerges a drink that is known affectionately as the Parish Priest—partly because of its appearance, with its black body and white collar, but also, one assumes, because of the succour it provides. The name it is now known by worldwide is, of course, Guinness.

Guinness is the product of a rich combination of hops, yeast, water and the all-important roasted barley brewed in a single barrel. The connoisseur will insist that numerous conditions have to be right to ensure the perfect pint: temperature, distance between cask and tap, consistency of flow, and, of course, the slow, gentle pouring of the stout from tap to glass.

ABOVE *The creamy white head and dense black body of a pint of Guinness have become an unofficial symbol of Ireland.*

LEFT *Guinness's health-giving properties have traditionally been championed in its often humorous advertising.*

It was in 1759 that the enterprising Arthur Guinness started brewing his own brand of 'porter', a drink already well established in England as a favourite tipple of porters. By the mid-19th century Guinness was hugely popular, and The Brewery, as the Irish refer to the drink's home, expanded to become the largest in the world. Today Guinness is brewed in over 50 countries and supped in 150, although there are many who insist that the Guinness brewed in Ireland has a distinctive taste unmatched beyond the country's shores.

Regardless of where it is brewed, Guinness has always been promoted as a wholesome drink: 'GUINNESS IS GOOD FOR YOU' was for many years a successful advertising slogan. Rich in iron, it was recommended to nursing mothers, while in parts of Africa it was believed to boost male virility. Others swear by an extravagant cocktail of champagne and Guinness—Black Velvet—as a cure for hangovers.

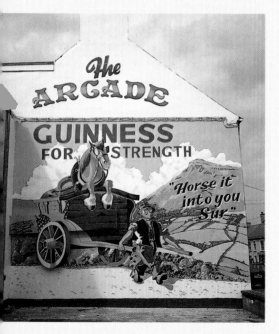

THE WILD COUNTRY

Next day I headed west along the coast for the wild country of Connemara.

On every journey I have undertaken, there is one place, one part of the country, that remains in my mind as superior to any other, a place that remains in my memory when the rest of the journey has become little more than a blur. On this journey through Ireland that place is the beautiful lake-and-mountain country of Connemara.

Summer was well into its stride as I came to Connemara. The first purple flush of heather was beginning to appear on the hillsides, the gorse was flaring in the hollows out of the wind, and the lanes were heavy with drooping fuchsia and bright orange montbretia. Even the bogs were looking their best, with a thatch of golden grass covering each like a blanket. All this stood out against a lush emerald-green backcloth and the loom of purple mountains.

I run ahead of myself; first I had to get to Connemara, and that took a day or two. Part of the attraction here in the west of Ireland is the desolation, and the road to Connemara is almost empty of people. I made good time along the coast road from Westport on another breezy morning, looking up to cloud-capped Croagh Patrick. The road rolls gently up and down beside the sea and leads to Louisburgh, a pretty little town or large village, once notorious as the home of the 16th-century pirate queen, Grace O'Malley.

Out here in the west of Ireland Grace O'Malley kept her own estate as Queen of the Western Isles and successfully ignored the English rule for decades. She built a castle on Clare Island and kept a fleet of ships in the bay to do her bidding, which meant preying on English shipping. If she needed laws she had the old Irish law—the Celtic *Brèhon* law—to fall back on. This was a code of ethics, suitable to Irish life, for it was based not on the edicts of a central power but on the wishes and needs of the community. It covered sanctions against the fostering of disorder and made provision for the settling of disputes by arbitration, all of which seems very sensible. It also permitted divorce at will: Grace O'Malley married several times and usually managed to retain the joint property after divorcing her husbands. Women held a high status under the *Brèhon* laws and this gave Grace enough confidence to act as an equal with the imperious English Queen Elizabeth I when the Queen complained about the O'Malley pirates.

Grace O'Malley's castle at Louisburgh is now in ruins, but the tale goes that after years of seizing English ships and pursuit by English admirals, Grace eventually sailed up the Thames to parley with Queen Elizabeth at Westminster. They struck a deal, by which Grace would hunt pirates off the coast of Clare as the price for keeping her lands. Grace is believed to be buried at the abbey on Clare Island.

My view south to the Twelve Pins of Connemara from the top of Croagh Patrick had been blocked by other mountains: the Mweelrea Mountains to the south and west, and the Sheeffry Hills which lie directly south, across the twinkling, water-logged plain of north Mayo. Southeast of there lay Joyce Country. This is a region of great beauty, but not an easy one to cross, being barred by hill and mountain, river and stream, dotted with lakes and carpeted with blanket bog.

ABOVE *A plaque bearing the O'Malley crest in Clare Abbey commemorates the famous pirate queen, Grace O'Malley. She ruled the 'wild west' of Ireland in the 16th century, and is said to be buried at the abbey.*

ABOVE *The tranquil waters of Lough Corrib, bathed in golden light from the setting sun.*

This part of Ireland, the land between Castlebar in the north and the city of Galway on the great bay, is virtually an island. To the west lies the Atlantic, while to the east the rest of Ireland is barred by two long loughs, Lough Mask and Lough Corrib.

In the 17th century these two loughs and their tributary rivers at first protected Connemara from the full fetch of the Cromwellian invasion, and they still protect this part of Ireland from the English language. Over here lies part of the Gaeltacht—the land of the Gael—where Irish is still, just, the common tongue of the country people, and where many of the people are descendants of those who were forced to flee here in the 17th century when the stark choice before them was flight or death, to 'Hell or Connaught'.

At the end of the previous century, during the Tudor planting period, the native Gael had been driven off the best land in Ulster and the east of Ireland. In September 1641 the dispossessed Irish peasants rose against their oppressors, first forming a league known as the Confederation of Kilkenny. The Protestants were greatly outnumbered by the Confederates, and they were quickly overwhelmed. There were, inevitably, atrocities. The best-remembered Catholic outrage against the Protestants took place on the bridge at Portadown in Ulster, when 100 Protestants, men, women and children, were hanged from the parapet, flung into the river to drown, or had their brains dashed out as they swam ashore. The Protestants of Ulster still remember this.

The Confederation of Kilkenny had the limited aim of repossessing the planted lands, but their confrontation with the current landowners eventually sucked the Irish Confederates into the English Civil War. Irish troops went to the aid of King Charles I and played a major part in all the King's battles, even though Irish soldiers captured by the Parliamentarians were routinely shot.

In August 1649, seven months after he had defeated and beheaded the King, Oliver Cromwell turned his attention to the rebellious Catholics of Ireland. What followed was so devastating that 'Mallacht Cromail'—the Curse of Cromwell—is an Irish imprecation to this day.

By 1652 all Ireland lay at Cromwell's feet, but he had still not finished with the Irish people. They were hunted across the moors and bogs like wild beasts, or deported or hanged or shot or beaten. Amnesty was eventually granted to Irish men of military age if they left Ireland for ever. Those who chose to remain were to be driven out of their homes and harried west beyond the Shannon into Clare and the stark boglands of Connaught—the present Mayo and Connemara—where they had to fend for themselves or starve. Their former lands were taken and sold to pay the cost of Cromwell's campaign, or given to Puritan veterans as a reward for their services.

Those who resisted were killed or imprisoned and then sent into bondage to Barbados. It was even a crime for a native Irishman to be found inside the walls of cities such as Dublin and Cork.

The migration had to be completed during the six months of winter and there was nowhere in Clare or Connaught for the people to go. There were no huts or habitations, no towns or villages, no shelter of any kind. The people could stay and die or go and starve. It was said at the time that in County Clare there were not 'trees enough to hang a man, water to drown him, or earth to bury him', while Connaught was, and is, the most unfertile of all the Irish provinces. Its present beauty cannot conceal the fact that it still provides a very thin living for the local farmers. The land is stony, the fields small, the soil scanty. Only sheep and goats can survive.

As for the people who took that trail of tears to Connaught, they simply vanished. Some, perhaps most of them, eventually filtered back across the Shannon, but tens of thousands simply disappeared, swallowed up in the moors and mists of this beautiful, desolate and tragic countryside.

ABOVE *A notorious example of sectarian violence in Ulster's history was the massacre of Protestants in Portadown in the early 1640s. It was partly in response to this event that Oliver Cromwell went on to persecute Irish Catholics.*

CROSSING CONNEMARA

From Louisburgh it is a good day's walk south to Leenaun, a small fishing port at the end of Killary harbour. Killary harbour is a ten-mile-long inlet off the west coast with a few curraghs, the traditional Irish punts or canoes, drawn up on the pebble strand. I walked south to Leenaun by the pass through the Sheeffry Hills and the Mweelrea Mountains, past Doo Lough.

ABOVE *Three fishermen carry their traditional fishing vessel, a curragh, to the water's edge ready for a day's work. Made from wood and canvas and waterproofed with black tar, these simple boats have been used by west-coast fishermen for centuries.*

Emerald-green mountains reared up ahead and the road rose and fell across a golden-yellow open moor littered with small lakes and streams. I walked south towards the pass for most of the morning and the mountains grew steadily closer. These are real mountains, tall and jagged, lush green from the rain-nourished moss but thickly dotted with sheep. So, gaping at the beauty about me, I entered Doo Lough Pass.

After Doo Lough comes Delphi, at the southern end of the pass, an unlikely name in such a setting, a pretty spot with a salmon fishery. The road then winds between the Mweelrea Mountains and Bengorm, a 2,303-foot-high peak, to the sea lough of Killary harbour. Here I turned east for Leenaun. The road is set above the sea and there was a seal dipping and diving for fish along the shore.

The road takes a hairpin bend round to Leenaun, past the point where the River Erriff flows into the sea. Here is another pretty spot, the river, dotted with fishermen, winding away into the backdrop of green hills. I had come about twenty miles that day, and therefore came to a much-needed halt at the Rock Café.

The Rock Café is one of those Irish places where you can get anything from a glass of beer to tractor parts. The local priest was in there, drinking Guinness and playing dominoes, and while I was drinking my tea two farmers drove up with tractor and trailer. The latter contained a large blackface ram, which whiled away the wait by butting the door of the trailer. Periodic thuds from the car park therefore played counterpart to my conversation with the farmers, as we sat at the bar and drank tots of Paddy, the local Irish whiskey, mixed into a toddy with hot water, sugar, lemon and cloves.

'That's a fine ram,' I offered as an opener. 'What sort of sheep do you run here?'

The green hills of Connemara are full of sheep, which are dotted over the moors or run or rest along the roadsides, or cover the mountains all the way up to the crests, so I was interested to know where they came from.

'We keep Scots blackface…they're hardy, and you can leave them on the hill whatever the weather.'

'Well, almost,' said the other. 'Unless we have the snow, but we don't have the snow very often.'

'You are not from these parts?' asked the first farmer, signalling the bar lady for another round of the hard stuff.

'No…I'm from England. Just here for a walk…a little holiday.'

I had given up telling people I was walking across Ireland. The Irish are great leg-pullers and most of them would not have believed me anyway.

'England, is it?' they marvelled. England was a remote place, somewhere men vanished to and never returned. 'Whereabouts in England is it?'

'Near London.'

'London, is it?' They thought about that for a moment, nodding the idea through before one of them asked, 'Do you keep sheep yourself?'

Did I look as if I kept sheep? Glancing in the mirror behind the bar I took in this wild-haired, wet fellow staring back at me, so yes, probably I did look as if I kept sheep. I got around that by discussing the matter of my lamb back on the Sperrins road in Ulster and the price I had been asked for it.

That interested everyone and the bar became animated. The price was difficult; my new-found farmer friends became very cautious over the price. Did I know if it was a ewe lamb or a ram lamb? Well, since I didn't, they couldn't tell if it was a fair price or not, and since I didn't have the lamb with me it was even more difficult. However, there was no money in the sheep these days, so I was better off without it. We all agreed on that.

Next day the Twelve Pins, or Bens, of Connemara came in sight—a barrier and a challenge. The Pins are mountains which rise to the 2,000- to 2,300-foot mark, and are dangerously attractive.

I longed to walk across them but I knew that they were a wet and springy slough of blanket bog. So I stuck to the road that leads south and skirts them.

BELOW *The snow-covered Twelve Pins of Connemara glint brightly in the sun. Even in the summer, however, the peaks look white: their quartzite stone has evolved over time into a light grey mineral called silica.*

CONNEMARA: A PRECIOUS WILDERNESS

LEFT *Connemara's landscape of bogs, mountains and lakes is wild and bleak, but possesses a haunting, unspoilt beauty.*

BELOW *The moorland of Mayo and west Galway is the only place in the British Isles where this pretty heather, St Dabeoc's heath, is found.*

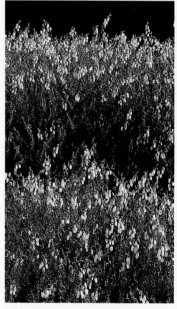

CONNEMARA NATIONAL PARK, a romantic land of granite mountains and myriad lakes and bogs, finds a fitting symbol in the graceful, agile Connemara pony. Roaming half-wild on the harsh coastal terrain, where pasture is scarce, the ponies grow hardy by grazing on a mineral-rich diet of seaweed and salt-tolerant grasses.

LEFT *The Connemara pony is descended from ponies that have lived in the area for thousands of years.*

Much of the 5,000 acres that make up Connemara National Park is covered by blanket bog and heath, creating habitats for red deer, a host of smaller mammals and a wide variety of birds, such as peregrines, merlins and stonechats. Rare marsh and moorland plants thrive in the park, including St Dabeoc's heath, a heather that grows nowhere else in the British Isles. Connemara was designated a national park in 1980, in recognition of its ecological importance and its breathtaking beauty.

Among the park's scenic wonders are a majestic gorge carved out by the Polladirk River and four mountains in the range known as the Twelve Pins: Bencullagh, Benbrack, Muckanaght and Benbaun, the highest in the range at 2,400 feet. Evidence of early human habitation can be seen in the remains

LEFT *The diminutive merlin is slightly smaller than its close relative the kestrel, but far rarer. Connemara provides it with a peaceful home.*

of 4,000-year-old tombs, and in cultivation ridges marking former grazing areas and arable fields.

In the 19th century much of the park lands formed part of the estate of Kylemore Abbey, a neo-Gothic mansion now run as a school by Benedictine nuns. Another part of the park was owned by one Richard Martin. Inspired, perhaps, by the wild and noble creatures around him, Martin was an early campaigner for animal rights, for which he earned himself the nickname 'Humanity Dick'.

Connemara is all rock and stream and blanket bog, as springy as a mattress, bouncing under your boots as you pass over it with water squirting up at every stride. This is fun for a while but you can't do the distance that way. Once off the road my feet were wet within twenty paces. Within 100 yards I would sink in to my knees. After half a mile of that I would crawl back to the road, where I would change my wet socks for a dry pair and set off once more for the south. That was a small inconvenience and did nothing to spoil the walk. I was almost alone out here in the wild, with just the occasional car and solitary fisherman to share this beauty with me and the sheep, and I liked it that way.

How people make a living here beats me, but it's lovely. I passed a few fishermen from Britain or Germany, say one every three or four miles, but otherwise there was not a soul to be seen in this empty landscape. The wind blows in constantly from the ocean, so there are few trees, and another result of this incessant breeze is that the gorse, instead of growing into tall bushes, survives here as ground cover, a yellow carpet clinging closely to the soil. It was now the end of July and the land was a tapestry of colours: purple heather, golden gorse, blue lakes and sky, green hills and yellow or red bog grass, great grey rocks and boulders spattered by green and yellow lichens, all of this picked out in that clear Atlantic light. Quite marvellous. I can think of nowhere so beautiful as Connemara in summer.

I got to Cashel on a wandering route from Killary Bay, coming round Tully Mountain and Ballynakill Harbour, then up the long track lined with piles of drying peat, past the old quarry by the River Traheen to Loughanillaun, and then over the moor by Cregg Hill, working my way round the radio mast on top—the best landmark for miles around—plunging into a stream or two and then passing over the River Owenglin.

The Owenglin is fast and shallow but varied, foaming over green rock at one point, dropping into deep, still pools a few yards further on. Like most of these west-coast streams, this is a salmon river, divided into beats, and there were more fishermen here, wading thigh-deep in the water or casting their flies from the banks.

I stopped for tea one afternoon at the Ballynahinch Hotel, where a great salmon lay breathing its last on the scales in the drawing room, and a day later I came slowly round the shore of the inlets off Bertraghboy Bay, and up the gravel path to the Cashel Palace Hotel. Five days from Louisburgh across this splendid Connemara countryside, and every one a delight.

At Cashel I went a bit up-market. The Cashel Palace Hotel is one of the great country-house hotels of Ireland and a very swish place indeed, but fortunately this is swish in the Irish fashion, which is to say they don't mind mud-spattered eejits turning up unannounced and standing in a spreading pool of water in their foyer. Deep down the Irish have a fondness for an eejit. Once my wet socks and anything else that needed a 'once-over-lightly' had been sent to the hotel laundry, I was sent a pot of tea and a plate of soda bread and scones. After a wild and windy day on the moors, all this luxury was delightful, as good a way as any to finish another day in Connemara.

ABOVE *The author found Connemara's boggy terrain heavy going, but the wild beauty of the place proved ample compensation for his soggy socks.*

ACROSS THE GAELTACHT

WHEN I GOT TO CASHEL I had been on the road for nearly four weeks. Hence the need for a small celebration and some time for a little assessment. This was longer than I would usually have devoted to such a distance. If I put my foot down, I can normally cover between 500 and 600 miles in four weeks, and Ireland is only just over 300 miles from end to end. This allows for the curious fact that Irish miles are, or at least were, much longer than English miles. The 'Irish mile' is 2,240 yards, the English mile is 1,760 yards. Nowadays they have converted to kilometres in the Republic, but many signposts give the distance in miles as well. Are these English or Irish miles, I would ask myself, and end up confused. Confusion arose because I seemed to be doing an awful lot of walking and making very little progress.

The reason is that Ireland is not the place to rush about in. Getting anywhere seems to involve going round a mountain or a lake, or up the road to the bridge over the river, and my original calculations had been based on the idea that I could nip across the tops and through the valleys like a leprechaun. As it was, I had a good two or three weeks to go unless the terrain became a good deal more helpful.

I was frequently confused in Ireland. When I arrived at Cashel I thought I was still in Connemara, but when I woke up the next day I found myself in Galway. This is because Connemara is not a county, but the name given to the western part of Galway. Also, a large part of this area, certainly in the south of Connemara and western Galway, is part of the Gaeltacht, so Irish names began to appear exclusively on the signposts. I was getting right into the heart of western Ireland now, well away from any form of tourist route.

I set off from the hotel next morning, but within half an hour I was lost. This is not hard to do in Ireland, for the maps are very little help. Indeed, one of the sights at every Irish crossroads is a driver brandishing a map and shouting at his wife. Perhaps it was the sight of one of these incidents that distracted me from paying closer attention to the route, for instead of cutting across the throat of the Ardmore peninsula and quickly hacking off the five miles to Gort, I found myself five miles south in quite the wrong direction. I was down near Carna on the coast before it registered that I had gone wrong.

Well, no matter. The Connemara countryside was just as lovely here. I became almost gleeful, not least because nobody knew where I was to within 100 miles. That brought a great sense of freedom; I strolled along, swinging my stick and shouting 'Mint sauce!' just for the hell of it and to worry the sheep.

LEFT *Undeveloped and desolate, Connemara's rugged coastline refreshes the eye and restores the spirit.*

Then I got fed up with roads and decided to cut into the hills for some soft ground and a decent walk. A long ridge runs north from Ardmore, back up to Gort, the sort of sharp-edged ridge that appeals to people like me. Besides, in spite of the bogs lurking up there, I had done enough on roads. This hill above Ardmore was a fine ridge, soaring like a wall to about 1,000 feet above the sea, and while I knew it would be boggy, I thought it would go. Go it did, and I nearly went with it.

The other purpose of climbing this ridge was to get a good view south, over Galway Bay and out to the Aran Islands. This whole coastline is a spectacular region, indented with bays and inlets, very wild and desolate, decorated offshore with a litter of small islands. The Aran Islands, which straddle the entrance to Galway Bay, act as a buffer to the full fetch of the Atlantic, and I hoped to get a view of them from the top to see if I could spot ferries hurrying from one island to another. If so, that meant that island-hopping down Galway Bay was a possibility, and I could save the time I must otherwise spend flogging round the shore.

Getting onto the ridge was easy enough, for a rough track ran up the east face of the hill. Once up I decided to keep well away from the edge and sploshed my way north, harried along by strong gusts of wind and rain. I saw a hare, and several large hawks hovered off the ridge, riding the wind. Black crows were blown past, flying down the wind like scraps of crumpled paper. It was a roaring day and I loved it.

Stone cairns dotted the various small peaks and I went from one to another as I tacked my way north. After days of trudging along roads, just to be up on a hill on soft going was exciting. Then it got rather too exciting.

I had walked nearly 1,200 miles in my current pair of boots, but never before on a really steep wet hillside, so maybe that was the problem. On the other hand, maybe I was too busy enjoying myself or just not paying attention to the footing. Whatever the reason I was walking down a steep slope close to the edge of the ridge when my boots shot from under me. Suddenly I was skiing. One leg shot off on its own, pushing the other leg into a knee-wrenching position, and I took a heavy fall. When I stopped rolling down the slope I was only a few feet from the edge of the cliff. I got up, somewhat shaken…well, all right, very shaken, took another step forward and did it again. But for my stick and the rucksack I would have toppled right over the edge. A great gap appeared at my side and scared the hell out of me. I rolled over and decided to crawl back to level ground. It seemed the safest way to get there.

The problem appeared to be the sloping, cut-away heels on my boots. Many modern walking boots have this feature: the idea is that the cut-away heel offers more protection from road shock than the sharp-edged-heel variety. This may well be true, and every little helps when walking on roads, but nothing is worse than walking on a steep hillside, unsure of your footing. It makes a chap nervous. Nor was this an isolated incident. I fell three or four more times when coming down the north face of this hill.

I got off the hill eventually and sat in the lee of a wall somewhere near Derryrush to rest my throbbing knee.

The sun came out, the wind dropped and I took an hour for another trawl through Irish history from the ever-growing library of books I had assembled in my rucksack.

THE TRIUMPHS AND TRAGEDY OF PARNELL

During my journey through Ireland I had begun to get the hang of Irish history, but what I still did not understand was *why* the Irish had not long since given up the struggle to get rid of the English. After all, the Scots—and I am a Scot—gave up biffing the Sassenachs (English) in 1603, by getting their own king on the English throne. They then took over most British institutions and ran large parts of the British Empire.

The Irish, on the other hand, don't want to manage anyone but themselves. That's what Sinn Fein means—'We Ourselves'—and this seems to sum up the nature of the Irish people. Because they are cheerful and friendly and easy-going, there is a tendency to think that the Irish are just like the other nations in that collection of countries we call the British Isles. But the Irish have eluded most of the formative influences that shaped Britain: the Romans and the Saxons, for example.

The Irish are therefore a distinct people—almost a tribe. They may look like other European people but their attitudes are different, and they like it that way. I once asked a friend of mine, Seamus Redmond, if it would have made any difference if the English had treated the Irish with more kindness over the centuries, but he shook his head. 'It would have made no difference what they did: we just wanted to be left alone.' Being left alone was the mission of the Fenians.

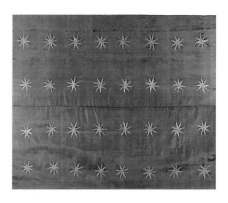

The Fenian Brotherhood—named after the 'Fianna', the Irish warriors of legendary times—was not formed in Ireland, or not exactly. The idea was Irish-American. By the middle of the 19th century, millions of Irish people had emigrated to America where, nursing their numerous wrongs, some of them set up a movement in 1859 to establish the Fenians in the 'Auld Sod' as an undercover organisation, sworn to evict the English from Ireland and establish a republic.

This aim soon made the Fenians vastly unpopular with the Catholic Church. The priests linked Republicanism with anti-clericalism, and urged the people not to support the movement. The Fenians staged an abortive rising in 1867, but when that failed they became involved in a much more popular movement, the Land League. The Land League was founded in 1879 with the sensible aim of land reform to benefit the tenant farmers of Ireland. The Land League enjoyed considerable success, partly because it was generally non-violent, not least because it had as its president a charismatic speaker and shrewd Parliamentarian, one of the great Irish statesmen, Charles Stewart Parnell, Member for Meath.

By the terms of the Act of Union, the Irish constituencies now sent 100 Members to the Westminster Parliament, enough to sway the voting in critical issues, and Parnell handled the Irish Party like a set of weights, putting their votes now with the Liberals and now with the Tories, not just ruthlessly or cynically, for he was a bigger man than that, but the votes usually went to whichever party would help Ireland. He even compelled the Westminster Parliament to buy the land of Ireland back for the Irish people, and where money failed to tilt the balance and achieve the sale, Parnell did not hesitate to act.

One of the most successful tactics used to squeeze out the consolidating landlords was the 'boycott'. This was first used against a certain Captain Boycott on lands for which he was the agent in County Mayo, and his name stuck to the process. 'Boycotting' meant sending the person involved to social and commercial isolation. No one would deal with him, speak to him, sell to him or buy from him. Even workmen were forbidden to work for him and, strictly enforced, the 'boycott' proved a powerful weapon. The Land Acts provided the money to buy out the landlords and, if they refused, a boycott would make them change their minds. Taken together, this was a situation few landlords could endure.

The Land Acts have had an enduring effect on the Irish landscape, which still supports a great number of small and only marginally economic farms. On the other hand, it has kept the land free from the clutches of agribusiness, besides creating a race of stubborn, decent, country people.

Having won this great victory for the tenants, Parnell then rode on the crest of this success towards his next aim—Home Rule.

Parnell almost got it. In 1886 his Home Rule Bill was introduced at Westminster. Then he made the fatal mistake of falling in love with a married woman, Kitty O'Shea, whose husband cited him in a divorce case—a great scandal for any public figure in Victorian times. He was execrated by the Irish Church, and the Irish Members rejected him as leader in 1890. Worn out with the struggle, Parnell died suddenly in 1891, and then, too late, his countrymen rushed to honour him.

He now has a statue in his memory at the end of O'Connell Street in Dublin where the inscription states the aims of his Home Rule policy: '*No man has the right to fix the boundary to the march of a nation.*' Under Parnell, the Irish nation had marched much nearer to their goal of independence. Had he lived longer and been supported, a great deal of the subsequent bloodshed might have been averted, for Parnell was both a Protestant and a landowner, a human bridge between the factions.

A LITERARY DETOUR

From my lodgings by the crossroads at Derryrush to the harbour at Rossaveel is a reasonable day's walk. My wrenched knee was still playing up, so I took my time over it, making a diversion to visit Patrick Pearse's cottage at Rosmuck,

RIGHT *The traditional whitewashed thatched cottage is a rare sight in Ireland today, but near Rosmuck the cottage of Patrick Pearse, leader of the Easter Rising, has been well preserved for posterity.*

partly because this is one of the few genuine examples left of west coast cottage architecture, and partly because Patrick Pearse is another Irish hero. Patrick Pearse and his brother William were both shot for their part in the Easter Rising of 1916.

Patrick Pearse spent his boyhood holidays over here in the Gaeltacht, where he strove to learn Irish. Pearse believed that if the Irish language were to die the people would lose their identity. He joined the paramilitary Irish Volunteers in 1913 and at Easter 1916 he led 2,000 Volunteers into Dublin and began the rebellion. As 'Commander-in-Chief of the Forces of the Irish Republic', he held the General Post Office against the British army for five days before surrendering.

Patrick Pearse's cottage is a small, snug, whitewashed building, quite unlike the modern bungalows that now litter the west coast of Ireland and do nothing to enhance the scenery. Some of their embellishments may comfort the occupiers but the effect is not pleasing. A bungalow with Doric columns at the door is a bunga-

low still, and only buildings like Patrick Pearse's cottage really look right in this wild Connemara landscape.

I had come out of the hills now and was on the open breezy plain on the north side of Galway Bay, crossing a countryside that was seamed with streams and rivers and dotted with ponds and lakes. It was quite beautiful and, even so close to Galway city, was still practically deserted. I was passed by the occasional car, or saw the lone fisherman here and there, but for the most part I was on my own, walking south towards the glimmer of the sea.

BELOW *Kenny's Bookshop in Galway is famed throughout the land as a treasure trove of books, both old and new; it also houses an art gallery.*

After Pearse's cottage I marched past the village of Costelloe, where a radio station broadcasts in the Irish language to the people of the Gaeltacht, down to Rossaveel, from where a fast ferry leaves for Inishmore, the nearest and largest of the Aran Islands. The service is irregular and I was damp and soon became cold with hanging about. I therefore found a B & B where I changed my wet clothes for dry ones. Then I took a bus into Galway, heading for Kenny's Bookshop.

The Irish are a literate people and I had heard a lot about Kenny's Bookshop, which is still run by the Kenny family, and is a book-lover's mecca. It extends over several floors and has new books, secondhand books and, at the back, an art gallery. Even better, the people behind the counter actually know about books and make a point of getting to know authors. Those walls not covered with bookshelves are plastered with the signed photographs of grateful writers whose books have flowed across the Kenny counters.

Words are the basis of Irish culture. Indeed, the Irish language—Gaelic—contains the earliest surviving collection of written European literature after Greek and Latin and dates back to the 5th century. Compared with Gaelic, the

ABOVE *The earliest surviving manuscript of Irish literature—Lebor Na Huidre or The Book of the Dun Cow—was written in Clonmacnoise before AD 1106.*

Anglo-Saxon tongue is an also-ran, but when the Irish use English they still seem inspired. I think this must go back to the bardic tradition, when Ireland was a land of poets and harpists. The Irish language went into decline when its use was suppressed under the Tudors. 'Hang all the harpers, wherever found' was one of Elizabeth I's most savage instructions, but it was probably a wise one, for the harpers sang the soldiers into battle as easily as any Highlander's pibroch.

Well, if Irish was suppressed, the Irish people have made good use of English. Think only of Wilde, Yeats, Shaw, Joyce, Beckett, Swift and Synge, to name just a few who have transformed the English tongue. Dublin has produced three winners of the Nobel prize for literature, and is the only city I can think of that devotes a day every year to the celebration of a literary character. This is Joyce's Leopold Bloom, and 'Bloomsday', held on June 16 every year, sees crowds crossing Dublin in period dress, celebrating Bloom's progress that day with copious draughts of red wine.

Galway is a big city by Irish standards, with a population of some 57,000. I had not been in a city for weeks and I found the traffic a problem. The traffic usually is

LITERARY IRELAND

WHEN OSCAR WILDE once remarked that 'we Irish are too poetical to be poets', he was not to know that during the 20th century Nobel prizes for literature would be awarded to the Irish poets W. B. Yeats (1923) and Seamus Heaney (1996) as well as to the Irish playwrights George Bernard Shaw (1925) and Samuel Beckett (1969). For a small country, Ireland has produced a disproportionate number of literary giants.

The first major Irish writer to express himself in English—as opposed to Gaelic Irish—was Jonathan Swift (1667–1745). Dean of St Patrick's Cathedral, Dublin, Swift was a brilliant satirist whose best-known work, *Gulliver's Travels*, is an ironic exposé of contemporary vices. The 18th century also saw a clutch of fine dramatists, especially Oliver Goldsmith and Richard Brinsley Sheridan, whose comedies still sparkle around the world.

Towards the end of the 19th century a number of Irish writers, led by W. B. Yeats, sought inspiration from Irish myth and folklore in a movement known as the Irish Renaissance. In 1904 Yeats helped found the Abbey Theatre in Dublin which, in 1907, shocked audiences with *The Playboy of the Western World*, a new play by J. M. Synge. Born in County Dublin, Synge had lived on the Aran Islands to

ABOVE *On Bloomsday—June 16—fans of James Joyce re-enact scenes from* Ulysses *and follow Leopold Bloom's route around Dublin.*

RIGHT *Contemporary novelist Edna O'Brien uses her experience of a convent education and Catholic upbringing in her work.*

a problem in Ireland, for the people like to park their cars in the middle of the road or stop there for a chat. Cars can come at you from several directions, so it pays to be wary and light on your feet. I explored the city unburdened, dodging about the lanes and byways, poking into the small shops. After the spaces of Connemara it made a change. This is the county town of Galway and the principal city of the old province of Connaught, and lies at the foot of the salmon-rich River Corrib. To the east of it lies the great limestone plain of Galway and Clare, running all the way south to the Shannon. Though it is a late addition to the list of Irish towns—it was founded in the 13th century by the Anglo-Norman de Burghs, or Burkes—Galway later became the foremost port on the west coast of Ireland when there were strong trade links with Spain. There are still fair-sized ships moored along the quays, but the city has never really recovered from the two savagings it received in the 17th century, first from Cromwell's army and then from the army of William of Orange in 1691.

I had a good afternoon in Galway, lunching in McDonagh's Fish Restaurant in Quay Street, where the McDonaghs have been buying and selling fish for four

LEFT *An outdoor production of* Gulliver's Travels *relates the story of the shipwrecked hero on an island of midgets.*

RIGHT *The Abbey Theatre now puts on well-received performances of the once controversial* The Playboy of the Western World.

get to know the life of the Irish peasant—a knowledge reflected in his work. But *The Playboy*'s cold scrutiny of Irish society and its 'immoral language' led to riots in the theatre. Audiences reacted angrily, too, to Sean O'Casey, whose *Juno and the Paycock* (1924) and *The Plough and the*

Stars (1926) critically examined Irish nationalism during the Troubles. The 1920s also saw the publication of *Ulysses*, the mould-breaking novel by James Joyce, who spent much of his life outside Ireland. Describing a day in the life of a Dubliner named Leopold Bloom, *Ulysses*

caused as much stir for its stylistic innovations as for its moral content.

In the late 20th century, Irish literature continues to flourish through such writers as Maeve Binchy, Roddy Doyle and Edna O'Brien. Born in County Clare, O'Brien is best known for her first three novels, *The Country Girls* (1960), *The Lonely Girl* (1962) and *Girls in Their Married Bliss* (1963), which explore the difficulties faced by young women growing up in an Ireland dominated by staunch Catholic values.

LEFT *Words appear to come easily to the Irish, and they have excelled in just about every literary form.*

generations, sitting in Eyre Square for a quiet read or sheltering from the rain in the 14th-century church of St Nicholas, which contains memorials to the Lynch family, who may have given their name to 'lynching'. The story goes that in 1493 the leader of the Lynch clan, Judge James Lynch, sentenced his only son, Walter, to death for murder. When no one could be found to carry out the sentence, Judge Lynch hanged his son himself.

I prefer the wide naves of St Nicholas to the more modern Roman Catholic cathedral of Galway, which was dedicated in 1965. Most of the old town of Galway lies between St Nicholas's and the docks around the Spanish Arch which was once the sea gateway through the town walls. Down here lots of narrow streets and alleyways are lined with little shops, cafés and bars to create a colourful area where the sound of street music is heard everywhere, played by local musicians on a great variety of instruments from flutes to drums.

ABOVE *Galway is a vibrant and colourful city. Young people in particular are attracted to its active folk scene and plethora of entertainment venues.*

Galway has been a great trading city since the 16th century, when there were strong trade links with Spain, and it is experiencing a revival today, partly from tourism. In and around Galway I often heard Gaelic spoken in the shops and streets and found it used on its own on shop fronts and signposts. I had even begun to get the hang of some of the Irish words. *Kill* or *cill* means a church, as in *Cill Chiaran* or, in English, Kilkieran; *cashel* means a castle and *slieve* a mountain.

Gaelic was the majority tongue in Ireland until the early years of the 17th century, and widely spoken in the countryside within living memory. It was even adopted as the national language after independence in 1921, but without success. Efforts are now being made to teach the language in schools and to use it in public on signs and documents.

The Galway Gaeltacht consists of the Aran Islands, the small villages of Connemara and southern Mayo and parts of the land along the north shore of Galway Bay. These areas are served by that Gaelic-speaking radio station I had passed on the road near Costelloe and by Gaelic summer schools which teach the tongue to people from all over Ireland. It is a gentle, lilting tongue, and I hope it never dies out.

THE ARAN ISLANDS

The three main Aran Islands, Inishmore, Inishmaan and Inisheer, lie like a barrier across the entrance to Galway Bay, presenting steep cliffs to the Atlantic. They are said to contain the last intact remnants of Gaelic culture. From photographs I could see that they were the most curious places, a great litter of stones supporting one of those tight-knit communities that seem quite common on the west of Ireland.

Another such Galway community, now dispersed, was the Claddagh, a community of fishermen who once lived on the beach—the Claddagh—close to Galway city near the present port. The natives lived in glorious isolation until quite recent times. One relic of the Claddagh folk is the Claddagh ring, a thick gold band which was handed down from mother to daughter, and examples of these can still be found in Galway shops. If the Claddagh folk have gone, those on the Aran Islands still preserve their identity. Or so I had heard.

The ferry trip out to Inishmore from Rossaveel took just forty minutes, and the voyage got fairly lively once we were out in the North Sound, beyond the shelter of Cashla Bay. Since we were running across the Atlantic swell the boat was soon plunging and twisting. Large waves sent their tops surging over the open decks, so I made my way inside.

Everyone there seemed to be adding

another tint to Ireland's famous forty shades of green. Everyone, that is, except four ladies of a certain age who were playing gin rummy at a table by the bar. The boat rolled, reared, shook, pitched and plunged and did everything but damned well sink, and still the ladies played on, unperturbed, a glass at each elbow, their cigarettes glued to their lower lips, eyes glinting behind their spectacles as they peered down at their cards. They were still hard at their game when we came into Kilronan Harbour on Inishmore and the rest of us staggered ashore.

It would be easy to get sniffy about the Aran Islands. I had been told tales of gnarled fisherfolk in thick-knit sweaters and sea boots, hauling in nets full of basking sharks and singing sea shanties. I had heard of local costumes and strange customs. But the Aran Islands today are not the turn-of-the-century backwater that legend has them to be. As the passengers tottered off the ferry, a horde of touts descended on us, offering bicycles for hire, minibus trips round the island or excursions about the town in a horse-drawn cart. The scent of horse manure hangs over Kilronan like a miasma, and the town centre is an alternating mixture of cafés, tourist shops and B & Bs, set along streets spattered with horse droppings. It is hardly romantic.

I headed for the tourist information office, to find out if I could island-hop down to Doolin and the Burren. I had seen Galway city and had no need to go back there, and if I could get south across the sea to Doolin it would save me a good two or three days' trudging round the shore of Galway Bay. My map showed ferries from Inishmore to Inishmaan and Inisheer, but no ferries from Inisheer to Doolin, although there were, I gathered, ferries from Doolin to Inisheer.

So far, constant badgering of the local people on this point had not enlightened me at all. Their best reply was a definite maybe. Now the girl in the tourist office

ABOVE The three inhabited Aran Islands of Inisheer, Inishmaan and Inishmore stretch out across the mouth of Galway Bay.

ABOVE Claddagh rings were traditionally passed down through the female line in families from the Galway coast and Aran Islands.

was equally vague, so I decided to island-hop down to Inisheer anyway and take my chances on getting across from there to Doolin. That decided, I found a B & B, dumped the pack and set off to explore the island.

The Aran Islands are buckling under the weight of visitors: the local guidebook by Pacella and Dara O'Conaola has sold over 50,000 copies and is reprinted every year. It is written half in Irish and half in English. From it I learned that Inisheer is two miles square, Inishmaan five miles square, and Inishmore about sixteen miles square. The total population of the islands is about 600. They work at fishing or ferrying and some do still dress in the traditional Aran garb of a tweed waistcoat called a 'vest', a knitted cap and rawhide shoes called 'pampooties'. I saw no one dressed like that nor any woman in a red flannel skirt and crocheted shawl.

I had not been ashore long on Inishmore when I discovered that the islands are one great fissured limestone plate. They are part of the Burren plateau which rises to the south of Galway Bay. Over the centuries the islanders have tried to improve and extend the soil with a mixture of sand and seaweed, but the wind blows

PAMPOOTIES AND GANSEYS

THE HARDY FISHERFOLK of the Aran Islands traditionally created most of their own clothing from local raw materials, particularly wool and hides. Tweed for coats and trousers was spun and woven by hand. Men protected themselves against Atlantic gales with grey-blue tweed trousers and sleeveless jackets worn over thick, white, woollen undergarments. Round their waists they wore tasselled belts woven from brightly coloured wools. The distinctive female costume was a red woollen skirt and crocheted shawl. Boots were a rare sight: much more practical for walking over the rocky terrain were 'pampooties'—shoes without heels, made from untanned cowhide and tied to the feet by laces. A well-used pair would last about a month.

Typical Aran dress can still occasionally be spotted. But it is the robust, intricately patterned 'ganseys', or sweaters, that are recognised as Aran far beyond Irish shores. Originally knitted by fishermen's wives from wool that was 'unscoured' (allowed to retain its natural greases for better waterproofing), the sweaters were often passed down from generation to generation of fishing families.

A traditional Aran knit usually incorporates three or four different alternating motifs. Cable patterns represent safety and good luck at sea; basket stitch reflects a hope of abundant catches for the fishing fleet; and the zigzag and trellis stitches depict the cliffs, stone walls and small fields of the islands. And according to legend, each family wove its own motif into a sweater—to help identify the wearer if he perished under the waves.

ABOVE RIGHT *An Aran Islander stitches a pair of pampooties (shoes) by hand.*

LEFT *This display of Aran sweaters, or ganseys, shows the variety of stitches used.*

it away. As a result the surface of the islands looks like the remains of a volcanic eruption. Great rocks are piled everywhere, and grass is in limited supply. The eastern side, by the port of Kilronan, is fairly flat, but on the seaward side there are cliffs, steep and fissured, and cut with ledges where the sea birds nest.

There is a walk, the Inis Mór Way, which runs for thirty-one miles around this island. This can be cut short by simply nipping across the narrow bits, and since Inishmore is about eight miles long but only two miles wide at its widest, I simply beat off the touts with the pony and traps and set off on foot.

I took a narrow track—called a 'roidin'—over to the cliffs by Dun Duchathair, a prehistoric stone fort from where I could see, across the ocean, the high Cliffs of Moher on the Burren. Then it was over to the church at Corruch which has a healing spring, and then back to Kilronan, with a lot of rubber sole and leather upper scuffed off my boots. The sharp limestone slabs of the islands play havoc with footwear.

Most of the visitors leave Inishmore on the early-evening ferry, but there were enough left to fill all the pubs to the doors. By Irish standards Kilronan is a bit short of pubs, having only three—Ti-Jo Mac's, and Ti-Joe Watty's sound authentic enough, but the American Bar seems somewhat out of place. I went to Ti-Jo Mac's and tried to get some stories from the locals. This was difficult as all the customers were visitors.

ABOVE *Dùn Aonghasa gives every appearance of being a victim of coastal erosion. In fact, it was ever thus: the prehistoric cliff-fort was defended on one side by semicircular walls and on the other by the raging waters of the Atlantic Ocean.*

I guess tourism is what really keeps the place alive. Everyone is first directed to the local cinema, which is tiny and shows only one film—Robert Flaherty's famous *Man of Aran*, which was processed in the fish-curing sheds. It was made in black and white in 1934, and shows the islanders mending nets and catching whale sharks and climbing cliffs to gather eggs and starving and drowning and generally having a terrible time.

I had already seen *Man of Aran*, so I revived myself with a few drinks and then took the guided minibus tour to the prehistoric fort at Dùn Aonghasa.

Dùn Aonghasa is one of the finest and most intact prehistoric fortifications in Europe. It starts on the cliff edge, about 200 feet above the sea, and consists of three defensive walls surrounding an inner keep, with a great cheval-de-frise of up-ended stones covering the open ground in front. This fort, and three or four others on the islands, are said to date back to the Fir-bolg people. These may never have existed, so it is more probable that they go back to early Celtic times, say 2,500 years ago. I had a look around, which did not take long, and then sat on the cliffs to watch the sea for a while, but 'rock fever' was already setting in. I took the minibus back to Kilronan and got mildly drunk.

ISLAND-HOPPING

The ferry came in more or less on time next morning, which is to say about half an hour late, and a gaggle of escapees filed on board, most of us hefting rucksacks or wheeling bicycles. It did not take long to discover that everyone else on board was either Swedish, German or French. I had noticed the night before that Englishmen were rarer than hens' teeth hereabouts. Rather more surprising was the fact that most of these people had been here two or three times before.

I had heard that to get ashore on the smaller islands you had to transship to a curragh, but the skipper told me that while that happened sometimes if it was rough or the tides were very low, there was now an all-tidal pier in both places and I was not to worry.

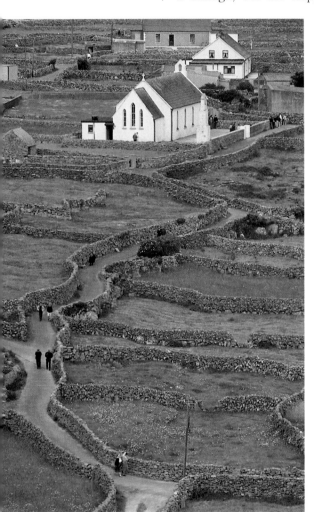

Life on the next island, Inishmaan, seems to lie in a belt about three miles wide across the middle of the island. As on Inishmore, there is a walk, the Inishmaan Way, which runs for five miles. I set off at a smart clip, past another stone fort and the cottage of Ti-Synge, where the playwright J. M. Synge spent every summer from 1881 to 1902. Synge set two of his works, *Raiders of the Sea* and *The Playboy of the Western World*, in the west of Ireland.

The most interesting thing hereabouts was a cattle trough with a sloping sill designed to catch rainwater, for apart from a few springs the island has no water. Beyond this, waymarks took me to the Cathaour Synge—Synge's Seat, where he used to sit and watch the waves sweep in from America. They were sweeping in today, sending great spurts of spray up the rocks and through the 'blowing holes' worn by the waves in the limestone. When a big wave got in a good blow at the rocks the ground actually shook.

I got back to the port at An Cora just in time to leap on the midday ferry to Inisheer. The locals call this island Inis Oirr, and it has the Inis Oirr Way, which runs about the north part of the island where, it said in the guide, the island largely consists of 'clints' (small hollows) and 'grykes' (crevices).

ABOVE *Islanders on Inisheer wind their way home from Mass along stone-walled roads. A lack of timber on the island means that fences have to be built from stone.*

Inisheer is another outcrop of the Burren, a bare, white, limestone slab, cast on the surface of the sea, but unlike Inishmaan it has water. There is even a well dedicated to St Enda, which never runs dry and is said to have healing powers. Be that as it may, the well water is cold enough to hurt your teeth.

In the spring, it says in the guide, this island becomes a carpet of flowers. Primroses and sea pinks cloak the cliffs, and rare plants such as the pyramid orchid are quite common. Now, in the middle of summer, the island was just a glinting white rock, broken up with miles of interlinked dry-stone walls. Its gaunt appearance apart, the island was bustling. Fat cattle chomped away at hay in the tiny fields, and the tourists were everywhere. There is even an airstrip, and the curragh fleet catches profitable lobsters for shipment to London. I suspect that in their own quiet way the local people are doing very well.

Inisheer is even smaller than Inishmaan. There are two or three churches and a scattering of houses on the north shore, and a small harbour. I went round the Inis Oirr Way. I saw the wreck of the steamer *Plassey*, which was tossed ashore here in 1960 and is quietly rusting away, and the well of St Enda, the patron saint of Inishmaan; it has to be excavated from the wind-blown sand from time to time. The only other notable features on the island were more troughs for collecting rainwater and stone pillars used for drying seaweed. There was hardly anyone about, except visitors, so I sat on the wall by the quay and worried about getting across the sea to Doolin.

I met a man who told me there would be no more ferries that day. Then I met another who said that there never were any ferries to Doolin and I should go back to Inishmore and try from there. At that moment, no fewer than two ferries came into the harbour from Doolin and the crews virtually fought each other for my custom. I went on board feeling smug, and an hour later I was sitting in O'Connor's pub in Doolin, cradling a pint of Smithwicks and grinning from ear to ear.

KARST COUNTRY

Doolin is about a mile inland from the harbour and straggles for 100 yards or so along the banks of the River Aille. The harbour is surrounded by those great limestone plaques I had got to know out on the islands, but otherwise this is farming country, where green fields are marked with ponds and cattle.

By reaching Doolin I had moved from County Galway into County Clare, the Banner Country, the place that has always been in the forefront of the fight for independence. Once across Clare, I would only have one more county to go.

Clare is a fairly flat county, bounded on the east by the Shannon and Lough Derg and to the west by the sea. There is a central limestone plain but mountains rise round the edges, most notably here on the Burren, which is a plateau of silver limestone rearing up 700 feet from the southern shore of Galway Bay. The word

ABOVE *Midsummer's Cavern, part of a maze of caves lying beneath the limestone surface of the Burren.*

'Burren' means 'the stony place', and that about describes it. This is karst country, bare limestone underpinned with caverns and underground rivers, covering a region of about 100 square miles, and running out on the coast at the escarpment above Ballyvaughan, or at the Cliffs of Moher, which lie just south of Doolin.

I had anticipated crossing the Burren on the Burren Way footpath, but was put out to discover that most of the Burren Way is yet another tarmac road, bearable for walkers but far more suitable for cycle tourists, who were cruising round it in great

numbers. It was becoming increasingly clear to me that Ireland is absolutely wonderful for the cycle tourist. There were cycle tourists in large groups led by a guide or in couples or families, even on their own.

Next morning I stepped out into bright sunshine under a sky full of white, puffy clouds and an air that smelt of the sea, and strode off up the Burren Way towards the Cliffs of Moher, five miles south of Doolin and one of the major attractions on the west coast.

When I came in across the car park, tourists were emerging in droves from the information centre and running the gauntlet of the traders on their way to the cliff edge. The car park was full of coaches. On the way up to the viewpoint of O'Brien's Tower there was a man with a dog and a donkey offering a photo opportunity, a man telling fortunes, people selling postcards, and three girls singing to the music of a harp. Above all this activity hung the smell of fried onions from the Shamrock Hamburger Stall. I plodded up the path to the cliffs.

The Cliffs of Moher are something to see. They drop a vertigo-inducing 700 feet sheer into the sea, and run for five miles, the steeper parts white with sea birds: puffins, guillemots, razorbills, even some choughs and ravens. How the birds survive the tourists beats me, for the flatter bits of the cliffs were like eroded terraces, full of people taking photographs from quite hazardous locations.

The wind on the top was sweeping in directly from America, strong enough to make me stagger or even stop my breath if I turned fully into it, and with the wind came the rain. I turned away from the sea and was blown downwind like a leaf, along the Burren Way to Lisdoonvarna.

Lisdoonvarna is Ireland's only spa. The description of the waters might put anyone off: 'sulphurous and chalybeate (iron) with elements of iodine and possessing radioactive properties'. Wonderful—you come for the cure and go home glowing in the dark! Several hotels advertise the cure but I have never cared for taking the waters and I arrived in the town centre after lunch gasping for a cup of tea. I found this in a café across from the Ritz Hotel, which advertised among its various attractions 'the best crack in town'. This statement was causing a certain amount of concern to a group of American visitors at a nearby table.

Lisdoonvarna is a holiday centre, one of those places that only comes alive when the tourists are in town, and, if it isn't careful, it will end up without any life of its own. Fortunately, even in midsummer, the bar at the Ritz was full of local lads with their noses stuck in the Guinness. There seemed to be plenty of young men about, which was a good thing because the traditional attraction of Lisdoonvarna is the Matchmaking.

Once a year men and women come from all over Ireland to Lisdoonvarna for the Matchmaking, or Bachelor Festival, to find themselves a mate. The young waiter in the tea shop told me that the Matchmaking Festival was really a great rave. Some women come all the way from America to see what they can catch. Hangovers mostly, if they were lucky.

The town still supports two active Matchmakers who will act for the families when a marriage needs making, arrange the wedding ceremony and even negotiate the dowry, not forgetting to take a commission before passing it on to the bridegroom's father. It all sounded very civilised, but I came here to cross the Burren.

THE STONY PLACE

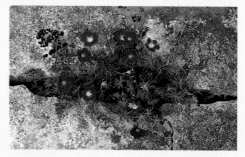

LEFT *Movements in the earth's crust caused the limestone of the Burren to fracture into the great, rough slabs we see today.*

BELOW *The bloody cranesbill, growing in a fissure, provides a startling splash of pink in the grey, seemingly lifeless landscape.*

LEFT *This dazzling gold collar, dating from about 700 BC, was found in 1930 at the Gleninsheen wedge tomb in the Burren.*

NORTHWEST County Clare is dominated by a strange lunar landscape—the Burren, a low, grey plateau of gentle hills, giant boulders, quick-filling lake beds and the occasional pasture and woodland. But the most striking and characteristic feature is a flat, fissured limestone pavement. The name 'Burren' is adapted from a Gaelic word meaning, all too aptly, 'stony place'.

Rainwater drains through the fissures (often emerging miles away in springs at the Burren's edge), and over the aeons has, together with glacial meltwater, dissolved pockets of limestone and so carved out a subterranean honeycomb of rivers, lakes and caverns. The most accessible of these cave complexes is the Aillwee Cave, a deep half-mile passage with large chambers, decorated with dramatic stalactite and stalagmite formations.

Bleak it may be, but the Burren is far from barren. In fact, it is famous as a botanical treasure house, displaying around 850 of Ireland's 1,200 plant species. Stunted hawthorn, juniper and

rowan trees maintain a stubborn foothold, ferns flourish in cave mouths, and in May wild flowers stipple the lakesides and adorn the crevices in the limestone. Thanks to the region's unique mix of microclimates, alpine, Mediterranean and even arctic plants can grow in close proximity. Nature lovers delight in the rock roses and spring gentian, limestone bugle and bloody cranesbill, mountain avens, eyebrights and almost two dozen different orchids.

The fauna is surprisingly plentiful too: a wealth of butterflies, such as the unique Burren green; skylarks and whooper swans; hares and feral goats. The rare pine marten survives in the patchy woods, and the caves accommodate

foxes, badgers and bats— and 'little people', apparently. As for real people, they have inhabited the region since the Stone Age. Witness all the prehistoric cahers (fortified farmsteads) and tombs, some of them 6,000 years old, as well as ancient artefacts such as stone axe heads and jewellery of bone or gold. From the Middle Ages and later, there are several ruined castles and churches. Today the region is home to a few hardy cattle farmers, and is the haunt of ever-increasing numbers of admiring tourists.

LEFT *Pine martens are at home in the bleak Burren, but these elusive creatures are rarely spotted.*

RIGHT *Structures such as the Poulnabrone Dolmen, which dates back some 4,500 years, testify to the Burren's long history of human habitation.*

It took the rest of the evening to get across the northern strip of the Burren and down to Ballyvaughan, where I found a B & B by the harbour. I had an hour or two to hang about before dinner, so I tried admiring the red, blue and yellow painted houses and the Galway 'Hookers', the traditional local fishing craft moored against the harbour wall. A coachload of French tourists were photographing the central road sign of Ballyvaughan, the one that had about thirty different sets of directions on it. I fell into Claire's Restaurant, where a lot of wine was consumed and there was some singing. Next day I felt very poorly.

On the way out next morning I flogged back up the hill from Ballyvaughan to the top of the escarpment, where I found myself at last on the road south across the main Burren plateau. After the Aran Islands the landscape of the Burren was familiar, a carapace of limestone littered with large boulders, divided here and there by dry-stone walls. It looks marvellously inhospitable. There is the occasional valley where trees, fields and small farms somehow manage to survive, but otherwise the plant life clings to crevasses in the karst.

The constant rain and the numerous springs that the Burren supplies have enabled life to exist in it since Stone Age times. The remains of prehistoric people have been found in stone forts and circles, in dolmens and standing stones. It is hard to see why people should make their life more difficult than it need be by attempting to scratch a living in such an inhospitable place, but presumably the attraction was security. No one in his right mind would envy someone who lived up here.

The first recorded habitation in these parts dates back to 1189 when a group of Cistercian monks founded an abbey near Corcomroe. The Cistercians, always eager to avoid soft living, usually chose remote spots for their foundations, so the Burren must have exerted a powerful appeal. They called their abbey Santa Maria de Petra Fertilis, St Mary of the Fertile Rock, which is a good description of the region as a whole.

The Burren covers an area of some 193 square miles and supports a wealth of wild flowers, such as the mountain avens, the spring gentian and over twenty species of orchid.

Wildlife is scanty but there are rare creatures such as the pine marten, and hawks circled in the sky as I passed the Aillwee Caves and then tramped down on a blazing day to the Burren Centre at Kilfenora.

Kilfenora lies five miles south of Lisdoonvarna. It has a few B & Bs and stands in fine open country, but the attraction here are the ruins of a 12th-century cathedral dedicated to St Fachtna. There are three high Celtic crosses in the graveyard and some carved tomb slabs depicting medieval bishops. The Burren Centre is full of information about the Burren, making the point that out here alpine and Mediterranean, and even arctic plants, somehow grow together. The best of the local flowers are on display in the spring, but even in midsummer there were enough to keep me happy: great hedges of fuchsia, wayside clumps of orange montbretia and hillsides bright with spreading yellow gorse. It was almost as good as Connemara.

ABOVE *Visitors to Ballyvaughan may have trouble making up their minds where to go, presented with this bewildering selection.*

CHAPTER SIX

THE FINAL LAP

ABOVE *Daniel O'Connell, the Irish barrister known as the 'Great Liberator', won civic freedom for Catholics with the Catholic Emancipation Act of 1829.*

I T TOOK ME TWO DAYS to walk across County Clare down to the Shannon. As I got further south and began to cross low hills, I could see ahead the twin pencil-thin towers of the power station at Killimer, from where the ferry crosses the Shannon for Tarbert.

I could have taken the long way round the Shannon estuary, past Limerick, but I liked the idea of a ferry ride. Eventually I hit the Shannon by Knock and walked round Clonderalaw Bay to Killimer. Here, on the north bank of the Shannon estuary, just above the ferry port, I dived into another pub and sat at the bar for a think. Once I crossed the river I would soon be in County Kerry. Valencia Island was in County Kerry, so I only had about 100 miles to go.

I could not leave Clare just yet, however, for Clare is a place that has played a significant part in Irish history. Although it lies a very long way from either Dublin or Westminster, it was the people of County Clare who elected Daniel O'Connell to Westminster in 1828, and Daniel O'Connell, the 'Great Liberator', is commemorated all over Ireland.

To talk about O'Connell we have to go back beyond Parnell and the Great Hunger to the tricky decades after the Act of Union in 1800. It was believed, at least in Ireland, that the Act of Union would give the Irish equal status with the English and the rights and privileges already enjoyed by the people of Great Britain. This belief was doomed to disappointment. They could send Members to Parliament, but Parliament refused to emancipate the Catholics. Catholics were barred from most of the professions and from all public office. Daniel O'Connell changed all that.

O'Connell was born in County Kerry in 1775 and educated in France. He left France when the Revolution broke out and went to London. The bloody excesses of the Terror turned him totally against violence as a means to political ends. He trained as a lawyer, returned to Ireland and founded the Catholic Association. In 1828 he entered Parliament as Member for Clare, where he immediately refused to take the required oath acknowledging the King as Head of the Church. From this defiance came the Emancipation Acts, which first gave the Irish Catholics a political voice. O'Connell then set out to gain the repeal of the Act of Union.

Matters came to a head in 1843 when tens of thousands of people attended meetings called by O'Connell to support the repeal of the Act. The government had him arrested. With the aid of a 'packed' jury full of Ulster Protestants, O'Connell was sent to gaol. The House of Lords ordered his release, but he emerged a broken man and died in 1847 at the height of the Great Famine, when the Irish had more to think about than liberation. His fame came later.

I was pleased to see the Shannon. This great river almost cuts Ireland in two. Since its course is slow and low-lying, from time to time it broadens out into great lakes. Here at Killimer the river is wide, and supports a certain amount of coastal shipping which steams up the river to Limerick. The ferry port at Killimer contains a couple of bars. Outside one of them is the bronze bust of the 'Colleen Bawn', Ellen Hanley, who is buried in the nearby churchyard.

AN ENCHANTING WATERWAY

IRELAND'S LONGEST RIVER, the Shannon, winds its 250-mile way southwestwards from the Iron Mountains in County Cavan down to the Atlantic beyond Limerick. For most of its length, the Shannon moves at a sedate pace through the pasture land of the central limestone plains, through a series of locks and loughs to the mud flats of the lengthy estuary. But for a stretch in its lower reaches, between Lough Derg and Limerick, it becomes more sprightly— so much so that, in the 1920s, a large hydroelectric station was built at Ardnacrusha, powered by a 100-foot plunge in the river's rechannelled waters.

A double lock was built here too, and a fish leap, to keep the river navigable for boats and salmon alike: vital, since both boating and fishing are immensely popular along the Shannon. Thousands of boats ply its routes each year, from simple canoes and yachts to luxury cabin cruisers. Other leisure activities include water sports such as windsurfing, and— on the river banks and lake shores—pony

trekking, birdwatching, hiking and cycling. And sightseeing, of course: idyllic villages and picturesque ruins— Bunratty Castle, say, or the monastic settlement of Clonmacnoise—brought about by Viking sackings, wars, or simply the ravages of time.

There is little industry along the banks, and the water was formerly renowned for its purity, nurturing otters and eels, and a wealth of bird life. But pollution, caused by sewage and agricultural effluent, has become a concern. Environmental policies are starting to have some effect, however, and look set to preserve the enchantment of the waterway.

ABOVE *Anglers on the banks of the Shannon in County Leitrim hope for a good catch.*

BELOW *The River Shannon has forged a path through Ireland's green landscape; here it flows past the monastery at Clonmacnoise.*

Ellen was just fifteen in 1819 when she met John Scanlan. Everyone knew he was a rotter and warned her against him, but she would not listen and married him. Scanlan soon tired of her. He eventually told a couple of his henchmen to take her out in a boat and drown her in the Shannon. This they did, but the body was washed ashore, the sorry tale came out and Scanlan was arrested, and subsequently found guilty. It is said that the horses drawing his carriage at first refused to take him to the scaffold, but he was hanged at Limerick in March 1820.

It's a sad tale and, to be honest, the dockside at Killimer is a sad place, overlooked by power stations and swarming with crows. I have never seen such numbers of crows as they have here in Ireland. They gather in black heaps under the roof eaves or hop about in flocks across the roads and car parks.

The ferry eventually came in and we swarmed aboard, several cars, many cycle tourists and the solitary walker. The ferry ploughed across the river, where I stepped ashore and turned upstream for the short walk into Glin. This led me along the banks of the Shannon into Tarbert, past the old lockup, the Bridewell, which is well preserved, and round the walls of the Glin estate and into the village itself.

The Fitzgerald family have lived here as Knights of Glin since the 14th century. Their medieval castle was destroyed on the orders of Elizabeth I in 1600, though the picturesque ruins still stand on a small hill overlooking the river. The new castle, which is a pleasant country house with towers and battlements on top, was erected in the

1780s and, times being what they are, the Fitzgeralds now open the house to the public.

I found a pub and settled down for the evening. I had crossed Clare and the mighty Shannon, stepped into County Limerick at Glin and now entered my last region, County Kerry. That was something to celebrate.

COUNTY KERRY

Kerry forms part of the old province of Munster and is best imagined like a hand laid out to the south and west. The palm is the limestone plain east of Tralee, and three of the fingers—the peninsulas of Dingle, Iveragh and Beara—probe the Atlantic. Hilly or mountainous, ringed with cliffs and offshore islands, these peninsulas are the great attractions of southwest Ireland and draw visitors by the tens of thousands. There is plenty of space down here in the southwest, though, and for most of the time I was still completely alone.

The main road south out of Glin leads over the moors to Abbeyfeale, a small town on the River Feale, but I had it in mind to visit Listowel, which

ABOVE *Glin Castle, where the Fitzgeralds have lived as hereditary knights since the 14th century.*

OPPOSITE *The Dingle peninsula, with its undulating mountains and green fields, reaches out into the Atlantic from southwestern Ireland.*

lies further downstream and is famous as a place for writers. I bent my track a little, turning west over the River Galey, which was foaming along, dark brown with peat, and so to the River Feale and into Listowel. This is a fair-sized town with a fair-sized church in the central square, which also contains an Art and Heritage Centre.

Listowel hosts an annual Writers' Week on the Whitsun bank holiday, when writers from all over the world come to mingle with their colleagues and talk about their work. I stopped for lunch there, sitting in a dark pub. Keane's pub is owned by John B. Keane—known hereabouts as 'John B.'—a successful Irish playwright. One of his plays, *The Field*, had just been made into a film, so there was cause for celebration in the bar, where John B. was drinking with the regulars.

Then it was south again, on over the moors on a narrow road across the Stacks Mountains into Tralee. Tralee stands at the landward end of the Dingle peninsula, at no great distance from the sea, and is linked to Dingle Bay by a ship canal. With the famous Killarney lakes and fells close at hand, Tralee was full of tourists, the streets jammed with cars and coaches.

IRELAND ON FILM

IRELAND'S BREATHTAKING countryside makes it an inspiring film location, and foreign directors have been shooting there since the 1940s. John Ford's classic *The Quiet Man* (1952) was filmed in his father's native Galway. David Lean's *Ryan's Daughter* (1970) was shot in west Kerry against a backdrop of stunning coastal scenery. The director employed locals as extras, and the village was touched by Hollywood glamour as it filled with the traffic of an international production—movie stars and crew, cameras and lights, period cars and limousines.

Irish film-making boomed in its own right towards the end of the 20th century. Irish director Jim Sheridan's *The Field* (1990), with a memorable performance by Richard Harris, deals with one farmer's stubborn refusal to sell a field to an

outsider who means to develop it, and whom he eventually murders.

Although the land has figured prominently in Irish films, the city features, too. In 1991 English director Alan Parker plucked a handful of unknowns from the streets of Dublin

ABOVE *Neil Jordan's 1996 film* Michael Collins *not only had an Irish director but also used an Irish actor—Liam Neeson, seen here on set in Dublin—in the title role.*

to belt out soul numbers in one of the decade's most boisterous musical hits, *The Commitments*. Neil Jordan, Ireland's most successful director, also set his film *Michael Collins* (1996) in Dublin. Collins, a man who used violence for political ends, is a figure who still arouses

The big event here is the annual Rose of Tralee competition, for which the streets are hung with fairy lights. This festival is open to girls of Irish descent from every country in the world, and they arrive by the hundreds in early August. What with the girls and their countless admirers, the event gives a real boost to the town's fragile economy.

It needs that kind of help, for, like a lot of Irish towns, Tralee is not that attractive. The parks and public buildings are fine but the main streets are narrow and full of poky little shops. William Mulchinock, who wrote the song 'The Rose of Tralee' in the last century, has a statue in the town park, and the town also supports the Siamsa Tíre, the National Folk Theatre of Ireland, which is dedicated to keeping Irish art and the Irish language alive. Indeed, Tralee is a very Irish town, so I decided to stay here for a couple of days before I crossed the Slieve Mish Mountains—the Ghost Mountains—which lie like a wall to the south of the town.

Tralee was a stronghold of the Desmonds until they were driven out in Elizabethan times. The Desmond story is told in an exhibition entitled 'The

passionate feelings. The Irish film censor gave *Michael Collins* a general release, despite its violence, because of the significance of its subject matter, but historians attacked the film for its inaccuracies and alleged glorification of the IRA. Whatever his liberties with historical facts, Jordan was keen to capture accurately the look of turn-of-the-century Dublin. Although the city retains its Georgian architecture, its 19th-century grime had long been cleaned

off, and smoke and filters were used to re-create a grey tinge.

But the high profile of directors such as Jordan ensures that the future of the Irish film industry is far from grey. Not only does the island continue to provide the scenic backdrop for international hits, it is now producing more and more successful films of its own.

MGM presents DAVID LEAN'S FILM of 'RYAN'S DAUGHTER'

RIGHT *Sarah Miles lit up the town of Dingle in Kerry when she and the rest of the crew arrived to film* Ryan's Daughter (1970).

LEFT *Richard Harris played 'The Bull' McCabe in Jim Sheridan's 1990 film* The Field, *a fable that explores the Irish people's attachment to their land.*

RIGHT *Alan Parker's film* The Commitments *was one of the biggest hits of the 1980s; its soundtrack album was in the Top Ten in both Britain and America.*

BELOW *John Wayne played the title role in* The Quiet Man (1952), *which was filmed in Galway. Locals were drafted in as extras for a marathon fight scene.*

Medieval Experience', where the visitor gets transported through the past. I also liked the splendid working Blennerville windmill and the little trains on the Tralee–Blennerville Steam Railway.

On the second day I took myself to Banna Strand, a few miles to the north. Banna Strand is a small village set behind a long, sandy beach, and the beach has two claims to fame. It was here they filmed *Ryan's Daughter*, and, more relevant to my underlying theme, this is the place where Sir Roger Casement landed from a German submarine on Good Friday in 1916. I found Sir Roger's rather battered memorial on the sand dunes behind the beach.

Born into an Ulster Protestant family in 1864, Sir Roger Casement became a diplomat and was knighted for his services as a consular agent. In spite of this background, Sir Roger was an Irish patriot. When the First World War began he followed the old rule that 'England's difficulty is Ireland's opportunity' and made his way to Germany. Having arranged for a shipment of arms he went ahead to Ireland in a German submarine, which put him ashore at Banna Strand. Then everything went wrong.

A British army patrol appeared and captured Casement in a wood behind the beach. The arms never arrived, and without them the Easter Rising had little chance of success. When it collapsed and the ringleaders were shot, Casement was taken to England, imprisoned in Pentonville and tried for high treason. By the law of the land he was a traitor to his country. Casement, however, believed he served another country, a country that had yet to come into existence—Ireland—and by that criterion he was no traitor at all.

Casement followed the path of other Irish patriots: rebellion, capture and trial, a speech from the dock, and the inevitable sentence and execution. Irishmen are good speakers, and these speeches from the dock must have been marvellous and tragic. Casement's speech seemed to sum up everything that was ever said about the state of Ireland under British rule, and since it put the case for Ireland far better than I could ever do, I reproduce part of it here:

ABOVE *In 1916 Sir Roger Casement, former British diplomat turned Irish freedom fighter, was declared an enemy of the King and hanged for his role in the Easter Rising.*

> Self-government is our right, a thing born in us at birth; a thing no more to be doled out to us or withheld from us by another people than the right to life itself—than the right to feel the sun or smell the flowers, or to love our kind. It is only from the convict these things are withheld…and Ireland that has wronged no man, that has injured no land, that has sought no dominion over others—Ireland is treated today among the nations of the world as if she was a convicted criminal. If it be treason to fight against such an unnatural fate as this, then I am proud to be a rebel, and shall cling to my 'rebellion' with the last drop of my blood. If there be no right of rebellion against a state of things that no savage tribe would endure without resistance, then I am sure that it is better for men to fight and die without right than to live in such a state of right as this.
>
> Where…men must beg with bated breath for leave to subsist in their own land, to think their own thoughts, to sing their own songs, to garner the fruits of their own labours—and even while they beg, to see things inexorably withdrawn

from them—then surely it is a braver, a saner and a truer thing, to be a rebel in act and deed against such circumstances as these than tamely to accept it as the natural lot of men.

Well, they hanged him, of course. What else could you do with a man who could speak like that?

CARAVANS AND BILLY GOATS

I had a job finding the right road out of Tralee to the Slieve Mish. Since the Slieve Mish are in plain sight, that may be hard to believe, but so it was. I eventually realised that I must follow the fingerpost labelled simply 'Viewpoint', which led me through the scattered suburbs and out onto a steep, narrow lane which eventually got me to the top of the range.

This is a sharp little mountain road up the Mish and, to be exact, it has two viewpoints. The one on the north face gave marvellous views over Tralee Bay and along the north shore of the Dingle peninsula, and from this viewpoint it is a short walk to Scotia's Glen and the stone slab of Scotia's Grave. Queen Scotia is said to be a daughter of an Egyptian Pharaoh who died in battle on the Slieve Mish in 1700 BC, after the legendary and most unlikely invasion of Ireland from Egypt, when the sons of Scotia fought and beat the native Da Danann people. The sons won but Scotia was killed in the moment of victory. It all sounds most unlikely to me.

From there I plodded on up the road to the southern viewpoint on the wind-racked crest of the hill and had my first view south to Carrauntoohil and the mountain range of the Macgillycuddy's Reeks. To the right lay Castlemaine Harbour, so somewhere in the lee of this hill—Knockmichael Mountain—must lie the town of Castlemaine. After that the plains began again and took me round the shore of Dingle Bay to the foot of the Reeks. That was my route to the end of this journey and it took me over Carrauntoohil, the highest mountain in Ireland.

BELOW *Touring the country in a horse-drawn caravan is a popular type of holiday in Ireland. But it is not beyond the bounds of possibility that the horse will need a little coaxing.*

The Slieve Mish stand like a long ridge at the landward end of the Dingle peninsula. There is a long-distance footpath here, the Dingle Way. This starts at Curraheen on the north of the peninsula and runs for ninety-five miles, right round the Dingle peninsula, and cuts off here along the Slieve Mish.

This Dingle footpath uses mountain trails and country roads, or 'borreens', and if I had not already settled firmly on a finish at Valencia Island, I would have followed it out to the west and enjoyed every step of it, for it is a well-established route, followed by hundreds of walkers every year. However, Carrauntoohil loomed ahead and I had to get over that before I could finish this walk.

I met a family with a horse-drawn holiday caravan. They were hauling the horse, which was hauling the caravan.

'We want to go over the hill to Tralee but the horse doesn't like hills,' said the wife.

'It doesn't even like slopes,' said the husband bitterly. 'We've spent a week walking around the flat bits of Kerry, dragging this bloody great horse. They don't put that in the brochures.'

They were not alone in having trouble with our four-footed friends. I passed several other caravans, all of them the wooden, round-roofed Gypsy kind, and everyone seemed to be walking beside their horse. Then, late in the afternoon, I turned a corner of the road and met two horses, both wearing white nosebags and trotting hard for Tralee. Further on, about a mile down the road, I found two horseless caravans drawn up off the road and two families running about blaming each other and screaming. When they stopped screaming I tried to be helpful.

'I think I've seen your horses, about a mile back...with white nosebags—right? They were trotting along happily and quite all right.'

This news did not go down too well. Everyone started screaming at me. Apparently I should have captured the horses and brought them back. The families ran off after their horses and I flogged on towards Castlemaine, the home of Jack Duggan—the 'wild colonial boy' of the old song:

There was a wild colonial boy,
Jack Duggan was his name.
He was born and raised in Ireland,
In a place called Castlemaine.

I've spent many an evening bawling out that song and I could hardly come all this way across Ireland without stopping in Castlemaine, where there would surely be a pub named Jack Duggan. After all, in Australia they have even named a beer after Castlemaine. There were several pubs in Castlemaine, and although none was named after Jack Duggan, I went into one and heard a man give a curious order: 'A Guinness, a Smithwicks, an Irish coffee, two Bush and a pint of milk.'

At Castlemaine I was down on the plains again, but not for long. There were mountains all around me now, rearing up green and dark. I went on to the town of Killorglin, which turned out to be jammed with people and the first place on this journey where I could not find a room for the night.

I found shelter at a B & B some distance outside the town, near Kilgobnet, and there I enlisted the entire family in my preparations for the following day's challenge—to climb Carrauntoohil.

This B & B would be my base camp for the assault on Carrauntoohil next day, with as much kit as possible left out of my rucksack. I went back into Killorglin in search of entertainment.

Killorglin is lively, even for an Irish town. I got there after dark when the clouds were sitting right on the rooftops and a thin, cold rain was falling, but the place was full of activity. Every bar was jammed with people, there was a band hard at it in every pub and all the restaurants were packed.

Most of the people here were young; I reflected, not for the first time on this journey, on how attractive Ireland must be for young people. There are lots of pubs, lots of chat, plenty of entertainment and, if you stick to hostels or B & Bs, plenty of cheap accommodation.

Killorglin is really not much more than a village. The population is scarcely more than 1,000 people, but it manages to support a dozen pubs as well as playing host to the annual 'Puck Fair and Pattern'. A 'pattern' is like the Breton 'pardon', the festival of the patron saint, traditionally held on the day of his death.

I had a good night. I went nipping through the rain from pub to pub, and had a good supper with a plate of soda bread that could have been cut with a chain saw. I might have stayed longer, because the town was winding itself up for a good Saturday night, but there was the lurking thought that tomorrow I had to get into the Reeks and up Carrauntoohil. When wisdom finally prevailed, I went back to bed at Kilgobnet and went to sleep listening to the sound of rain pelting hard against the window.

FÊTING KING PUCK

KILLORGLIN, A SMALL TOWN in County Kerry, is famous in Ireland for its Puck Fair, a combined livestock fair and festival that takes place over three days every August. On the first day—the Gathering—people come in from all over the countryside, bringing their goats, sheep, cattle and horses for the second day's market, the Puck. There are other events too, including duck-racing, but at the centre of the festival is an unusual rite dating back to Celtic times: the young men of the town capture a large wild billy goat from the surrounding hills, parade him through the town and install him on a 10-foot-high platform in the town square. The goat is named King Puck, and he stays on his platform throughout the festival, his horns decorated with ribbons, rosettes and a crown, eating the finest of vegetables and looking down on the often rowdy booze-up below.

The drinking is the main event of Puck Fair, and there are probably more sales of whiskey and Guinness than of animals. For three days and nights Killorglin is an open town. Shops, cafés and pubs are on the go 24 hours a day as the local people drink, sing and dance while King Puck presides.

The origins of Puck Fair are obscure, but one tale has it that King Puck is installed on his comfortable platform as a reward for the time when stampeding goats gave warning of an approaching English army. But it is more likely that the fair has its origins in a pagan harvest festival, dedicated to a Celtic god named Lug, to whom King Puck would have been sacrificed on the final day, the Scattering. In these more humane times, however, he returns to his herd, having had a taste of the high life.

LEFT *For three days in August, one wild billy goat gets a taste of the high life after being crowned King Puck at Killorglin Puck Fair.*

CLIMBING CARRAUNTOOHIL

At 3,414 feet, Carrauntoohil is a bulky, sharp-summited peak, the pride of Macgillycuddy's Reeks, the range that occupies the high ground at the landward end of the Iveragh peninsula and the Ring of Kerry.

ABOVE *Carrauntoohil in the Macgillycuddy's Reeks is Ireland's highest peak. Its jagged summit, which touches the clouds, presents a forbidding sight to climbers.*

The Reeks used to be called Na Cruecha Dubha—the Black Stacks—which fails to explain where the 'Reeks' came from, though the Macgillycuddys were a local family who lived on the banks of the River Laune. As for Carrauntoohil, like a lot of things in Ireland, the name is spelt in various ways, and it took me quite a while to realise that Carrauntoohil and 'Corran Tuathail' were the same mountain.

The previous day, when I came over the Slieve Mish, they had looked splendid in the evening light, sharp-edged against the sky. That was yesterday. Today they were covered with cloud, rain was spattering against the window, the wind was up and I felt like death. This was surprising, as I had drunk very little the night before.

I spent several hours mooching round the B & B, holding my throbbing head, crunching aspirin and drinking cups of coffee. From time to time I picked up the half-empty rucksack, which still seemed to weigh a ton, and looked out at the rain.

When I finally declared that the best answer was to sweat it out on the hill, my hosts offered me a lift to the start of the walk just a mile or two down the road. I needed all the help I could get, so I accepted the offer gratefully. The entire family piled into the car and came to see me off at the foot of the mountain.

There is a waymarked trail up Carrauntoohil. It begins in the yard of a small farm set in a valley between two peaks with unpronounceable names, Cloghfaunaglibbaun and Knocknafreughaun. A plaque on the wall here remembers the crew of a US transport plane that crashed into the Reeks in 1943. Half a dozen cars were parked by the sign, indicating that I would have some company on the hill.

A pair of long, furry ears projected above the wall, and as I began to clamber into the hard-hitting gear, a donkey clip-clopped into the yard and poked me hard in the back with his nose. I fended off the donkey and compared my own map with one on the wall. The wall map advised that to the top of Carrauntoohil and back would take four hours. It was now mid-afternoon, so I would have to press on hard if I was to be down again before dark. (I might as well add that I think that four hours up and down is an optimistic estimate for anyone other than a mountain goat, but my critical faculties were not functioning too well at the time.)

As I set off up the Hags Glen I could see the long scar on the face of the mountain, a mile or so up the valley, that had to be the Devil's Ladder, the main way up. The Ladder looked very steep and long, but that narrow track up the face of the cliff had been worn away by boots, so clearly it could be climbed. The Ladder is, in fact, a gully, 600 feet high and not a place to fall in, but if others could climb it, I could.

The walk in to Carrauntoohil is pleasant. The path is a clear track leading up an open valley and begins across a small stream. Then I was out in the open, with the Purple Mountain on my left, Carrauntoohil ahead and the River Gaddagh foaming away in a ravine to my right. The rain was coming down in vertical sheets, and streams were foaming across the track.

Dressed for the worst and feeling ghastly, I met a group of schoolchildren coming down after two nights camping on the mountain.

'What was it like?' I asked.

'Great,' they chorused. 'Brilliant.'

They were soaked to the skin. How could it have been brilliant?

'Tough?' I asked. 'Wet and cold? Bit of a challenge?'

'Easy-peasy.'

BELOW *Low, black clouds hover menacingly above Purple Mountain.*

Their teacher, who was bringing up the rear, was a bit less sanguine. 'Visibility on the top is now about zero,' he said. 'Watch your step, especially on the Ladder coming down.'

I crossed the River Gaddagh once or twice, picking my way across on wet boulders, sploshed across a couple of bogs, and was already very wet when I reached the jumble of rocks called the Hags Teeth and found myself at the foot of the Ladder. The path there leads between two lakes which occupy much of the land at the foot of Carrauntoohil. Lough Gouragh and Lough Callee are no great size but they feed the River Gaddagh.

I could see by now that the Ladder was an almost vertical rock-and-scree slope, with a stream running down the face. On a wet day it doubles as a waterfall. My raingear was proof even against Irish rain, but jets of water were shooting over the rocks and when I took a handhold, the stream shot smartly up my sleeves and down my back. Within minutes I was soaked to the skin. As a bonus, small rocks and stones, loosened by the rain or by other climbers ahead, also came bouncing past. That apart, I had no energy. I took a few paces, ran out of puff, stood hunched under the rain to get my breath back and took another few paces.

Since I knew enough to realise that the hill was not the problem, I finally concluded that I was ill.

There is a rough route up the Ladder, a path of sorts made by countless other walkers, but this route sometimes disappears. On a day of low cloud and pelting rain any route would be hard to make out, but I just plodded on, picking handholds where I could, scraping off the mud, watching the water flow into my boots and wishing I was twenty years younger. I eventually got to the top of the Ladder, but getting there took more than twice the time I had allowed.

Even worse, everyone I passed was heading down and giving me worried looks. Over the last few yards up the Ladder the route left the rock behind and led through a narrow gully of earth and mud. On the lip of this gully a family sat in the rain eating sandwiches.

ABOVE *The Devil's Ladder (part of which is seen in the middle of the picture) is the recommended route up Carrauntoohil, but it is an arduous climb at the best of times. The author attempted it in the worst of conditions.*

'That was a tough one,' I said to the family as I flopped wearily onto the grass. 'Where's the summit?' Since I had been at it for hours I expected the summit to be in sight.

They looked surprised. 'You're not there yet,' said the father. 'It's another forty minutes or so…up there in the clouds.'

My heart sank.

I lay there for a few minutes. Then the family urged me to get a move on as the day was getting late, so I left them at a fast clip, which slowed to a stagger within yards.

The path from the Ladder to the summit of Carrauntoohil runs uphill over rough ground and is marked by stone cairns. I plodded painfully on, head butting into the pelting rain, exchanging greetings with younger walkers, who came bounding down out of the mist in a shower of stones.

'Keep going,' cried one.

'It's not far now,' said another.

Like a lot of mountains, Carrauntoohil has false crests. Every so often, looking up from my bent-double position over my walking stick, I would see what appeared to be the top of the mountain, a curving, grey line in the mist up ahead, and think, I've done it! Then, as I staggered upwards, another dim crest would appear behind that, then another and another, endlessly upwards.

The finish eventually came in sight. The summit of Carrauntoohil is marked by a tall, green-painted metal cross, and I was very glad to see it. I shrugged off my rucksack and wandered about the hilltop. Then I decided to start down.

Getting down was painful. When I got back to the top of the Ladder I was already quite shattered. I sat down on a rock, pulled my boots off and poured out a stream of peaty brown water. Then I put on dry socks and squeezed my feet back into the boots again. That done, I picked up my stick and rucksack and started down.

From above I could see a fairly obvious route. It was wet and muddy and took a lot out of me, but in about an hour I was at the bottom. I limped off across the plain and over the river as fast as my trembling legs would carry me.

I got back to the farm at eight o'clock. Night was now beginning to fall, but there was a car in the car park. Not everyone is willing to offer a lift to a soaking wet, muddy eejit with a rucksack, so God Bless Ireland, where people are kind. These were walkers who had returned to the car park half an hour before, and they were drinking hot toddies from a Thermos and as tired as I was. They all swore they would never do it again, and we had a dram or two while we agreed on that.

Back at the B & B came the divestment. This took time and help from the family to peel off my wet, muddy clothes. Then came the ecstasy of a hot bath and dry garments. Even after that I didn't feel too good.

I sat on the sofa that evening, declining all offers of food, drinking endless cups of tea, shivering and sweating. It finally occurred to me that the 'Bug-That-Was-Going Around' had stopped going around and pounced on me. I certainly felt like death as I crawled into bed. Even so, I was determined not to stop now. In another day I could be on Valencia Island.

VALENCIA

I felt all right next morning. My clothes were dry and I had slept like the dead. Then, halfway through breakfast, I began to disintegrate. Getting into the gear took a great deal of time, and someone else had to pick up the rucksack and hold it while I backed into the straps like a tired old plough horse. This was bad enough but I began to feel really shaky as I said goodbye to my hosts, who stood watching anxiously in the doorway as I plodded off down the drive. Within half

ABOVE *The author finally made it to the cross that marks the summit of Carrauntoohil.*

ABOVE *The circular Ring of Kerry route takes in countryside teeming with life and colour, as well as golden beaches and tranquil lakes.*

an hour I was definitely ill again, but no matter. I had a bug, not bubonic plague. A hard day would not kill me, and I only had about thirty miles to go.

Given another lifetime I could spend an entire trip just sauntering round the Ring of Kerry. This is a road that runs round the Iveragh peninsula through all the beauty spots, a route that will take the traveller right round the coast and back to Killarney through the Killarney National Park. There is also a footpath, the Kerry Way, the Republic's longest waymarked trail, which runs round the Iveragh peninsula, right out to the far west point and back to Killarney—a total distance of 134 miles.

This path follows tracks and green roads with some tarmac sections here and there, and a number of drove roads or 'butter' routes which once took sheep or produce to market. The Kerry Way flanks the Ring of Kerry road but lies inland, keeping to higher and hopefully drier ground, and I hoped to pick it up as soon as possible. There were also remains of the old railway line that once ran out to Valencia, and although the track has gone, the bridges and embankments remain; so what with one thing and another I had the possibility of dry going for the last part of my journey…but now it had to rain.

I was in no state to hang about. I marched as fast as I could to pick up the Kerry Way and then cut north, sometimes on roads, sometimes on the Way itself, across the col between Coolroe and the Giant's Seat—two small hills which overlook Dingle Bay—to stumble down to the Ring of Kerry to the café at the Mountain Stage.

From here I could follow the Way or the railway, or the road west. There was not much to see, for the cloud base was just above the telegraph poles and the visibility restricted by great drifts of rain. My temperature was now over the 100° mark, but with coffees in the occasional wayside café and a few hot toddies in every open pub, I got along well enough. I veered right up the coast road, driven on by a gusting wind.

This brought me along the Ring of Kerry road to a point near Daniel O'Connell's country house at Moneyduff, and here I swung left for Cahersiveen, a straggling village surrounded by fuchsia bushes. I was striding along, my head lowered against the gusts. Then the offshore mist lifted for a moment as the wind shredded it, and there, across the rooftops and the wave-tipped Sound, lay the green hump of Valencia Island.

I had thought that, with a name like that, Valencia must be named after some Armada galleon that had come to grief here in 1588, but

ABOVE *The town of Cahersiveen has a quiet and laid-back air, but for all that it is the main shopping centre for the Iveragh peninsula.*

not so. Scores of galleons wrecked themselves down this coast, from Antrim and Malin Head to the Blasket Islands, but the Spaniards who survived never had the time to give their names to anything. Those who got ashore had a hard welcome from local people. Even if they had wished to be hospitable the English prevented it.

The Governor of Connaught declared that anyone sheltering a Spaniard would be declared a traitor. Some 10,000 Spaniards were therefore slaughtered on the beaches or pushed back into the sea to drown, and those stories that trace the dark-haired Irish people of the west back to some Spanish survivor are simply fancies, nothing more.

Valencia Island takes its name from Beal Innse, the name for the channel that is now Valencia Harbour. This lies at the landward end of the island, which is most easily reached over a bridge further west at Portmagee. However, there was a short cut for people on foot, and I had no intention of walking one step further than necessary. I veered off the Ring of Kerry and down a minor road to Reenard Point, following the signs marked 'Ferry'.

BELOW *The author and ferryman Mickey Dore set out for Valencia Island after a couple of medicinal drinks in the local pub.*

The first person I met at Reenard Point was Mickey Dore, the ferryman, who was wrapped in bright yellow fishermen's oilskins and clearly looking for trade. He told me he could whip me over to Valencia Island in no time, as long as the tide was right. The tide would be right for an hour or two yet, and it was time for a nip of something on a soft day like this. I agreed and we went to the pub.

The Point Bar by the slipway at Reenard Point is a friendly pub run by Bridie O'Neill, who is a fine-looking woman for someone who had eight children by the time she was thirty-one. There were children everywhere, running among the tables, ducking under the counter, chattering like jays. The drinkers included visiting French fishermen trying to hire a boat.

I sat at the bar talking to Bridie and Mickey while they poured various remedies down my throat, all suggested by their grandmothers. Most of these contained lavish amounts of whiskey. I translated for the Frenchmen who wanted to go shark fishing off the Skelligs, and picked feebly at a grilled trout, until Mickey said that the tide was falling and we would have to be off. One boat ride and five miles after that and my walk would be over.

Mickey took my elbow and helped me down the seaweed-slimy slipway onto his open launch. Then we were off across the Sound.

This ferry crossing lies at the narrow landward end of the Portmagee Channel and runs across to Knights Town on the island. Knights Town, the island capital, was the former home of the Knights of Kerry, local lords like the Knights of Glin, and the town once supported a large monastery. John Paul Jones, the Scottish privateer who preyed on English shipping during the American War of Independence, often came into Valencia to rest his crew ashore before another foray up the English Channel, but those dramatic days are long gone. Knights Town today is a quiet little fishing port.

Getting ashore at Valencia was not easy. The falling tide kept Mickey's

ABOVE *Knights Town on Valencia Island, five miles from the author's final destination.*

launch well off the pier, and we finally made it by climbing over a series of trawlers. The state of my health meant we had to go to the pub, which naturally was crowded on this wet day. My condition was explained and various cures were suggested. These were then consumed, and there was some singing. It was mid-afternoon before I could set off on the last short walk to Bray Head. A number of people had offered me a lift, but this last bit I had to do by myself. It was quiet in Knights Town with no one about, and only the sound of the rain pattering on my rain gear to break the silence.

I left the carousing behind me and plodded up the western road. The wind was tearing towards me between hedgerows thick with fuchsia, and on I went, ever

more slowly, through Chapeltown to the Bray Headland. Low cloud hung along the coast, and nothing moved on sea or land except a small ferry which was ploughing back up the Portmagee Channel after an excursion to the Skelligs. I was quite alone at the end of my walk, and I liked it that way.

Past Chapeltown the country became more bumpy, but the road eventually brought me to the little village of Clynacantah, then swung back, and a track pointed west to the end of my journey, a mile further on across the wind-tugged grass.

So I went on through the grey day on the wet road above the heaving ocean to the end of my journey, and I kept going until I could go no further. I felt ghastly but that was just the illness, and I was contented enough to shrug that off for a few moments as I flopped down on the wet grass on the western tip of Ireland, and looked out at the ocean.

Out there, beyond the tip of Bray Head, lay America, 3,000 miles away. At my back lay Ireland, a country I hardly knew six weeks before, but where I now felt quite at home.

I would like to say that my walk had led me to some philosophical conclusion about this fascinating, friendly and frustrating island, but no thoughts came to me at the time, except that my journey had been a happy one. Ireland has its problems, God knows, but this is a light-hearted country. You would have to be a great pessimist to walk among these cheerful people and end up gloomy.

Only later did it occur to me that Ireland is not a place of the head but a place of the heart. It is a waste of time trying to understand it. You have to feel it and let your feelings take over. When people ask me why I enjoyed it, words won't do. I end up saying that they will have to go and feel it for themselves. ■

HIGHLIGHTS

The best that Ireland has to offer

ABOVE *Majestic Errigal Mountain, at almost 2,500 feet, is the highest mountain in the Derryveagh range in Donegal (see page 157).*

RIGHT *This elegant bronze statue of the great Irish poet and playwright W. B. Yeats graces the town of Sligo (see page 141).*

BELOW *The fishing port of Dingle (see page 138) has a large number of bright and attractive shops, cafés and pubs to entice visitors.*

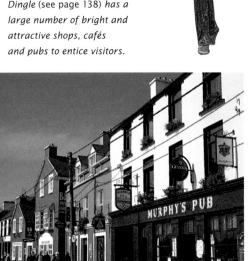

ABOVE *Passengers once travelled in style in this 1883 tram, now at the Ulster Folk and Transport Museum (see page 149).*

BELOW *A display at Dublin's Guinness Hop Store (see page 152) shows coopers making barrels for storing the famous drink.*

RIGHT *A plaque in Dublin's Westmoreland Street celebrates James Joyce's novel* Ulysses, *which is set in the city (see page 142).*

BELOW *A classical folly and ornamental lily pond form the centrepiece of the Italianate gardens at Ilnacullin (see page 147).*

CONTENTS

ABOUT THIS SECTION

THE FOLLOWING PAGES contain a wealth of infomation to help you plan your own Irish trip. You may wish to follow the ambitious example of Robin Neillands and travel by foot, using one of the walking trails listed on page 158. For the less energetic there are easier ways of getting around: for example, by one of the many pleasure craft that ply the island's waterways, listed on page 159.

With two official languages at their disposal (English and Gaelic), the Irish are great talkers, and many are world-famous for their way with words. Meet the wordsmiths and other celebrated Irish folk from page 163. A calendar of events can be found on page 169: details of exact dates should be sought from tourist offices, listed on page 168. Where appropriate, entries are followed by grid references for the map opposite.

Heights in feet
3,000 / 2,000 / 1,500 / 1,000 / 500 / 250 / 0

CITIES, TOWNS AND VILLAGES

Armagh/Ard Mhacha F3

The seat of both Protestant and Roman Catholic primates of Ireland, Armagh has two fine cathedrals on opposing hills. The city also boasts graceful Georgian architecture around an oval mall, constructed in local rosy limestone. Ireland's only planetarium is now a high-tech visitor attraction. An 18th-century Observatory commands good views of the city below as well as the heavens above. The placid fruit orchards around Armagh belie the political violence that has recently bedevilled this part of Northern Ireland.

Belfast/Béal Feirste G2

Despite the buffeting Northern Ireland's capital has had from its economic and sectarian troubles, no visitor leaves Belfast without a sense of its energy and resilience. A fine harbour setting with many green spaces adds to its appeal, and open countryside can be reached in minutes from the centre. It has a smaller population than Dublin, but is more industrialised; linen, engineering and shipbuilding all once brought great prosperity. Its museums, especially the Ulster Museum, are among Ireland's best. The Waterfront Hall, Conference and Concert Centre is an ultra-modern multipurpose venue for business and entertainment events. Belfast hosts a year-round programme of sports and cultural events, including one of Britain's brightest arts festivals. (*See also feature on page 30.*)

Blarney/An Bhlarna C8

Blarney's most famous asset, the Blarney Stone (*see feature on page 144*), can be found on the battlements of its ruined castle. Behind the castle is Blarney House, in Scottish baronial style. Grandly furnished and studded with family portraits, it has fine landscaped grounds. Blarney's crowds find further diversions in its many pubs and craft shops. A huge commercial enterprise called Blarney Woollen Mills occupies a restored 19th-century textile factory.

Cashel/Caiseal D7

A limestone rock erupts bizarrely from the lush agricultural fields of the Golden Vale. Poised on it are the spiky outlines of the fortified early Christian buildings that make Cashel one of Ireland's foremost visitor attractions. At the foot of the hill are the Brú Ború Heritage Centre, dedicated to the celebrated 10th-century Munster king Brian Ború; a Dominican friary; and the remains of a Cistercian abbey. Also in the town, Cashel Palace is a fine Queen Anne house, formerly a bishop's residence and now a luxury hotel.

Clifden/An Clochán B5

The grey spires of Clifden's rival churches pierce the horizons of a 19th-century market town huddled beneath the peaks of the Twelve Pins. Clifden's role as the capital of Connemara brings it many visitors. Craft shops and music bars occupy a number of the colourful buildings in the town centre.

The Sky Road northwest of the town runs past stunning coastal views. The Connemara Pony Show attracts large crowds in August.

Cobh/An Cóbh D8

Formerly called Queenstown, this appealing little port is set on an island in Cork Harbour. Millions of Irish emigrants set sail from Cobh during the famine years. The surrounding deep water enabled large ships to berth: the ill-fated *Titanic* anchored just outside the harbour before setting off across the Atlantic. Slim-spired St Colman's Cathedral makes a flamboyant statement in French Gothic style, and the Queenstown Story exhibition recounts the story of Irish emigration as well as that of the *Titanic*.

Cork/Corcaigh C8

The Republic's second city (*pictured below*), Cork started life as a monastery founded by St Finbarr in AD 650. Cork's Gaelic name means 'marshy place', and today the city centre rests on reclaimed marshland encircled by waterways and bridges. Towering over it stands the richly ornamented French Gothic cathedral (1870), while the famous Bells of Shandon peal out from St Anne's on its northern flanks. Cork presides over a magnificent natural harbour and some of Ireland's most beautiful coastal scenery. Bow-fronted Georgian houses grace the central quaysides, and while waterborne commerce has declined, Cork's cultural life thrives, especially in the university quarter. The Crawford Art Gallery, the Gaol Museum and an annual jazz festival interest many visitors.

Dingle/An Daingean A7

The popularity of this colourful fishing town in the far west is boosted by the scenic peninsula that trails beyond it towards the Atlantic, and in recent years by a friendly dolphin called Fungie who has taken up residence in Dingle Bay (*see feature on page 159*). Archaeological antiquities abound in the surrounding countryside, and although there are few compelling monuments within the town itself, Dingle's craft shops, music pubs and seafood restaurants have a raffish charm. The Oceanworld Aquarium features local species. Boat trips are advertised in summer, many featuring Fungie.

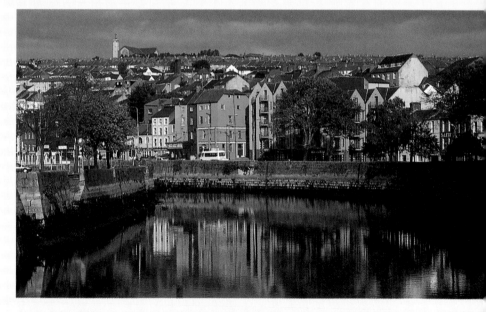

ABOVE *Colourful houses on the waterfront are reflected in the River Lee at Cork. Much of the commercial activity of the Republic of Ireland's second city takes place around the quays.*

THE WORK OF ANGELS

ABOVE *The introductory page to the Gospel of St Matthew from the Book of Kells. The early medieval book contains the four Gospels.*

WHEN THE historian Gerald of Wales stared at an illuminated manuscript in 1185, he was so astonished by its beauty that he declared it to be the work 'not of men, but of angels'. Scholars still debate whether what he saw was the *Book of Kells*. But, of all Ireland's medieval manuscripts, this has the greatest claim to be of divine origin.

The book presents the four Gospels in an elegant Latin script. Its glory lies, though, in its illuminations, which include portraits of Christ and a wealth of swirling, decorative spirals, foliage and animals. Pages were made from vellum—calf or lamb's skin—and scribes worked with ink made from soot or crushed oak apples. Illuminators used natural colours, such as green from treated copper and blue from lapis lazuli.

Exactly who created the book and where remains a mystery. It may be the work of monks from the monastery founded at Kells by St Columba in the 6th century, but many believe it was begun at Iona and brought to Kells after a Viking raid in 806. Since the 17th century the book has been at Trinity College, Dublin, but there are copies in Kells town hall and the church that now stands on the monastery site. In 1999 a new version of the book was begun to celebrate the millennium, with contributions from 155 Gaelic poets and artists.

This small town has bequeathed some other treasures to the nation: no fewer than five high crosses, a 100-foot-tall round tower and St Columba's House—a 9th-century corbelled church, all of which provide echoes of Kells' illustrious monastic past.

Donegal/Dún na nGall D2

This small town at the mouth of the Eske dates back to Viking times, and has had a tumultuous history. A former O'Donnell stronghold, its present layout round a central 'diamond' was designed by the English planter Sir Basil Brooke. He also remodelled Donegal Castle from a medieval tower house into a Jacobean mansion. Ruinous Donegal Abbey dates back to O'Donnell times. The town is famous for its tweed, which is still manufactured locally.

Downpatrick/Dún Pádraig G3

Named for its associations with Ireland's most illustrious saint, Patrick, this Northern Irish market town has an interesting museum housed in the 18th-century county gaol, where the courageous United Irishman Thomas Russell spent his final days. Several of the old prison cells can be seen. A parallel exhibition in the gatehouse relates the story of St Patrick, who was buried, according to legend, in the churchyard of the Protestant Down Cathedral. Other notable buildings include the courthouse, the customs house, almshouses and judge's lodgings.

Drogheda/Droichead Átha F4

This Norman port makes an ideal excursion base for exploring the battle sites and antiquities of the River Boyne. Relics of its long and significant past are scattered on either side of the estuary. Catholic and Protestant churches (both called St Peter's) in the town centre on the north bank display respectively the shrine of St Oliver Plunkett (executed for treason at Tyburn in 1681) and a tomb depicting the decomposing bodies of its two occupants. The Millmount Museum of local history is housed in the officers' quarters of a military garrison on the south bank.

Dublin/Baile Átha Cliath F5

(See pages 142–3)

Ennis/Inis C6

The county town of Clare stands on the River Fergus. Well placed for exploring the Burren, and easily reached from Shannon Airport, it makes a popular touring base. It has become a centre for traditional music, and regular folk festivals are held in the town. Well-restored shop fronts and pubs characterise its narrow streets. A prominent landmark is a ruined Franciscan friary, decorated with carvings.

Enniskillen/Inis Ceithleann E3

A causeway setting on Lough Erne's wasp waist enhances this pretty Fermanagh town. Enniskillen is a great boating and fishing centre on the Shannon–Erne waterway. Trips to lake islands and visits to limestone caves feature in its tourist literature. The lake-shore castle, famed for its quaintly turreted Watergate, houses a heritage centre and a Regimental Museum. Two prestigious military regiments are associated with the town: the Inniskilling Dragoons and the Royal Inniskilling Fusiliers. In 1987 one of the IRA's worst atrocities took place during a Remembrance Day ceremony, when 11 people were killed.

Galway/Gaillimh C5

One of Europe's fastest-growing cities and the largest urban community in the west, Galway feels as friendly as a country village. Once a flourishing port, it is now a thriving business and industrial centre. Music, theatre, a host of sporting and cultural events, excellent restaurants, crafts and bookshops, and an Oyster Festival are just some of its attractions. The quaint old streets between Eyre Square and the waterfront blend Anglo-Norman and Gaelic features. Reminders of prosperous trading days can be seen in the Spanish Arch by the harbour, while the Claddagh on the west bank was once an Irish-speaking fishing community. Galway's eye-catching modern Roman Catholic cathedral arouses mixed reactions. In spring, the Salmon Weir Bridge is a popular place to watch the fish leaping to their spawning grounds on the River Corrib.

Kells/Ceananas F4

(See feature above)

CITIES, TOWNS AND VILLAGES (CONTINUED)

ABOVE *Kinsale is home to one of the most picturesque harbours in Ireland. The town has a rich maritime history, and today plays host to several international sailing and fishing events.*

Kildare/Cill Dara E5

The shrine of Ireland's racing fraternity stands on the northern fringes of the Curragh, a limestone plain where thoroughbreds regularly test their paces on the verdant turf. The town centre is dominated by St Brigid's Cathedral, founded by the saint in 490. Just outside Kildare, the National Stud and neighbouring Japanese Gardens make a memorable visit. The racecourses of Leopardstown and Punchestown lie within easy reach.

Kilkenny/Cill Chainnigh E6

Visitors besiege this delightful county town all summer. Its historic buildings are unusually well preserved. A doughty Norman fortress guards the River Nore, a stronghold of the Butler family. The stable block opposite houses the enterprising Kilkenny Design Centre. Central sights include the 18th-century Tholsel (city hall), the Shee Almshouses (home of the Tourist Information Office), Rothe House Museum (a Tudor merchant's house), and St Canice's Cathedral with its round tower and 16th-century tombs. A spicy local legend tells of Alice Kyteler, a 14th-century witch accused of poisoning several husbands.

Killarney/Cill Airne B8

Tourism first hit Killarney in the 19th century, and now it's very big business. All summer, the town heaves with visitors, and with such outstanding sights and scenery on its doorstep, it's easy to understand its popularity. Within the town, the tall-spired St Mary's Cathedral was designed by Pugin. Just outside, Muckross House is an elegant mock-Tudor mansion in superb grounds. Jarveys (pony traps) take a breathtaking loop through the Gap of Dunloe.

Kinsale/Cionn tSáile C8

Crowds pour in during Gourmet Week, and for international sailing or angling events, but at any time of year this gorgeous little south-coast seaport (*pictured above*) is understandably popular. Historic interest combines with a superb setting on the wooded Bandon estuary, dotted with yachts and faced by tall, slate-roofed houses. Two star-shaped forts guard the harbour entrance, and in the town centre St Mulrose Church and Desmond Castle catch the eye amid picturesque streets and excellent restaurants. The Old Courthouse, now a regional museum, is a good place to learn about the fateful Battle of Kinsale (1601) or the sinking of the torpedoed *Lusitania* off the Old Head of Kinsale in 1915.

Knock/An Cnoc C4

(*See feature on page 155*)

Limerick/Luimneach C6

Straddling the River Shannon's southernmost bridging point, with an international airport on its doorstep, Limerick endures regular traffic jams. Scene of bitter battles between English and Irish forces in the 17th century, this former silversmithing and lace-making centre is now one of the Republic's largest and most important cities. A revitalised waterfront adds new zest to the centre. Restored 18th- and 19th-century buildings in Castle Lane house several visitor attractions. Near by at Thomond Bridge is the formidable medieval King John's Castle. Inside is an entertaining multimedia history exhibition. The Hunt Museum in the Custom House displays a splendid collection of Celtic antiquities. St Mary's Cathedral, a 15th-century Protestant church, contains fine misericords—rare in Ireland.

Lismore/Lios Mór D7

A single unmissable landmark dominates this peaceful little angling town in the Blackwater Valley—the huge and romantic-looking Lismore Castle. The building is private (it is the Irish seat of the Dukes of Devonshire), but the gardens can be visited in summer. This small town has two cathedrals: the Protestant one contains a fine tomb and a Burne-Jones window. Until the Middle Ages this was an important monastic centre and one of the greatest seats of learning in all Europe. The town's history is told in the heritage centre.

Londonderry/Derry/Doire E2

Even the name of this Northern Irish city provokes fierce arguments between Catholic

and Protestant communities. Ceded to the livery companies of London in 1613 as a plantation settlement, it acquired its 'London' prefix. Most people call it simply 'Derry', the anglicised version of the name given to it by its founder St Columba, meaning 'an oak grove'. The city centre, encased in sturdy walls, suffered the longest siege in British history in 1688–9. A handsome example of 17th-century architecture, Derry is gradually emerging from its troubled past into a revitalised cultural and commercial centre.

Roscommon/Ros Comáin D4

This thriving market town is mainly Georgian and Victorian in character. A Dominican priory stands at the south end of town; a gaunt Norman fortress guards the north. The county gaol in the centre employed a female executioner during the 18th century. The formidable Lady Betty, who once faced the rope herself, volunteered for the post and carried out her duties unflinchingly for over 30 years. Near Roscommon, the Strokestown estate encapsulates the lifestyle of the Anglo-Irish gentry.

Sligo/Sligeach C3

Sligo's most celebrated residents were the poet W. B. Yeats and his artist brother Jack, who are commemorated in the County Museum and Art Gallery. An annual international summer school draws in more creative talent, and visitors scour the environs of the town in search of Yeatsian landmarks such as the flat-topped hill of Benbulbin or the lake isle of Innisfree. In the centre of town the ruined Sligo Abbey dates from 1252. Traditional shop fronts and pubs line the streets of the town.

Tralee/Trá Lí B7

Immortalised by the romantic ballad and the Rose of Tralee festival based on it, Kerry's county town makes great efforts to entertain visitors. The Ashe Memorial Hall houses the county museum and a trip back in time to medieval Tralee called Kerry the Kingdom. In summer the Siamsa Tíre folklore theatre stages performances of Irish song and dance. Just outside Tralee at Blennerville, a working windmill, a steam railway and the Jeanie Johnston Visitor Shipyard have become popular attractions. The town makes a good springboard for exploring the Dingle peninsula.

Waterford/Port Láirge E7

Renowned for its glass industry (*see feature on page 153*), Waterford is a major seaport

HISTORY AND MUSIC IN WEXFORD

LEFT *Wexford Festival Opera Chorus perform the tragi-comic opera* Šarlatán *by Pavel Haas.*

ORIGINALLY FOUNDED by Vikings as a trading port, Wexford is now more famous for its international opera festival than for any trade. The town's name derives from the Norse Waesfjord ('muddy harbour'), and the River Slaney—at whose mouth the town stands—had to be dredged from medieval times until the 19th century, when the harbour finally silted up. Inside the town, Norman walls screen a main street bristling with alleyways—some with gruesome memories. The 12th-century Selskar Abbey allegedly witnessed Henry II's whispered

penance for the murder of Thomas à Becket, while the Bull Ring was the scene of Cromwellian atrocities in 1649.

On a brighter note, each autumn the town hosts Wexford Festival Opera, which has gained an international reputation for staging less well-known or long-forgotten works—preferring, for example, Puccini's *Manon Lescaut* to his *Madame Butterfly*, or Verdi's *Aroldo* to his *Aida*. Begun in 1951, the festival was the brainchild of a local opera-appreciation group and found a home at the Theatre Royal. At first, this Victorian theatre lacked dressing rooms and a bar—visiting divas had to dress and make up in their hotels, and theatregoers spent the interval in nearby pubs, where specially fitted bells warned them when to take their seats. The theatre was finally renovated in 1960, by which time the festival had grown to include recitals and talks in addition to the main fare of three operas—to appeal, it has been said, to the mind, the heart and a sense of fun.

along the River Suir. Founded by invading Vikings in 853, the city became an Anglo-Norman stronghold in medieval times. Sections of walls and watchtowers still stand, an authentic setting for the city museum. Several churches are worth exploring. Locally made crystal chandeliers grace some of Waterford's civic buildings. Treasures of Waterford, a museum housed in a restored granary on the quayside, contains medieval statuary, archaeological artefacts and an exhibition on the history of glass-making.

Westport/Cathair na Mart B4

This delightful town is one of Ireland's best examples of Georgian planning. Designed in the 1770s by James Wyatt as a companion piece to the local 'big house', its tree-lined Mall and wide, orderly streets make a charming scene at the head of island-scattered Clew Bay. The restored

harbour buildings house stylish apartments, galleries, restaurants and shops. Six miles southwest, the sacred mountain of Croagh Patrick looms to 2,510 feet.

Wexford/Loch Garman F7

(*See feature above*)

Youghal/Eochaill D8

This walled seaport by the mouth of the River Blackwater has a distinguished collection of historic buildings: a four-storey clock tower bestriding the main street, the Dutch-style Red House (1710) and 15th-century Tynte's Castle. St Mary's Church contains an elaborate monument commemorating the Earl of Cork and his enormous family of three wives and 16 children. Sir Walter Raleigh was once mayor of Youghal, and it is said that the first potato planted on Irish soil grew in the grounds of his gabled manor, Myrtle Grove.

DUBLIN

PEOPLE TEND *to fall in love with Dublin. It could be the legendary friendliness of its inhabitants that wins affections; it could be a matter of geography, the compactness which makes it so easy to move around, the Liffey coursing ceaselessly through its heart; or it could be the sheer energy of a university city, teeming with youth and ideas. To list all of Dublin's manifold attractions would require a whole book. Here, then, is Dublin in miniature, a selection of places to visit that will give you a flavour of the fair city. Further sites of interest in Dublin will be found listed in other sections of Highlights (e.g.* **IRELAND'S HERITAGE**, *page 148).*

Christ Church Cathedral
Christ Church Place ❹

A Protestant church since the Reformation, Christ Church was first commissioned in 1172 by Strongbow, Ireland's first Anglo-Norman ruler, on the site of an earlier Viking church. Though claimed as Dublin's oldest building, its Gothic lines were radically reshaped during the 19th century, when the building fell into poor repair. Inside is the Strongbow Monument, a medieval lectern and some 13th-century floor tiles. The crypt contains a strange ragbag of curios, including the mummified bodies of a cat and a mouse which apparently got stuck in an organ pipe.

Dublin Castle Dame Street ❺

The River Poddle meets the Liffey below the gardens of Dublin Castle, forming the 'Dubh Linn' ('dark pool' in Norse) from which the city gets its name. Located in the heart of the historic city, the castle was for many centuries the power base of English rule. The Anglo-Normans built a stronghold here in the 13th century. The Record Tower still remains, though most of the present structure dates from the late 18th century. The ornate Chapel Royal is in 19th-century Gothic Revival style. Today the palatial viceregal State Apartments provide a venue for official functions; at other times, guided tours take place.

DUBLIN, CITY OF CULTURE

LEFT *Trinity College, Dublin, where generations of Irish intellectuals have been educated.*

RIGHT *The logo of the Abbey Theatre, renowned for promoting the work of Irish playwrights, depicts Cuchulain, the mythical Irish hero.*

WHEN DUBLIN was designated European City of Culture in 1991 it seemed to herald the start of an economic and cultural boom that has made the city the envy of Europe. From buskers and pavement artists in Grafton Street to the high culture of the National Concert Hall and the Museum of Modern Art, Dublin has become a crucible of creative endeavour. Symbolic, perhaps, of this cultural renaissance is the transformation

of Temple Bar from a neglected riverside district of 18th-century buildings to a buzzing hive of bars, bistros, nightclubs and cinemas.

Dublin first gained its reputation for elegance and culture in the 1700s. This was the era when dandies and rakes swapped gossip in coffee houses, when palatial buildings such as the Custom House and the Four Courts were raised and when Trinity College was turning out brilliant graduates, including the philosophers Bishop Berkeley and Edmund Burke. Indeed Trinity, spread over a 40-acre site in the heart of Dublin, continues to be the city's intellectual powerhouse,

LEFT *A statue of Oscar Wilde, 19th-century playwright and novelist, reclines on a stone seat in the middle of Merrion Square; it was at No. 1 that Wilde lived during his childhood.*

training the academics, artists and politicians of the future.

Of all the arts, it is surely literature for which Dublin is most famous. Birthplace of a host of eminent writers—from the reforming Jonathan Swift to the notorious Oscar Wilde, whose brilliant career ended in scandal and imprisonment—Dublin features in the work of James Joyce, Flann O'Brien and Roddy Doyle, among others. It can also boast its own Writers Museum, as well as the famous Abbey Theatre. Opened in 1904, ruined by fire in 1951, and rebuilt in 1963, the Abbey has a fine reputation for encouraging home-grown talent, including J. M. Synge, Sean O'Casey and Brian Friel.

In music, too, Dublin has a vibrant tradition. It was the venue for the premiere of Handel's *Messiah* in 1742 and, more recently, has been the home or nurturer of numerous rock and pop acts, such as U2, Sinéad O'Connor and the Cranberries. And all over the city, pubs and bars hum at night with traditional music 'sessions'—when fiddlers, pipers and other musicians spin out hypnotic reels and jigs.

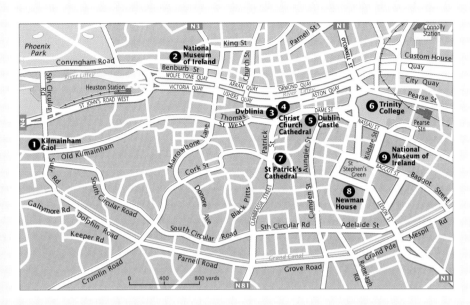

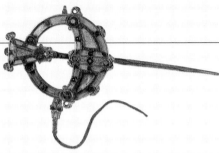

ABOVE *The Tara Brooch is one of many Celtic treasures housed in Dublin's National Museum. The gold, amber and enamel brooch dates from the 8th century* AD.

in the nave is the Chapter House door, housed in a special exhibition case. The hole cut in it shows where the Earl of Kildare made peace with his enemy Ormonde by 'chancing his arm' in 1492. Next to the cathedral stands Archbishop Marsh's Library, a fascinating example of a 17th-century academic reading room.

Dvblinia St Michael's Hill ❸

Housed in the neo-Gothic Synod Hall next to Christ Church Cathedral, this exhibition re-creates Dublin's history from Anglo-Norman times to the closure of the monasteries in 1540. An audiotape tour leads visitors through life in medieval Dublin with tableaux, city models and a 'hands-on' Medieval Fayre. The ground floor contains an exhibition of medieval artefacts excavated during building works at nearby Wood Quay. St Michael's Tower offers an excellent vantage point over the modern city.

Kilmainham Gaol
Inchicore Road, Kilmainham ❶

The grim setting of Ireland's largest unoccupied prison gives visitors a vivid insight into penal history, as well as the momentous events that have shaped modern Ireland. After being decommissioned in 1924 (its last prisoner was Eamon de Valera), Kilmainham now contains an excellent museum. The central hall of metal stairways and wired galleries makes a dramatic starting point to a guided tour past the dark cells where political internees of various rebellions were held, finishing at the Stonebreaker's Yard where the leaders of the Easter Rising were executed by firing squad in 1916.

National Museum of Ireland
Kildare Street ❾ and
Collins Barracks, Benburb Street ❷

Housed in an imposing neoclassical building dating from the 1880s, the National Museum is the merged assembly of several different

collections. Artefacts date from 7000 BC to the present day, and include Celtic treasures such as the Tara Brooch (*pictured above right*), the Ardagh Chalice and the great Cross of Cong. Exhibitions on prehistoric and Viking Ireland help to relate the museum's bewildering riches within set periods. One section deals with the struggle for Irish independence. A newly opened site devoted to decorative arts and social history occupies the stern Collins Barracks on the north bank of the Liffey.

Newman House
85–6 St Stephen's Green ❽

This magnificent building comprises two of Dublin's most splendid Georgian houses, recently restored to their original spectacular plaster work and interior decoration. The building was originally the site of Cardinal Newman's Catholic University. Celebrated former residents include the Jesuit poet Gerard Manley Hopkins, who was Classics Professor from 1884 to 1889, and James Joyce, who studied for his degree here at the turn of the century. Book ahead for a tour.

St Patrick's Cathedral
Patrick's Close ❼

Like the other ancient cathedral in Dublin, Christ Church, St Patrick's is an Anglican establishment. It stands on an ancient site legendarily associated with Ireland's patron saint. St Patrick's was Ireland's first university from 1320 to 1520. Its most famous incumbent dean was the great scholar and satirist Jonathan Swift, who is buried in the cathedral beside his beloved Stella. An arresting feature

Trinity College ❻

Ireland's oldest and most famous university dates from 1592, when it was founded by Queen Elizabeth I on the site of an Augustinian monastery right in the heart of the city. Many of Ireland's most celebrated writers were students here, but Catholics have only been admitted in the last 36 years. The stately college buildings ramble over a secluded 40-acre site, enclosing squares and gardens. The biggest single attraction for visitors is the magnificent Old Library, which houses the great illuminated manuscript known as the *Book of Kells* (*see feature on page 139*); a popular multimedia show called The Dublin Experience is on display in the Arts Building during the summer.

BELOW *Kilmainham Gaol was a prison for 130 years; the only inmates now are willing ones, entranced by the grim history of the building.*

CASTLES AND STATELY HOMES

Bantry House Bantry B8

In the mid-18th century, this fine mansion passed into the hands of the White family. In a superb setting overlooking Bantry Bay, its formal Italianate grounds are as grand as the house. Tapestries and portraits deck the

interior, along with many unusual treasures and curios. When adverse winds dashed Wolfe Tone's plans to attack Bantry with a French invasion fleet in 1796, Richard White (who had organised volunteers to defend the bay) was ennobled by a grateful George III. Descendants of the Earls of Bantry have owned and lived in the house ever since. An exhibition in the stable block entertainingly recounts the invasion story.

Blarney Castle Blarney C8

Ruinous towers and a square, battlemented keep are all that remain of Lord Blarney's tower house, built in 1446. Undeterred, visitors flock here, hoping that some of the magic of silver-tongued Cormac MacDermot MacCarthy, whose eloquent prevarications exasperated Queen Elizabeth I, will rub off if they suffer the indignity of kissing the Blarney Stone (see feature, right).

Bunratty Castle Bunratty C6

Renowned for its twice-nightly medieval banquets, complete with singers, Bunratty Castle was built in 1425 on a site used by Vikings as a trading post. The present building is 15th century, and was formerly owned by the O'Briens, Earls of Thomond. A collection of 15th- and 16th-century artefacts re-creates the mood of the times. Within the castle grounds is Bunratty Folk Park (see page 148).

Cahir Castle Cahir D7

Cahir's formidable fortress on a rocky island in the River Suir provides an impressive

backdrop for swashbuckling films such as *Excalibur* (1980). The powerful Butler family became its keepers from 1375. Throughout later centuries, the castle expanded into its present complex layout, comprising three successive walled wards guarded by an outer barbican. The great hall was restored in Victorian times. Exhibitions and an audiovisual presentation provide an overview of the historical and archaeological sites in the area.

Castle Coole Enniskillen E3

Unquestionably one of Ireland's grandest neoclassical houses, Castle Coole is a masterpiece by James Wyatt. Flanked by colonnades and pavilions of Portland stone, the main house contains furnishings and

craftsmanship of the highest order. The first Earl of Belmore, who commissioned the house, was virtually bankrupted by its cost, and it was his son who completed the decoration in Regency style around 1820. Among many dazzling rooms, the sumptuous oak-floored saloon is especially superb.

Castletown House Celbridge F5

Desmond Guinness and the Irish Georgian Society rescued this palatial country house in 1967, and gradually it has been restored to authentic period grandeur with contemporary furnishings and decorative schemes. Originally built for William Conolly, Speaker of the Irish House of Commons, in 1722, it was substantially renovated by Lady

KISSING THE BLARNEY STONE

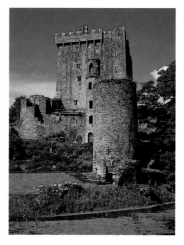

LEFT *Blarney Castle was built in 1446 as a fortress for the MacCarthys. The keep is still imposing today.*

LEFT *A tourist contorts himself uncomfortably to kiss the Blarney Stone, said to confer eloquence.*

head hangs below a parapet in which the stone rests above a hair-raising drop. One quick peck will apparently suffice for the stone to work its magic.

THE IDEA THAT a person can be given the gift of the gab simply by kissing a block of stone may seem a flight of fancy. But the Blarney Stone, set in the battlements of Blarney Castle, is said to do exactly that. The tradition that the stone can inspire the tongue-tied to speak fluently and flatteringly goes back at least to the 19th century, and to this day it attracts queues of visitors.

This fount of verbal inspiration is actually a mute limestone slab. To reach it, visitors must climb more than 80 feet to the top of the roofless keep. There, by the edge, with a guide securing you by the legs, you lie on your back so that your

The word 'blarney' was coined in the 16th century, when Lord Blarney— Cormack MacDermot MacCarthy—was asked by Elizabeth I to demonstrate his allegiance to her. But 'with fair words and soft speech' the suave lord deferred for so long that the exasperated Queen blurted out: 'Blarney! Blarney! What he says he never means. It's the usual Blarney!' The link between the stone and its verbal powers has been lost in the mists of time. But the connection was definitely known to the 19th-century wit and versifier Father Prout, who wrote that it was: 'A stone that whoever kisses/O, he never misses to grow eloquent.'

ABOVE *The Gothic rear façade of Castleward House; the front of the house is in classical style.*

Louisa Conolly, who lived here from 1758. Its treasures include a long gallery with Pompeiian friezes, rococo stucco work and a print room full of Italian engravings. The multi-arched memorial in the grounds is known as Conolly's Folly.

Castleward House Strangford G3

This strange hybrid mansion on the shores of Strangford Lough reflects the diverse opinions of its 18th-century owners, Lord and Lady Bangor. His tastes were classical; she preferred Gothic. They disagreed over other things, too, and eventually parted. The differing styles of front and rear façades continue throughout the house, but successfully evoke a personal and fascinating family home. Lady Bangor's boudoir was modelled on the fan-vaulted chapel in Westminster Abbey. Exhibitions below stairs re-create life on a Victorian estate.

Florence Court near Enniskillen E3

The former home of the Earls of Enniskillen enjoys a beautiful hilly setting. It dates from the mid-18th century, and stands in fine

grounds with walks and nature trails. Disaster struck in 1955 when a fire gutted the main building, but quick-witted workmen saved some of the priceless rococo ceiling plaster by piercing holes in it to allow water from fire hoses to escape. The interior has been meticulously restored using family heirlooms. In the grounds is an ancient yew tree which has been propagated all over Ireland.

Kilkenny Castle Kilkenny E6

This Norman stronghold of the Butler family has dominated the city of Kilkenny for over 800 years. During that time, its original

medieval structure has undergone many alterations, especially in Victorian times. After falling into disrepair, the building is now in state care and has been extensively restored. Its finest room is the long gallery, which boasts a sky-lit hammerbeam roof and a host of family portraits. Formal terraced gardens surround the castle, with parkland beyond.

Malahide Castle Malahide F5

Apart from a brief period of Cromwellian dispossession, the Jacobite Talbot family lived at Malahide for nearly 800 years until 1976. The building is romantically authentic and in remarkable condition, showing how a stern, early medieval fortress evolved into a delightful domestic residence. Ireland's only example of a medieval Great Hall is hung with portraits, part of the National Gallery's collection. All 14 members of the Talbot family who breakfasted in the hall on the morning of the Battle of the Boyne perished that day. The splendid 260-acre grounds contain an astonishing 5,000 varieties of exotic plant species. The Fry Model Railway is Ireland's largest working miniature railway, with handmade models dating from the 1920s.

Muckross House near Killarney B8

Though in Elizabethan style, this gabled, creeper-covered manor (*pictured below*) dates from the 1840s. Originally built for Henry

Herbert, MP for County Kerry, it was donated to the nation in 1932. Set in a magnificent location amid the lakes and mountains of Killarney National Park, Muckross House is one of Ireland's most visited tourist attractions. Elegantly furnished rooms are used for various exhibitions. In the grounds, the Muckross Traditional Farms recreate a bygone way of rural life. The gardens are especially beautiful in late spring, when the rhododendrons and azaleas are in flower.

Ormonde Castle Carrick-on-Suir E7

Elizabethan mansions are rare in Ireland, and this is an exceptionally fine example. Nestling in a wooded park on the site of a 15th-century fortification, Ormonde Castle displays the classic mullioned windows and gabled roofs of its period. It was commissioned by Black Tom, 10th Earl of Ormonde, a keen royalist and a favourite of Elizabeth I.

Parke's Castle near Dromahair D3

A romantic location on Lough Gill near the Yeatsian isle of Innisfree ensures this fortified plantation manor receives plenty of attention, but it's a fascinating building in any terms. Built on the site of a 16th-century tower house in 1609 by an English settler who became a local MP, the house has been magnificently restored using original building methods and materials, preserving many distinctive

BELOW *Ivy-clad Muckross House looks Elizabethan, but in fact dates from the reign of Queen Victoria. In fine weather, the gardens are a delight; if it rains, head for the folk museum in the grounds.*

CASTLES AND STATELY HOMES (CONTINUED) | GARDENS

features. Photographs and documents displayed inside show how the work was carried out. The three-storey house looks like a small castle keep, and is protected by a walled and gated enclosure known as a bawn.

Russborough House near Blessington F5

Designed by the great Palladian architect Richard Castle for Joseph Leeson, later Earl of Milltown, Russborough expresses the confident stance of the Anglo-Irish ascendancy during the mid-18th century. No expense was spared to decorate the granite house with glorious stucco by the Lafranchini brothers. Views stretch beyond an artificial lake towards the Wicklow Mountains. When the house changed hands in 1952, Sir Alfred Beit, heir to the De Beers diamond fortune, chose it as a fitting setting for his art collection. In 1974 Russborough hit the headlines when 16 paintings temporarily disappeared into IRA

hands. The house is beautifully maintained and also contains fine furniture, tapestries, carpets, porcelain, silver and bronzes.

Strokestown Park House Strokestown D4

For 300 years up until 1979, Strokestown was the family seat of the Pakenham Mahon family. The original farmhouse was remodelled by Richard Cassels during the 1730s in the fashionable neoclassical style. Now managed by a local enterprise, this magnificent Palladian mansion gives a fascinating insight into the life of the gentry and their tenants in this part of Ireland. The Famine Museum situated in the old stables of Strokestown Park displays contemporary documents relating to the administration of the estate during the Great Famine of the 19th century. The fully restored four-acre walled pleasure gardens are also open to the public.

GARDENS

NOT WITHOUT REASON *is Ireland called the Emerald Isle, and the reason is, of course, rain. Gardeners have exploited the damp, mild climate to maximum effect, and Irish gardens come in a dazzling variety, from the formal and elegant to riots of subtropical colour. Here are some of the most impressive examples.*

Butterstream Trim F5

Praise has been heaped on this wonderfully imaginative garden. Yet unlike some of Ireland's greatest gardens, which have matured for hundreds of years, Butterstream

dates only from the early 1970s. Carefully orchestrated plantings in a series of interlocking 'rooms' produce a maze of restrained theatrical surprises. A plantsman's garden with true designer magic.

Glanleam Subtropical Gardens
Valencia Island A8

Remote-controlled gates glide open mysteriously as visitors approach this extraordinary domain on the tip of Valencia Island. The former estate of the Knight of Kerry houses a mature and beautiful collection of exotic species, thriving in the mild west-coast climate. Palms, tree ferns and bamboo groves weave a dense subtropical jungle, but spectacular vistas of Valencia Harbour and the mountains of Kerry appear between the undergrowth. To enjoy these lush surroundings at greater leisure, book a night or two's accommodation at Glanleam House.

Glenveagh Castle Gardens
near Church Hill D2

The remote and beautiful national park of the Derryveagh Mountains makes a spectacular setting for these luxuriant gardens on the shores of Lough Beagh. Laid out by Cornelia Adair in the 1890s, they were perfected by Henty McIlhenny, an Irish-American art dealer from Philadelphia. The grounds incorporate a wide range of elements, from an Italian

VICTIMS OF THE TROUBLES

DURING THE TROUBLED times of the early 1920s, significant numbers of Anglo-Irish country mansions were torched by the IRA, who saw them as symbols of oppression. Although some were rebuilt, many others were left to crumble, with ivy and nesting birds replacing chandeliers, silk wallpaper and well-stocked libraries.

   The heyday of the country mansion, or 'big house', came in the 18th century. These houses gave security and comfort to a Protestant gentry always under real or imagined threat from their Catholic tenants. But landlords were often too poor to maintain their demesnes. Other houses became sitting ducks during the Troubles.

LEFT *Tyrone House—ivy-clad and roofless— was left to dilapidate after the IRA gutted it during the civil war in the 1920s.*

Among those torched was Castle Bernard, where the owner's wife touchingly sang 'God Save the King' as she watched the inferno. At Mount Shannon, near Limerick, it is said that the intense heat melted the marble staircase. Other targets included Lord Castlemaine's mansion of Moydrum Castle, and Woodstock House—perhaps the finest Georgian house in County Kilkenny.

   After the formation of the Irish Free State and, later, the Irish Republic, landowners' attempts to restore or maintain their homes were hampered by inimical tax laws and official indifference. But in 1958 the founding of the Irish Georgian Society began to change the climate of opinion with a programme of restoration. Although Ireland still lacks a properly funded guardian of heritage properties, such as Britain's National Trust, tax concessions in the late 1970s and the formation of the National Heritage Council in 1988 have given conservationists a degree of optimism for the future.

terrace garden full of statuary and terracotta to a walled garden of vegetable and fruit plots fringed with box hedges. Much of the grounds are set in woodland dense with rhododendrons, azaleas and eucryphias.

Heywood Ballinakill E6
Most keen gardeners have heard of Sir Edwin Lutyens, whose association with Gertrude Jekyll produced many wonderful country house gardens. This 18th-century park was redesigned by Lutyens himself in the early 20th century. After decades of neglect, Heywood has once again been carefully restored and is now regarded as one of Lutyens's most elegant garden masterpieces. Architectural features (pools, steps, pergolas and lime walks) frame a sequence of tranquil spaces.

Ilnacullin Garinish Island B8
Boats from Glengarriff transport visitors to this magical island garden from March until the end of October. Designed by Harold Peto for a Belfast-born MP in 1910, the garden blends classical form with a superb collection of tender species from all over the world. The achievement is even more remarkable considering the barren, infertile soil (despite its beautiful location) of the original site.

Japanese Gardens Kildare F5
The unusual gardens at the National Stud near Kildare were created in Edwardian times, when oriental themes were much in vogue. The celebrated exponent Tassa Eida and his son Minoru designed the gardens for Lord Wavertree. Pathways lead through a sequence of landscaped rocks, waterways and hills, symbolising a journey through life, starting with the cave of birth and passing through learning, marriage, tribulation and wisdom to the gateway of eternity.

John F. Kennedy Arboretum near New Ross F7
Over 4,500 different species of trees and shrubs in a constantly expanding collection covering more than 600 acres commemorates the late President Kennedy, whose ancestors hailed from nearby Dunganstown. Designed as a scientific as well as ornamental collection, each specimen is clearly labelled and recorded on a grid system. Two botanical walks lead through the trees, one through conifers, the other through broad-leaved genera. A visitor centre explains the organisation and history of the arboretum.

ABOVE *Powerscourt House was burnt out in 1974 but the gardens, adorned with terraces, flowerbeds and mosaics, remain immaculate in their glorious setting below Great Sugar Loaf mountain.*

Kilruddery House near Bray F5
These formal gardens are considered the best example of French classical horticulture in Ireland. Laid out in the 1680s by one of the master gardeners of Versailles, it is easy to see where the influences lie. More naturalistic embellishments were made in the 19th century. Precisely planned parterres and statuary flank a geometric scheme based on canals, a large circular pool and tree- or hedge-lined walks. A sylvan theatre is one of its most unusual features.

Mount Stewart Grey Abbey G3
The subtropical microclimate of Strangford Lough encourages the rampant vegetation of these splendid gardens, now in the care of the National Trust. The gardens were designed during the 1920s as a foil to the palatial home of the Marquesses of Londonderry. Formally designed Italian, Spanish and sunken gardens surround the house, while the Shamrock Garden combines Irish motifs, including the Red Hand of Ulster. The octagonal Temple of the Winds, a Greek-inspired banqueting pavilion, surveys the lough from the grounds.

Mount Usher Ashford F6
In pleasing contrast to some of the grand, formal gardens of Ireland's big houses, Mount Usher dates from a less symmetrical era. Planted in the natural style favoured by the great Victorian landscaper William Robinson, it dates back to the mid-19th century. The 20-acre gardens straddle the banks of the River Vartry, linked by suspension bridges and mini-cascades. Most of the 4,000-odd species are exotic shrubs and trees, particularly spectacular in spring and autumn colour.

National Botanic Gardens near Dublin F5
These gardens were established in 1795 on the south banks of the River Tolka. They are now Ireland's foremost horticultural institution, dedicated to conservation, education and research. Varied exhibits include rockeries, borders, ponds, Victorian carpet bedding and rose gardens. Extensive glasshouses create ideal growing conditions for alpines, orchids, ferns and palms. Pride of place is taken by Richard Turner's magnificent mid-Victorian curvilinear range in elegant cast iron.

Powerscourt House Enniskerry F5
The scale of this monumental demesne (*pictured above*) is truly breathtaking. Designed with superb vistas towards the Great Sugar Loaf mountain, the gardens were originally commissioned in 1731, but a century later they were extensively remodelled under the talented direction of Daniel Robertson. Sweeping terraces, statuary and ornamental lakes sheltered by specimen trees cover a vast sloping site. Sadly, the great house, which these gardens were designed to complement, was gutted by fire in 1974.

IRELAND'S HERITAGE

JUST AS the Clearances are a recurrent theme in so many Scottish museums, so the Famine figures large in Ireland. Dozens of institutions commemorate it, but numerous other aspects of Irish history and culture are amply and fascinatingly evoked, too, from fine art in Dublin to the foaling unit at the National Stud.

Avondale House Rathdrum F6

Charles Stewart Parnell was one of Ireland's greatest political leaders, and his birthplace is the best place to find out more about him. Built in 1779, the Georgian mansion was bought by the state in 1904, when it became

an important centre for Irish forestry. Many beautiful walks pass through the estate's 500 acres of woods and parkland. The house is now a museum dedicated to Parnell's struggle for Irish Home Rule, and the love affair with Kitty O'Shea that ruined his career. There is a good audiovisual presentation, and a letter from Parnell to Kitty makes poignant reading.

Ballincollig Gunpowder Mills Heritage Centre Ballincollig C8

In the 1880s the Royal Gunpowder Mills were among the largest employers in the Cork region. The water-powered mills were established in 1794, and came into their own a decade later when Napoleon posed a serious threat to British interests. The complex covers an extensive site with buildings scattered along a canalised stretch of the River Lee. A heritage centre shows the day-to-day working of the mills and the many skills—such as coopering, millwrighting and carpentry—that were required in addition to manufacturing explosives.

Bunratty Folk Park Bunratty C6

This painstaking re-creation of Irish rural life at the turn of the 20th century is enormously

popular. The Folk Park contains almost an entire village, including eight farmhouses, shops, a pub, a water mill and a blacksmith's forge. In the holiday season, costumed staff demonstrate traditional crafts and trades, such as bread-making, weaving and knitting, to visitors. The whole site covers 26 acres next to Bunratty Castle (*see page 144*), and includes a tearoom.

Burren Display Centre Kilfenora C6

This information centre in a Burren village, run as a cooperative by the villagers themselves, presents an informative exhibition on the geology and biodiversity of this extraordinary limestone landscape (*see feature on page 114*). Books, models, displays and an audiovisual show reveal the unusual flora and fauna that colonise the bare rocks, as well as some of the history of the region. Next to the visitor centre stand the ruins of St Fachtnan's Cathedral.

Derrynane House near Caherdaniel A8

Visitors interested in the 19th-century patriot and statesman Daniel O'Connell should take a look at his former home while touring the Ring of Kerry. Derrynane House dates from the 17th century, and is now a museum containing O'Connell memorabilia, original and period furnishings and a collection of family portraits. An elaborate table of walnut and Irish oak graces the drawing room. A short film captures a glimpse of O'Connell's charisma. The extensive grounds sweep down to the coast.

Down County Museum Downpatrick G3

The stern setting of an 18th-century gaol adds to the impact of two excellent exhibitions inside. The grim, dark prison cells once incarcerated the leader of the United Irishmen, Thomas Russell, convicted and executed here in 1803 for taking part in Robert Emmet's abortive uprising. In complete contrast, the St Patrick Heritage Centre sorts out some of the facts from the fiction about the life of Ireland's patron saint, who began his mission near Downpatrick in the 5th century.

Irish Agricultural Museum near Wexford F7

The restored farmyard of a splendid Gothic Revival mansion, Johnstown Castle (now used as an agricultural institute), provides the setting for this engaging collection of old-fashioned farm implements, veterinary

equipment and domestic bygones. The transport section traces the transition from horse-drawn to motorised vehicles. Reconstructed workshops in the outbuildings show how work tools would have been arranged and used by wheelwrights and other artisans. An exhibition tells the story of the Great Famine.

Irish Museum of Modern Art Dublin F5

The museum is housed in a remarkable 17th-century military hospital (*pictured above*). Dating from 1680, it was designed as a home for wounded soldiers. The baroque chapel contains fine glass, woodcarving and an astonishingly ornate ceiling. In 1991 the lofty wings of the residential quarters were converted to house the national collection of modern art, which is set in chilly grandeur against ice-white walls. A self-service restaurant and a programme of performing arts are additional plus points. Combine it with a visit to Kilmainham Gaol (*see page 143*) just beyond the gates.

Irish National Heritage Park Ferrycarrig F7

This attractive open-air museum on reclaimed marshland overlooking the Slaney estuary offers an informative and coherent gallop through several thousand years of Irish history. Woodland trails link a series of 14 different sites illustrating how Stone Age settlers, Celts, Vikings and

ABOVE *The building in which the Irish Museum of Modern Art is housed is almost as remarkable as the collection itself. The former hospital is Ireland's best example of 17th-century architecture.*

Normans lived. Full-scale replicas of homesteads, sacred sites, burial places and fortresses stand in naturalistic settings. Costumed craftsfolk demonstrate ancient skills. A water-powered horizontal mill shows how corn was ground as early as the 7th century, and a Viking boat yard displays a typical raiding ship.

Jameson Heritage Centre Midleton **D8**
These handsome 18th-century buildings make an enjoyable visit, especially for whiskey-lovers. Midleton is the largest distillery in Ireland, part of the Irish Distillers group, producing several brands including Jameson and Tullamore Dew. An excellent, well-arranged tour takes in historic sections of the complex—maltings, granaries, warehouses and an enormous still with a capacity of 30,000 gallons. Sampling sessions take place in the bar (there's a coffee shop if you prefer). (*See also Old Bushmills, page 153.*)

King John's Castle Limerick **C6**
The solid drum towers of Limerick's medieval Norman fortress are reflected in the Shannon at Thomond Bridge, dramatically floodlit at night. The well-restored interior houses a lively walk-through exhibition on 800 years of the history of Limerick and Ireland. Excavations in the foundations have

unearthed pre-Norman dwellings, and in the courtyard stand replicas of siege machinery with handy explanatory notes. Documents discovered in the castle include the diary of a soldier at the terrible Siege of Limerick, which took place soon after the Battle of the Boyne (1690).

National Stud Kildare **F5**
Anyone with the least interest in horses or racing should make a pilgrimage to this state-run bloodstock farm just outside Kildare. Founded at the turn of the century by the eccentric Lord Wavertree, the stud is most interesting during spring and early summer, when new foals gambol in the fenced paddocks and brood mares arrive to be coupled with some promising resident stallion. Guided tours explore the stallion boxes, foaling unit and an equine museum containing the skeleton of the great steeplechaser Arkle. Veterinary research is carried out at the centre.

Peatland World Museum
near Rathangan **E5**
A visit to Peatland World provides an opportunity to experience the story of Ireland's last wilderness, the great Bog of Allen of the central plain. Exhibits at the museum show how raised bog was formed,

explain how peat was used, both domestically and in industry, and highlight the importance of peatland conservation. Guided walks are available by arrangement.

Ulster–American Folk Park
near Omagh **E2**
A generous endowment by the Mellon Foundation has transformed the boyhood home of the Pittsburgh banking magnate Thomas Mellon into an imaginative open-air theme park, tracing the passage of Ulster emigrants to the New World during the 18th and 19th centuries. Guided walks lead visitors from the placid sylvan setting of a typical Ulster village with its weaver's cottage and dour Presbyterian meeting house to the traumatic sea crossing and struggle for survival of those early settlers in their new homesteads. Traditional thatched buildings, American log houses and a full-scale emigrant ship have been reproduced to bring a bygone era back to life. A genealogy database encourages visitors to research family ties.

Ulster Folk and Transport Museum
Holywood **G2**
The huge grounds of Cultra Manor provide a suitable setting for an ambitious folk park, consisting of dozens of typical Ulster buildings dismantled and re-erected here. Exhibits include mills and farmhouses, rural and urban cottages, shops and a school. Demonstrations of local crafts are held within the furnished interiors. Gallery exhibitions on domestic, social and agricultural life set the scene. The transport museum covers Ulster engineering triumphs and tragedies ranging from the Irish Railway Collection to the gull-winged De Lorean sports car, and Harland and Wolff's ill-starred commission—the 'unsinkable' *Titanic*.

Ulster Museum Belfast **G2**
During the 1920s, the municipal collections moved to this spacious four-storey building in the grounds of the Botanic Gardens, and now form a fitting museum for Northern Ireland. Exhibits range from geology and botany to antiquities and fine and applied arts. Most memorable, perhaps, are the sections devoted to Ulster's tempestuous history (related with admirable impartiality) and the galleries on Belfast's industrial history. One section displays wonderful gold and silver jewellery recovered from the Armada ships that sank off the north Antrim coast in 1588 (*see also feature on page 38*).

ARCHAEOLOGICAL SITES

THE ANCIENT PEOPLES *of Ireland have left abundant evidence of their occupation, in the form of standing stones, tombs and dolmens. Some, like Newgrange, are substantial constructions that date back more than 5,000 years and reveal intriguing insights into the people who built them; others appear as no more than a scattering of stones in a field, whose original purpose we can only guess at.*

Beaghmore Stone Circles
near Cookstown **F2**
Enigmatic stone alignments and circles bestrew a remote stretch of open moorland in the Sperrin foothills. Their purpose is obscure,

but they are believed to date from between 2000 and 1200 BC, and one theory suggests they may have served as some kind of solar calendar. The individual stones are quite small, less than four feet high, but the extent of the formations is impressive. Round cairns used as burial mounds have also been discovered. The site was unearthed in 1945, having survived many intervening centuries protected by a thick blanket of peat.

Browne's Hill Dolmen near Carlow **E6**
The capstone of this megalithic monument is believed to be the largest of its kind in Europe, weighing in at around 100 tons and probably dating from about 2000 BC. Dolmens or portal tombs consist of several huge boulders delicately poised in a table-like formation. Almost certainly they were the burial places of important dignitaries, but they may have had some unknown ritual purpose too. Other good examples can be found on the Burren (Poulnabrone Dolmen), near Carlingford (Proleek Dolmen) and in the Mountains of Mourne (Legananny Dolmen).

Brúgh Na Bóinne near Slane **F4**
The farmland of the Boyne Valley is scattered with dozens of neolithic monuments. A visitor centre at Donore acts as the starting point for exploration of two of the most spectacular passage graves, Newgrange and Knowth. Newgrange is covered by a large, grassy mound about 33 feet high and faced with

striking white stones. An entrance leads inside the chamber where stone basins for the ashes of the dead can be seen. Once a year during the winter solstice, the rays of the sun illuminate the interior of the tomb. Knowth, a mile or two west of Newgrange, has some remarkable neolithic carvings.

Carrowkeel Passage Tomb Cemetery
near Ballinafad **D4**
On a remote limestone peak (1,057 feet) in the Bricklieve Mountains, with panoramic views of Lough Arrow, lie 14 neolithic passage graves dating from about 2500–2000 BC. These corbelled cairns are similar to those at Newgrange, but the burial chambers are orientated to the summer rather than the winter solstice. Near by are the remains of about 50 late Stone Age huts, possibly belonging to the same community that constructed the passage tombs. This site is rather tricky to find; look for a single-track lane from Castlebaldwin (not recommended in bad weather).

Carrowmore Megalithic Cemetery
near Sligo **C3**
Just outside Sligo town stands this remarkable collection of Stone Age tombs, once one of the most extensive in Europe. Through the centuries the site was damaged by unsupervised quarrying; even more scandalously, there were recent plans to submerge it beneath a rubbish dump, but fortunately the restored site is now protected and has a visitor centre. Over 40 passage graves, dolmens and stone circles survive, scattered over a wide area among the old quarry workings. Cremated remains have been discovered in many of the burial chambers.

Céide Fields Ballycastle **F1**
The bleak, empty boglands of northwest Mayo apparently supported a thriving population during the Stone Age, as this elaborate field system shows. Several square miles were enclosed by walls to grow crops and raise cattle. Gradually these primitive farmlands were covered by bog, which preserved them from the elements for several thousand years. From the viewing platform at the visitor centre, excavated sections of the bog clearly show the ancient field patterns; finds from the site are on display inside. There is also an audiovisual presentation.

Drombeg Stone Circle
near Ross Carbery **C9**
Signposted from the Glandore road west of Clonakilty, this fine example of a stone circle

dates back to about 150 BC. The 17 standing stones enclose an arena about 30 feet across, in which charred bones were buried. At the winter solstice, the setting sun shines on the flat altar stone by the entrance to the circle. A *fulacht fiadh*, or Stone Age cooking pit, can be seen near by. Water heated by stones from the fire was used to cook large pieces of meat.

Dùn Aonghasa Inishmore **B5**
The best-known of the Aran Islands' ancient promontory fortresses stands on a remarkable site above sheer cliffs. Three concentric horseshoe walls shield it from marauders, but it remains pitilessly exposed to the elements, and the only escape is via a suicidal 200-foot drop to the waves. These days a regular procession of sightseers troops up the steep, stony path from the harbour road. No one seems certain how old the fortress is, but it dates from between the Bronze and Iron Ages.

Eamhain Macha/Navan Fort
near Armagh **F3**
West of Armagh city lies the Navan Fort, a massive earthwork crowning a hilltop. In pre-Christian Celtic times, Navan was known as Eamhain Macha, the ceremonial centre of the kingdom of Ulster, for ever linked with legends of the great warrior Cuchulain and the Red Branch Knights. A multimedia experience in the Navan Centre re-creates the history of this evocative site from earliest times. In about 100 BC a huge wooden structure was built on the mound, perhaps 130 feet across. For some ritual reason, one supposes, it was burnt, then covered with earth.

Grianán of Aileach near Fahan **E1**
This impressive circular monument commands a lonely hilltop vantage point overlooking Lough Swilly and the Inishowen peninsula. Stone walls about 16 feet high enclose a grassy space about 75 feet across. A small entrance gate allows access to the tiered interior. It is believed to date from the 5th century BC. Theories abound as to its original purpose, but it may have been some

IRISH CRAFTS AND WORKPLACES

kind of pagan sun temple. Later it was used as a stronghold by the O'Neills. It was restored (rather too tidily) in the 1870s. A visitor centre in a deconsecrated church in Burt gives some more background.

Hill of Tara near Navan F4

This sacred hilltop site commands exhilarating views over the surrounding countryside. Grassy hollows and hummocks show evidence of occupation from many different periods. Early inhabitants lived here in the Stone Age, but Tara's greatest days spanned the period from about 500 BC to AD 500, when it was the centre of Celtic Ireland and the seat of its pagan High Kings. Its power waned

after the arrival of Christianity, but it retains a firm grasp on nationalist imaginations even today. In 1843 the Catholics' champion Daniel O'Connell held a massive political rally here. An interpretative centre clarifies the defensive earthworks, including the Royal Enclosure, and Cormac's House, where the inauguration stone of the High Kings is kept.

Lough Gur Interpretative Centre near Limerick A1

This crescent-shaped lake south of Limerick city covers one of Ireland's longest-inhabited sites. When the lake was partly drained in the 19th century, excavated remains dating back over 5,000 years were removed in cartloads. Megalithic tombs and standing stones bestrew the surrounding area, where pre-Celtic settlers farmed. An interpretative centre housed in thatched Stone Age-style huts displays local finds (implements, weapons, etc.) and background information on the lifestyle and rituals of the ancient lake-dwellers.

Newgrange See Brúgh Na Bóinne

THE IRISH, *like any substantially rural population, have long depended on their own ingenuity to make things for themselves. Some crafts have grown into large businesses, such as the Parian China firm in Ballyshannon; others, such as lace-making, remain cottage industries. Big or small, a craft factory or workshop makes for a stimulating visit, and many have souvenir shops—a spade from Patterson's Spade Mill would make an unusual gift!*

Ardara D2

The little village of Ardara near the Blue Stack Mountains has a long tradition of making handcrafted tweed. Mechanised cloth-making takes place locally, but there has recently been a great revival of interest in traditional methods. Old-style hand weaving is still carried out in the homes of local people, as it has been for centuries. Ardara has numerous tweed and knitwear shops, and one or two of the larger stores (e.g. Triona Design or John Malloy) offer tours and demonstrations of hand-loom weaving. Ardara's heritage centre fills in more background about the weaving industry.

Avoca Handweavers Avoca F6

Ireland's oldest surviving hand-weaving mill, dating from 1723, is still a thriving enterprise. Avoca Handweavers produce bright tweeds in jewel-like colours, mostly for women's fashions. Much is now manufactured on modern machinery, but visitors to this neat riverside complex of white cottages can still watch old looms in action. Large showrooms display an extensive range of finished goods and other crafts.

Belleek Pottery Belleek D3

Practically straddling the border between Northern Ireland and the Republic, this handsome 19th-century building produces some of Ireland's most prized and instantly recognisable china. Parian ware is named after the Greek island of Paros, whose pale,

translucent marble the china resembles. Belleek's speciality is a delicate, ornamental style called basketware—cream-coloured, lattice-patterned and decorated with flowers. A visitor centre and museum display some eye-catching historic pieces. An audiovisual presentation, gift shop and guided factory tours are laid on for visitors.

Burren Perfumery and Floral Centre near Corrofin C6

A remote house in the ghostly limestone wilderness of the Burren is an unlikely setting for a working perfumery. For over 25 years this fascinating centre has extracted essential oils by traditional methods from dozens of varieties of flowers, ferns and mosses. They are then blended into cosmetics, fragrances and aromatherapy products. There is an audiovisual presentation and photographic exhibition on different types of Burren flora, and also on display is a traditional still capable of distilling oils from over 1,000 pounds of plant material at a time.

Burren Smokehouse Lisdoonvarna B6

EU regulations on food hygiene preclude tours round the processing rooms these days, but visitors can find out from demonstrations and an audiovisual presentation how Atlantic salmon is cold smoked over charred oak chippings. The secrets of this ancient craft are alleged to date back to Celtic times. Gourmet products are on sale at the centre (trout, mackerel and eel as well as salmon). The century-old Roadside Tavern next door offers more extensive tastings. A worldwide mail-order service is available.

Carrickmacross Lace Gallery Carrickmacross F4

County Monaghan has a long tradition of lace-making, and Carrickmacross is the oldest centre in Ireland. The craft was first introduced in the early 19th century by a rector's wife who learned her skills on her Italian honeymoon (my, was she bored!). A lace-makers' cooperative runs this gallery, where exquisite pieces of handmade lace are displayed, and the craft is demonstrated. Typical Carrickmacross lace features fine loop work incorporating Irish emblems such as harps and shamrocks. Other centres of Irish lace-making include Clones, Kenmare and Limerick.

IRISH CRAFTS AND WORKPLACES (CONTINUED)

ABOVE *The Old Bushmills Distillery, situated on the River Bush, was granted a licence to produce whiskey in 1608, making it the oldest such establishment in the world.*

Connemara Marble Factory Moycullen C5

The attractively mottled greenish stone known as Connemara marble is carved into a surprising range of souvenir products in this small village. You may not want to lug your own gravestone home, but jewellery, ashtrays, figurines and paperweights make appealing and portable presents. Worry beads are a factory speciality.

Donegal Craft Village Donegal D2

This village-like complex of studio shops just outside the town on the main N15 Ballyshannon road makes a good place for souvenir hunting. Modern, purpose-built premises provide an attractive showcase for local artisans and craft workers—potters, weavers, silkscreen printers, jewellers, etc. There's no charge for entry to the village, where there is easy parking. Visitors can usually see some craft work in progress.

Donegal Parian China Ballyshannon A1

Here, at the garrison town of Ballyshannon, a large modern factory welcomes visitors for free tours and a perusal of its showroom, where local products, made from china known as Parian ware, are on display. An audiovisual presentation explains the production process.

Foxford Woollen Mills Foxford C4

The visitor centre at this historic woollen mill opened exactly a century after a single-minded nun, Agnes Morrogh-Bernard (1842–1932), first set up the weaving enterprise in 1892 in an attempt to staunch emigration. This small country town on the River Moy is now a popular touring destination. A tour round the mill shows local craftspeople busy at work on Foxford's high-quality rugs, blankets and tweeds, along with plenty of background about the history of the factory. Ancillary attractions include a restaurant, art galleries and a jewellery workshop.

Guinness Hop Store Dublin F5

The black stuff with the 'foamous' top (as James Joyce put it) probably evokes Ireland more than any other product, though the recipe was modelled on 'porter', a London beer. This warehouse visitor centre near the world-famous Dublin brewery provides a detailed and entertaining exhibition on the historic product, ending with a tasting session in the bar: the Liffey-side premises where the modern version of Arthur Guinness's original beer is produced is the largest brewery in Europe. The profits have financed many charitable projects. (*See also feature on page 90.*)

Irish Linen Centre Lisburn F3

Northern Ireland's linen industry is given a new lease of life in this award-winning attraction opened in 1994. A self-guided tour through re-created factory scenes tells the story of the textile from its earliest origins. A spinner's cottage, a beetling engine (where the flax fibres were hammered to a smooth surface) and a weaving workshop are on display. Expert weavers still produce damask linen in traditional ways on restored 19th-century looms. Linen products are on sale in the shop.

Irish National Knitting Centre near Buncrana E1

Irish knitwear can be found all over Ireland these days, far from its traditional home on the Aran Islands. Increasingly, it is produced mechanically, but this small centre near Buncrana on the Inishowen peninsula keeps alive the time-honoured cottage industry skills of hand-knitting—albeit by computerised patterns. Home workers from both sides of the Irish border are trained to knit the classic honeycombs, plaits and blackberries which find their way into sweaters and hats. Knitting tuition holidays are organised. A small exhibition includes features on spinning and natural dyes.

Kilkenny Design Centre Kilkenny E6

The old stable block of Kilkenny Castle was imaginatively converted into a complex of craft studios during the early 1960s. Today it has achieved widespread recognition as one of Ireland's foremost centres of artistic and design talent. Visitors can watch a great variety of craft work in progress, while the large, airy showrooms display the finished products on sale. Items include leather goods, knitwear, ceramics, jewellery and glass.

Louis Mulcahy's Pottery Ballyferriter A7

This attractive pottery close to the village of Ballyferriter makes a good place to stop on a tour of the Dingle peninsula. These light, stylish galleries make ideal showrooms for the distinctive, chunky ceramics produced on site, which are particularly noted for their unusual decorative glazes. A coffee shop gives visitors the chance to try out some of the products on tables inlaid with ceramic tiles.

Magee's Donegal D2

Still owned and run by the family that first established the business in 1866, Magee's is a local legend, manufacturing the high-quality, hard-wearing tweed, for which this part of Ireland is famous, in soft, natural, peaty colours. The premises stand right in the heart of town. Some of the original wooden hand looms are still in use, but more advanced technology produces the majority of the textiles. A thriving export trade distributes bales of cloth and tailored men's garments to many parts of the world. Visitors are welcome to join short, free tours during opening hours (closed Wednesdays).

Old Bushmills Distillery Bushmills F1
Northern Ireland's famous whiskey hails from the world's oldest continuously run distillery, on the outskirts of the town. Sir Thomas Phillips was first granted a licence in 1608, though the 'water of life' was probably produced here well before that. Bushmills is now part of the Irish Distillers Group, which produces the popular blended whiskeys Jameson and Blackbush, but it is also famous for its aged single malts. The distillery tours are an immensely popular tourist attraction—with a tasting, of course. Reservations are advised in high season.

Patterson's Spade Mill Templepatrick F2
The last water-powered spade mill in Ireland still turns out a great variety of turf and garden spades using original equipment. The plant was founded in 1919. Spade-making was once an essential rural craft: Ireland has no natural coal or oil reserves and only limited forests, so peat-cutting, now almost exclusively mechanised, was until postwar times the only way many people could obtain fuel for cooking and heating. Visitors can see the spades being made and buy the finished products.

Roundstone Musical Instruments Roundstone B5
The charming village of Roundstone stands at the foot of Errisbeg on the southern coast of Connemara. Near by is one of the best remaining stretches of blanket bog. The village contains a number of craft enterprises, most unusual of which is this musical instrument workshop, open seven days a week. Various simple traditional instruments are on sale: most typical is the *bodhrán*—a hand-held goatskin drum (*above*). Plenty of pubs in this part of Ireland offer music and allow you to hear the instruments in action.

CRYSTAL CLEAR

WHEN GEORGE and William Penrose established their glass-making business in 1783, little did they know that Waterford Crystal would become prized the world over. Using a secret formula, the Penroses created a lead crystal glass with spectacular properties: thick enough to cut deep patterns into, the crystal refracted light with a brilliance that made it sparkle like diamonds. Original Waterford Crystal was a smoky blue colour, and although collectors will pay large sums for such pieces, the manufacturers worked hard to produce the clear crystal sold today.

Waterford Crystal flourished, but by 1851—the year it won several gold medals at the Great Exhibition in London—heavy taxation forced the business to close. Almost a whole century passed before glass-making returned to Waterford. In the 1940s Irish independence spurred an Irish crafts revival, and as part of this revival a small glass factory opened in 1947. Master craftsmen trained up young apprentices to use the traditional tools and techniques, and Waterford was

ABOVE *Ornate Waterford Crystal, delicately crafted by Ireland's master cutters, graces homes across the world.*

LEFT *A master blower exerts all his skill and energy to turn the raw material into the right shape and size of glass or bowl.*

soon producing high-class crystal once more. By the 1980s it was the largest manufacturer of hand-crafted crystal in the world.

The key craftsmen in the crystal-making process are the blowers and cutters. The blowers skilfully transform globules of molten crystal into the clearest glass using simple hollow iron rods, handmade wooden tools and their sheer puff; while the cutters, with their steady hands and sharp eyes, grind delicate shapes into the crystal to create beautiful and complex designs.

RELIGIOUS SITES

Boyle Abbey Boyle D4
Founded in 1161, this Cistercian abbey in the centre of Boyle was a sister house of Mellifont (*see entry on page 156*). It survived repeated raids and political suppression remarkably intact, and much of it can still be seen, including cellars and kitchens as well as the church and cloisters. Gothic and Romanesque features are preserved in the 12th-century church, housing some quaint carvings. In 1659 it was fortified. A visitors' centre in the old gatehouse tells the story of the abbey.

Clonfert Cathedral Clonfert D5
The Church of Ireland Cathedral of Clonfert stands beside the Shannon near a lonely expanse of Midland bog. Its most famous feature is a superb Romanesque doorway dating from around 1200, one of the most ornately decorated anywhere in Ireland. A triangular tympanum of human heads carved from stone surmounts a rounded archway teeming with geometrical, animal and plant details. The tiny cathedral was built on the site of a much earlier monastery founded in 563 by St Brendan, the great navigator whose transatlantic voyages may have predated Columbus. He is believed to be buried here.

Clonmacnoise near Shannonbridge D5
These medieval ruins occupy a tranquil site beside the River Shannon. The monastery was founded by St Ciaran in the mid-6th century, and became one of the most influential in Ireland as a place of scholarship and artistic talent until its final desecration by English forces in 1552. Some of its greatest treasures are now on display in Dublin's National Museum, including a decorated crozier of gold and silver, and the early Irish illuminated manuscript, the *Book of the Dun Cow*. The complex contains the stone shells of the cathedral and eight churches, two round towers and several carved crosses. A visitors' centre houses finds from the site in replica beehive huts. On St Ciaran's Day (September 9) pilgrims circle the ruins three times.

Cong Abbey Cong B5
Cong Abbey was an Augustinian foundation established by Turlough O'Connor, a 12th-century King of Connaught and High King of Ireland. An earlier monastery had existed on the site since the 6th century. Residual structures include fine carved doorways in transitional style (wavering between Romanesque and Gothic), a chapter house and restored cloisters. Most unusual is an ingenious fishing house poised over the river.

ABOVE *The Gallarus Oratory is a curious little church shaped like an upturned boat; probably dating from the 7th or 8th century, its dry-stone masonry is still remarkably intact.*

Bait was rigged on a line attached to a bell in the kitchens, and when a fish was hooked, the bell rang. Cong's most precious asset is an ornate processional cross, now on display in Dublin's National Museum.

Croagh Patrick near Leckanvy B4
At 2,510 feet, this regular conical peak dominates the countryside around Clew Bay. It has been a place of ritual worship for thousands of years. In 441, St Patrick allegedly fasted and prayed here for the 40 days of Lent, and it subsequently became Ireland's holy mountain. Pilgrims and penitents make an arduous ascent to the mountain-top chapel at the end of July, some barefoot. Apart from blisters, rewards of a climb (weather permitting) are splendid views. Folklore asserts that Patrick rang a bell from the summit and all the snakes of Ireland fled from the country.

Devenish Island near Enniskillen E3
Close to Enniskillen, where Lower Lough Erne constricts to a causeway, this tiny islet has aroused interest for centuries. During the 6th century the scholar-monk St Molaise founded a great centre of learning here, which survived Viking and Norman raids and stayed influential until the 17th century. Among its most interesting features are the Teampull Mór (a church dating from 1225), and St Mary's Priory, a much later Augustinian

church constructed during the 15th century. Best-preserved feature is the defensive round tower, which stands over 80 feet high. Boat trips run from Enniskillen in summer.

Gallarus Oratory near Ballyferriter A7
This tiny, boat-shaped church on the Dingle peninsula (*pictured above*) is one of the best-preserved early Christian buildings in Ireland. It stands isolated in a small, walled field on the treeless slopes overlooking Smerwick Harbour. Its precise age is uncertain; it has been variously attributed to periods anywhere between the 6th and 12th centuries, but is most probably from the 7th or 8th. Skilfully constructed in dry-stone masonry, it still keeps out the rain after 1,000 years.

Gartan Lough
near Glenveagh National Park D2
This beautiful spot near Glenveagh National Park is the supposed birthplace of one of Ireland's greatest and most charismatic saints: Columba (Colmcille in Gaelic, meaning 'the Dove of the Church'). To find out more about him, head for the Colmcille Heritage Centre on the lake shore, where an interpretative exhibition places the saint's extraordinary life against the perspective of Celtic Christianity during the 6th century. The nearby Natal Stone, where Columba is said to have been born in 521, is revered for its healing powers.

Glendalough near Laragh F6

The innate beauty of a lake-and-woodland setting in the Wicklow Mountains makes this important monastic site one of the most evocative anywhere in Ireland. Glendalough was founded by St Kevin, a hermit scholar-monk, in the 6th century. Despite repeated attacks by Vikings and Norman forces, it survived until the Dissolution of the Monasteries in 1539. Most of the buildings are very early, dating from the 8th to 12th centuries. They include an intact round tower, a simple church with a chimney-like belfry called St Kevin's Kitchen, and the scattered remains of several other church buildings, monk cells, crosses and gravestones. A visitor centre interprets the site, and way-marked walks lead round the ruins.

Holy Cross Abbey Holycross D6

The great treasure of this Benedictine abbey is a splinter of that ubiquitous object of Christian veneration, the True Cross. During the Middle Ages, this sacred relic made Holy Cross a famous place of pilgrimage, and the riches thus endowed on the church resulted in a late Gothic masterpiece. The present cruciform 15th-century building was constructed by the Cistercians who took over the abbey in 1180. During the last 30 years Holy Cross has been extensively restored and is once more a shrine for Catholic pilgrims. Inside is a rare wall painting of a Norman hunting scene and some impressive stone carving.

Jerpoint Abbey near Thomastown E7

These handsome, square-towered ruins are easily spotted by the roadside southwest of Thomastown. Many of the domestic parts of this fortified Cistercian monastery have vanished, but some lively sculptures of courtly life and strange beasts adorn arcades, capitals and tombs in the church. Carved figures clearly show details of the clothes and armour worn in the 15th and 16th centuries. Jerpoint was founded by a Celtic king in about 1160, and passed into the hands of the Earl of Ormonde after the Dissolution of the Monasteries.

Kells F4

The famous illuminated manuscript from Kells Monastery is now kept in the Old Library at Trinity College, Dublin (*see feature on page 139*), but a facsimile is on view in St Columba's Church in Kells. The community was first set up by St Columba during the 6th century, but it expanded during the 9th, when monks fled here from Iona after Viking

attacks. Near the church stand St Columba's house (a stone-roofed oratory), a round tower, and several carved high crosses. One of these was moved to the marketplace and used as a gallows during a 1798 uprising.

Kilmacduagh near Gort C6

From a distance, this remote monastic site looks a bit like a rocket launching-pad against the wan limestone of the Burren. A surreally tilting round tower pierces the skyline, distracting passing motorists who think their eyes are playing tricks. Fields near by enclose a simple, roofless cathedral or tempeall and a scattering of smaller dependent churches.

The tempeall, originally pre-Norman, was modified in Gothic style, while the Abbot's House to the northeast (recently restored) dates from late medieval times.

Knock C4

(See feature below)

Lough Derg D6

In the middle of this remote lake, a small island has been a pilgrimage site since medieval times. Today the islet is entirely covered with buildings, including hostels and a substantial basilica. Each year from Whitsuntide to the Feast of the Assumption

---

THE MIRACLE OF KNOCK

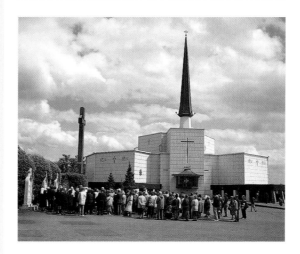

ABOVE *Religious icons in all shapes and forms can be bought at souvenir shops in the holy village of Knock.*

LEFT *The basilica at Knock, which Father Horan built in 1976 to accommodate pilgrims to the Holy Shrine.*

THREE FIGURES, bathed in a shimmering light, mysteriously hovered beside the village church wall; beside them a lamb and a wooden cross were also visible. It was this scene that no fewer than 15 people claimed they witnessed on August 21, 1879, in the small community of Knock, in northwest Ireland. The figures, which the villagers recognised as the Virgin Mary, St Joseph and St John the Evangelist, appeared for two hours; their glow engulfed the whole church and was said to have been visible from miles around.

Since this miraculous event, devout Catholics have flocked in their thousands to Knock to pray at the Holy Shrine. A hundred years on the local parish priest, Father James Horan, began to

invest all his energies in getting Knock recognised as one of the world's most important Marian shrines. One of his first projects, in 1976, was to build a huge 20,000-seat basilica as a much-needed alternative to the small village church.

Perhaps Horan's greatest coup, however, was when Pope John Paul II accepted his invitation to attend the centenary celebration of Knock shrine. In 1979 the first ever papal visit to Ireland caused shock waves of delight throughout the country. Horan's last achievement was also phenomenal: in 1986 an airport opened near Knock to provide easy access to the shrine for worshippers from the four corners of the world. It was named not after the town, but after the humble priest with big ideas.

RELIGIOUS SITES (CONTINUED)

WILD IRELAND

(June–August), pilgrims arrive for a penitential three-day stay. They undertake an all-night vigil, eat and drink nothing except black tea and dry bread, and walk barefoot around the island, praying at various shrines. The regime is based on the legend that Station Island, like Croagh Patrick (*see page 154*), was where St Patrick once spent a Lenten fast. Outside the pilgrim season, other visitors are welcome.

Mellifont Abbey near Drogheda F4

Not far from Monasterboice (*see entry below*) are the ruins of Ireland's first Cistercian monastery, founded in 1142 by St Malachy, Archbishop of Armagh. The abbey's design shows many similarities to the French monastery at Clairvaux, where the abbot was a friend of St Malachy. The most impressively preserved section is a 13th-century octagonal lavabo, a fountain where the monks washed before meals. Parts of the cloisters and chapter house also remain. William of Orange used Mellifont as his headquarters during the Battle of the Boyne in 1690.

Monasterboice near Drogheda F4

A rural graveyard near Drogheda contains the well-preserved ruins of a 5th-century monastic settlement founded by St Buite, a disciple of St Patrick. The most remarkable features of this site are its 10th-century high crosses, among the best of their kind in Ireland. The one known as Muiredach's Cross has the clearest decoration. The sculpted biblical scenes are carved in deep relief, and include David and Goliath, Cain slaying Abel, and the Last Judgment. The west face contains scenes from the life of Christ. Two other crosses, ruined churches, a round tower and a pre-Gothic sundial can be seen near by.

Rock of Cashel Cashel D7

During St Patrick's mission in the 5th century, this rocky stronghold was the seat of the Kings of Munster. Convinced by Patrick's use of a shamrock leaf to interpret the doctrine of the Holy Trinity, King Aengus became Ireland's first Christian ruler. From the 12th century Cashel flourished as a religious centre rather than a political power base, until Cromwell's Ironsides massacred its inhabitants in 1647. The main surviving buildings include the roofless ruins of the Gothic cathedral, and next to it Cormac's Chapel featuring beautiful Romanesque carving. The oldest and tallest structure on the Rock is the round tower, with an entrance safely above ground level. The 15th-century Hall of the Vicars' Choral now houses a museum containing St Patrick's Cross.

St Columb's Cathedral Londonderry E2

This Protestant cathedral was the first to be founded anywhere in the British Isles after the Reformation. The original building was constructed between 1628 and 1633, but extensively modified during the 19th century. Anyone who wants to understand the North's

turbulent history should visit the Chapter House Museum, where the keys to the city once seized by Derry's Apprentice Boys are held. The cannonball in the vestibule was fired by James II's army during the terrible siege of 1689, carrying a note dictating terms for surrender. The defiant reply 'No Surrender' has echoed down the centuries.

St Michan's Church Dublin F5

Unremarkable from the outside, this mainly 17th-century church on the north bank of the Liffey attracts visitors with a taste for the macabre. Deep in its vaults lies a collection of ancient mummified corpses, some thought to belong to leaders of the 1798 rebellion. St Michan's has other less ghoulish points of interest: the penitent's pew is where wrongdoers publicly confessed their offences; and spectacular woodcarving showing fruits and musical instruments can be seen above the choir Handel is said to have played the church's organ.

Shrine of St Oliver Plunkett Drogheda F4

The Catholic church of St Peter's in Drogheda is renowned for its unusual shrine. In July 1681 the much-respected Oliver Plunkett, Archbishop of Armagh and Primate of All Ireland, was executed for treason at Tyburn in London, after false allegations that he had been involved in a plot to undermine British rule in Ireland. Plunkett's severed head, blackened by flames, was embalmed and brought back to Ireland, where it can be seen in the church. In 1976 he was canonised for his refusal to recant his Catholicism.

WITH A POPULATION *of just 5 million and an area little more than one-third the size of mainland Britain, Ireland abounds in open spaces, where nature has wrought the landscape into breathtaking forms. Here you will find some of the most exhilarating scenery in the British Isles. In high season you are unlikely to have it to yourself, but it will enthrall you nonetheless.*

Beara Peninsula B8

Often overlooked by visitors in favour of the better-known Ring of Kerry or Dingle peninsula, Beara (half in Cork, half in Kerry), amply repays exploration in fine weather. The coastal route takes in glorious views around Bantry Bay and the Kenmare estuary, trickling past the desolate copper-mining landscapes of Allihies. Highlights include the luxuriant Derreen Gardens at Lauragh, and Dursey Island, reached by cable car. Even more spectacular is the steep climb via the Healy Pass through the Caha Mountains.

The Burren C6

(*See feature on page 114*)

Cliffs of Moher B6

A five-mile curtain of dark cliffs guards the Burren coast of Clare near Liscannor, plunging dramatically from a height of 650 feet. Sea birds squabble on precarious ledges of black shale and sandstone. A well-signed car park with a commercialised visitors' centre makes it a popular tourist spot, but the best way to absorb this awesome natural spectacle is to walk along the coastal path, taking great care not to stray too near the crumbling edges. O'Brien's Tower is a Victorian folly and viewing point. On clear days the Aran Islands and the mountains of Connemara are visible.

Connemara National Park B5

(*See feature on page 96*)

Giant's Causeway F1

Legend says the Ulster giant Finn MacCool built the causeway as a stepping stone to Scotland, but geologists incline to the notion that this crystalline mass of hexagonal basalt columns was formed by the cooling of volcanic lava about 60 million years ago. Today, Ireland's most recognisable landmark is classed as a World Heritage Site and a nature reserve in the care of the National Trust. A visitors' centre fills in the background to this extraordinary phenomenon, and in summer a shuttle bus takes visitors down the steep hill to the rocks.

Glenveagh National Park D2

Grand glacial valleys carve through the moorlands and mountains of central Donegal. The symmetrical cone of Errigal Mountain (2,466 feet) is the highest of the Derryveagh range. Lough Beagh and the Poisoned Glen are other natural features around the estate of Glenveagh Castle, where Ireland's largest herd of red deer roams. Woodland of native oak and birch persists in scattered patches; spruce and rhododendron are more recent imports. Self-guided nature trails and a visitor centre encourage further exploration through this magnificent 25,000-acre park.

Killarney National Park B8

During the height of the tourist season, Killarney is anything but peaceful, but the grandeur of its scenery is truly unmatched.

 Three interconnected lakes reflect a dazzling backdrop of Ireland's highest mountains, its largest area of natural woodlands and substantial stretches of bog, all cloaked in luxuriant vegetation. Highlights of the park include the Muckross Estate and the glacial pass called the Gap of Dunloe, a popular touring route. Ladies' View and the Meeting of the Waters are two of the best vantage points.

Lough Neagh F2

Covering about 150 square miles, this vast expanse of water is the largest freshwater lake in the British Isles, and a wetland site of international importance. Mostly very shallow, its margins are fringed by reed beds and marshland, so access to the waterfront is relatively difficult. Huge numbers of waterfowl overwinter here, especially grebes and swans. Lough Neagh is also famed for its eels, which are fished from Toome on the northern shore. The southern shores consist of peat bog; an exhibition at the nature reserve of Peatlands Park explains the bog-land environment.

Mourne Mountains F3

These evocative granite hills enjoy a flattering coastal setting on County Down's southeastern extremity. Few of its peaks exceed 2,000 feet, but the range is immensely popular with walkers, birdwatchers and geologists. Local rocks are full of unusual minerals and semi-precious gemstones. Road access is limited, but walking trails through heather and cotton grass run to Slieve Donard, highest point at 2,796 feet, and along the Silent Valley, where reservoirs enclosed by the Mourne Wall (a scheme to alleviate unemployment) supply Belfast's water.

Slieve Bloom Mountains E5

Unusual habitats of mountain blanket bog and coniferous woodland extend over much of Ireland's largest national nature reserve. These low hills add light relief to the flat Midland counties, and while the area cannot be described as spectacular, it is quietly attractive. Minor roads across the range give motorists access to scenic vistas, while the Slieve Bloom Way is a 19-mile circular walking trail through glens and hills. Parts of the bogland are treacherous: keep to the marked tracks.

Strangford Lough G3

When the tide turns, 400 million tons of sea water race through the narrow neck of this landlocked inlet (*pictured below*) like agitated champagne, forming a shallow basin of drowned drumlins (glacial hills). It's an important marine wildlife reserve owned by the National Trust. Scenic roads run close to most of the shoreline, and a convenient ferry carries passengers and vehicles across the straits known as the Strangford Narrows. For more information on local species, visit Exploris, the Portaferry aquarium. The National Trust properties of Castleward House and Mount Stewart House stand by the waterfront (*see entries on pages 145 and 147*).

Wicklow Mountains F6

Just south of Dublin's urban tentacles, the rounded peaks of these eroded hills make a strange, bleak scene. Great Sugar Loaf's granite cone pierces the skyline close to the coastal plain, but further inland are wilder summits divided by lonely tracts of heath and bog, misty glens and glacial lakes. The region's remoteness offered many safe hiding places for rebels during periodic uprisings against English rule. In 1800 the Military Road was constructed to provide access through the mountains. Today this road and the Wicklow Way walking trail make exhilarating touring routes—though they can be dangerous in bad weather.

ABOVE *The smooth-shaped islands of Strangford Lough, known as drumlins, were left by advancing glaciers during the Ice Age. The name comes from the Gaelic for 'small hill'.*

WALKS, DRIVES AND WATERWAYS

THERE IS *an infinite variety of ways to tour Ireland. Walking allows one to see the countryside close to, and the walks listed here are among the best. If the weather turns wet, as it so often does, then the car comes into its own; beware the notoriously unreliable road signs, and be prepared for heavy traffic in the most scenic areas. Barge or longboat holidays and trips are increasingly popular.*

WALKS

Burren Way B6 & C6

This spectacular trail leads from Ballyvaughan near Galway Bay past the Cliffs of Moher to Liscannor, a distance of about 26 miles. It takes hikers on lanes and hill paths through the exciting limestone landscape of northwest Clare known as the Burren (*see feature on page 114*), best seen in early summer when an astonishing range of lime-loving plants colonise the cracks between the bare rocks. The shale peak of Slieve Elva offers a completely contrasting floral habitat of boggy, acidic soils where heather flourishes. Walking on the Burren can be hazardous: it's easy to slip and twist an ankle.

Ulster Way

A magnificent 500-mile long-distance footpath through all six counties of Northern Ireland takes walkers to the heart of its most beautiful areas, some of which are inaccessible by road. The route is easily split into more manageable lengths. Much of it is coastal, passing through well-known tourist areas such as the Mourne Mountains, the Glens of Antrim and the Causeway coast, but trails also lead beside Lough Neagh, across the Sperrin Mountains and through the Lakes of Fermanagh.

Western Way B5

This 18-mile trail begins at Oughterard on the shores of Lough Corrib and leads through the spectacular scenery of Connemara National Park, taking in superb views of mountains, lakes, coast and blanket bog. Fiord-like Killary Harbour is especially magnificent; so too are the mountains known as the Twelve Pins (or Bens) in the heart of Connemara. The southern section follows the placid, verdant shoreline near Cashel. This route is graded as 'easy to medium' in difficulty, but follow the route carefully: the wilder parts of Connemara can be dangerous, especially in bad weather.

Wicklow Way F5 & F6

This dramatic trail was the first long-distance footpath established in the Republic. At over 80 miles, it is still one of the longest and most varied. Starting in Marley Park, just outside Dublin, it climbs rapidly through the Dublin hills, then switches back through the wild glens of the Wicklow Mountains down to Clonegall in County Carlow. Parts of the route are difficult to follow, so good maps are essential. It is not advisable to attempt this walk alone in misty or wintry conditions.

SCENIC DRIVES

Dingle Peninsula A7 & B7

Whichever way this rugged 100-mile coastal tour between Castlemaine and Tralee is tackled, it starts quietly enough, skirting huge and glorious beaches around Inch or Stradbally. Grandest scenery lies towards the western end, around Slea Head (*pictured below*) or over the Connor Pass. These Irish-speaking extremities are peppered with minor antiquities: beehive huts, Iron Age forts and ancient churches. Film buffs will recognise the seascapes around Dunquin and the Blaskets as the backdrop to *Ryan's Daughter*.

Donegal Coast C2 to D1

Almost any of Donegal's peninsulas offer the stunning seascapes featured on postcards and holiday brochures, though parts of Ireland's westerly coastline have been disfigured by obtrusive modern housing. Highlights include the Slieve League coast, where Europe's highest sea cliffs plunge to the waves, and the lonely Glengesh Pass, which takes a roller-coaster ride to Ardara. Further north lie the Rosses, speckled with glinting pools and scattered islands. Neighbouring Horn Head, Rosguill peninsula and Fanad peninsula compete for scenery prizes, while the quieter Inishowen peninsula sparkles most spectacularly at Dunaff Head and Malin Head.

Glens of Antrim F1 & F2

A 54-mile coastal drive between Larne and Ballycastle leads past nine of these rugged, fertile valleys, which slice through a complex geological layer cake to the sea. The Glens make popular playgrounds for walking, angling, golfing and many other outdoor activities, but the route can easily be driven in a day, allowing several detours from the A2. 'Capital of the Glens' is Cushendall, where three of the glens converge at a sprucely kept village. Near by

ABOVE *Dry-stone walls crisscross Slea Head on the Dingle peninsula, while dotted here and there are the circular, corbelled stone buildings known as beehive huts.*

THE DINGLE DOLPHIN

LEFT *Fungie acrobatically welcomes a boat to his playground in Dingle Bay.*

SWIMMING WITH DOLPHINS is a popular holiday pastime in the warm waters of the Caribbean, but for those prepared to brave the cold Atlantic waves this activity is also available in Ireland. Twenty-one species of Cetacea, or whales—dolphins included—can be found off the Irish coast; and in Dingle Bay a lone, wild, bottle-nosed male dolphin has made his home.

Local fishermen first spotted Fungie, as they named him, in 1984. Two years later two divers from Cork began to spend almost every weekend swimming with him. Within months Fungie trusted the divers completely, and would make it difficult for them to leave at the end of a swim.

Word soon spread about Fungie the friendly dolphin, and before long Dingle was transformed from a sleepy coastal town into an eco-tourist centre. Hordes of people visit Dingle in the hope of glimpsing Fungie performing his acrobatics, or even to swim alongside him. Over the years he has provided not only entertainment, but inspired poetry, assuaged grief and healed hurt.

Dolphin-watching is popular elsewhere in Ireland. The Shannon estuary is fortunate in being one of only six places in the whole of Europe where there is a large resident population of bottle-nosed dolphins; records of dolphins in the estuary date back to the 1800s. Fungie has chosen to live a more solitary life, yet his sustained stay in Dingle Bay and continued contact with humans makes him the most sociable independent animal ever recorded.

---

lie the ruined 13th-century Layde Old Church and Ossian's Grave, a Stone Age burial site. Cushendun, a postcard-pretty conservation village, huddles at the mouth of wild Glendun. Glenariff, 'Queen of the Glens', plunges through a forest gorge laced with waterfalls.

Ring of Kerry A8 & B8
The coastal road around the edge of the Iveragh peninsula is probably the most popular touring route in Ireland. Avoid the worst convoys by setting off early and heading clockwise. The usual starting points are Killarney or Kenmare. A detour to Valencia Island makes a rewarding side-trip; alternative routes lead across the interior past the Caragh lakes or Macgillicuddy's Reeks. The natural scenery is a varied, often breathtaking mix of lakes, mountains, coast, islands, subtropical vegetation and bogland.

South Cork Coast B9 & C9
Southern Cork possesses some of Ireland's most idyllic coastal scenery. A leisurely drive pottering round its intricacies (preferably in fine weather!) is guaranteed to leave lastingly favourable impressions. Between Kinsale and Bantry minor roads trickle through charming fishing villages mirrored in calm, sheltered inlets (Ross Carbery, Glandore and Unionhall). Beyond, tantalising green fingers of land reach towards Atlantic breakers frothing on dark rocks. Sandy beaches alternate with estuarine mud flats where wading birds rummage for food. Best bits include the eerily peaceful tidal lagoon of Lough Hyne, the lively crafts villages of Skull and Ballydehob, and Baltimore's salty harbour on Roaringwater Bay. Crookhaven and Goleen weave a special spell on the rugged Mizen Head peninsula, where a lighthouse linked by a suspension bridge guards Ireland's southwesterly extremity.

BOAT TRIPS

Dolphinwatch Carrigaholt B6
While not quite as popular as Dingle's resident dolphin, Fungie (*see feature, left*), the sea mammals of west Clare are becoming increasingly well known. A school of about 80 bottle-nosed dolphins lives in the lower reaches of the Shannon estuary, and trips from Carrigaholt on the Loop Head peninsula take visitors out to watch them feeding and socialising during the summer months. Book ahead for a two-hour trip.

Grand Canal D5, E5 & F5
Two major canal systems run through County Kildare. The Royal and Grand Canals were constructed in the 18th century to link Dublin with the Shannon and Barrow rivers. Disused after the arrival of steam power, Ireland's inland waterways have recently been revitalised by a new enthusiasm for leisure boating. From the quayside of the 19th-century village of Robertstown, barge cruises show something of the Grand Canal, accompanied by candlelit dinners at the imposing hotel, built in 1801, by the waterfront.

Shannon–Erne Waterway D4 & E3
This imaginative, recently completed project links Upper and Lower Lough Erne in County Fermanagh with the River Shannon, creating Europe's longest navigable recreational waterway (*pictured below*). It is now possible to sail unhindered from Belleek in Northern Ireland to Limerick in the Republic, a cheering piece of cross-border cooperation. From Upper Lough Erne, the restored Ballinamore–Ballyconnell Canal (abandoned in the 1860s) glides through a series of locks and lakes to join the river near Carrick-on-Shannon, a major cruiser base. The system combines modern engineering and picturesque Victorian stone bridges.

ISLANDS OF IRELAND

LEFT *A tourist ferry departs Tory Island. Today's islanders welcome boats from the mainland, but in 1884 they were not so hospitable, invoking their god to sink a gunboat coming for taxes.*

about 700 makes a living mainly from summer tourism and fishing. The principal village of Leabgarrow is known for its pubs, whose licensing hours seem exceptionally flexible. In July and August the population swells with Irish-language students and the atmosphere is especially lively.

Blasket Islands A7 & A8
From Slea Head on the far west of the Dingle peninsula, the Blasket Islands seem tantalisingly close. But the last permanent residents left Great Blasket in 1953, ending a unique way of life which inspired a fertile literary tradition. Accounts of the islanders' idiosyncratic culture are exhibited at the Blasket Centre in Dunquin. Boat cruises visit the islands from Dunquin and Dingle in summer, though there is no scheduled ferry service.

Clear Island B9
The coast of southwest Cork shatters into dozens of fragments. Clear Island—reputed birthplace of St Ciaran—is the southernmost of Ireland's islands, at the entrance to the aptly named Roaringwater Bay, and an hour's exciting sail from Baltimore. An Irish-speaking population of about 150 live permanently on the island, but migrant songbirds attract many ornithologists. Beyond Clear Island is the Fastnet Rock, westerly target of the biennial yacht race from the Isle of Wight.

Clare Island B4
In the 16th century Clare Island was the lair of the fierce pirate queen Grace O'Malley. Grace died in 1603, the same year as her great adversary Elizabeth I, who respected her sufficiently to receive her at court. Grace is said to be buried on the island in a tiny Cistercian abbey. Her story is recounted in the Granuaile Centre in Louisburgh, on the Mayo mainland. The hilly, boggy island is popular with walkers and wildlife lovers. Ferries depart from Westport harbour and Roonah Quay all year round.

Inishbofin A4
The exiled Abbot of Lindisfarne, St Colman, chose this remote fastness as a refuge during the 7th century. A medieval church occupies the site of his original monastery. A ruined pirate castle near the harbour has romantic

I RELAND'S MANY ISLANDS *make for interesting day-trips… or longer ones: swiftly changing sea conditions can mean that the boat that took you out on millpond-still waters is unable to make the scheduled journey home. Islands often preserve an idiosyncratic way of life— witness the Aran Islands, where the inhabitants have their unique farming methods and famous knitted woollens. And with numerous migratory birds using islands as stopping-off points, keen birdwatchers can have a field day.*

Achill Island A4 & B4
Tethered to Mayo's ragged coastline by a road bridge, Achill is no longer strictly an island, though at over 13 miles long, it is Ireland's largest offshore landmass. The Atlantic Drive makes a popular touring route, writhing past rocky headlands and dazzling beaches. Inland, the scenery consists of moorland, bog and mountains. Water sports and shark-fishing trips are advertised in the main village of Keel, where the dramatic Cathedral Rocks plunge to an idyllic 'Blue Flag' beach.

The Aran Islands B5 & B6
Inishmore, Inishmaan and Inisheer are the eroded remains of a limestone ridge near the mouth of Galway Bay. Making a living on these treeless, storm-swept rocks is difficult, and many younger islanders emigrate in search of work. For visitors, however, these bleak landscapes and the islanders' traditional ways of life are compelling. Ferries and light aircraft serve the islands in summer from Doolin and all year from the Galway coast (weather permitting). Inishmore is the largest and most visited island, measuring about eight miles long. At its harbour village, Kilronan, the Aran Heritage Centre shows how the islanders create their tiny walled fields with the help of seaweed and sand, and fish the rough seas in frail-looking boats called curraghs. A classic documentary film, *Man of Aran* (1934), is regularly shown. (*See also feature on page 108.*)

Aran Island C2
A 25-minute boat-trip from Burtonport on the scenic Rosses headland takes visitors to this sizable rocky island. A resident population of

OUTDOOR PURSUITS

associations with a Spanish pirate, and was later a Cromwellian garrison. Visitors enjoy walking, diving and wildlife—the island is one of the last Irish habitats of an increasingly rare bird, the corncrake. Ferry access is from Cleggan.

Rathlin Island F1

Rathlin lies just under an hour's boat ride from Ballycastle and supports a resident population of about 30 families who raise livestock for export. Strongly influenced by Scottish culture, Rathlin has had a violent history beset by Viking and pirate raids. Bull Point's volcanic stacks are a well-known spot for birdwatching, and Bruce's Cave is where the Scottish King Robert the Bruce learned a spidery lesson in perseverance.

The Skelligs A8

The jagged pinnacles of Great Skellig (*pictured below*) and Little Skellig make an unforgettable sight off the Iveragh coast. The Skellig Experience Centre (on the Valencia causeway near Portmagee) tells the story

of the islands. This amazingly inhospitable location housed an early Christian community for six centuries. Today the Skelligs are left to the sea birds.

Tory Island D1

In 1884 a British gunboat set off from the mainland to collect the islanders' unpaid taxes, but the inhabitants invoked the dark forces of Balor, a malevolent Celtic god, and *The Wasp* sank before reaching the shore. Tory Islanders still pay no tax and delight in their resilient spirit—a much-needed characteristic on this craggy outpost (*pictured above left*), often cut off by storms for weeks on end. A school of Primitive-style painters emerged here to popular acclaim during the 1960s. Their work is on view at the Dixon Gallery in West Town. Erratic boat services run mainly from Bunbeg.

IF YOU CAN'T BEAT *the weather, you might as well join it. With its glorious scenery—made all the more glorious by the infamous rain—Ireland is a great place for lovers of the outdoors. Don a pair of waders and stand mid-river fishing for salmon; or wrap up in your waterproofs and take an invigorating ride through the mountains. Once you've had your fill of rain, watch others getting soaked to the skin playing an exciting game of Gaelic football, while you stay warm and dry in the stadium.*

Birdwatching

Ireland has fewer breeding birds than Britain, but its migration routes see many unusual transitory species. The rasping call of the corncrake (*pictured right*) can still be heard in a few remote westerly habitats, while Little Skellig hosts one of the world's largest gannetries. As first winter landfall for many Arctic species, Ireland's wetlands invite significant colonies of rare geese and swans. There are over 60 bird sanctuaries in Ireland, some with hides and facilities for interested visitors. For more information, contact the Irish Wildbird Conservancy in Dublin, or the Belfast branch of the Royal Society for the Protection of Birds.

Equestrian activities

Ireland is a great place for horses and those who love them. There's a race meeting somewhere in Ireland on over 230 days a year, and the cumulative sums of money that change hands in betting shops beggar belief. Famous flat-racing venues include the Curragh in County Kildare, home of the Irish Derby. Steeple-chasing (National Hunt racing over

fences) is held at Fairyhouse, Punchestown and Galway, and major races are great social events. Hunt meetings, show-jumping competitions and gymkhanas take place all over the country, and polo is played at Phoenix Park in Dublin. The diverse, uncongested countryside offers countless possibilities for trekking and trail riding; no region lacks riding stables, and colourful events such as the Connemara Pony Show or the Ballinasloe Horse Fair attract many visitors.

Romany caravans make an unusual and classically Irish way to enjoy horse-power. Five companies, all in the Republic, belong to the Horse-Drawn Caravan Federation, and publish a leaflet (available from Bord Fáilte) about hiring a caravan and looking after the horse. Suggested routes cover the flatter parts of Ireland, and designated places to stay provide overnight facilities (caravans have no driving lights or bathrooms, though they generally have simple four-berth folding beds inside).

Riding facilities are widely available. Some centres provide or organise accommodation, allowing riders to take part in lengthy trails, either from a single base or on a planned route staying in different places each night.

Gaelic sports

(*See feature on page 162*)

Golf

Ireland offers keen golfers the experience of a lifetime. The current tally of 350-plus golf courses is constantly expanding. Many are internationally renowned, varying from spectacular coastal links to challenging modern designer courses in parkland settings. Championship courses include the Republic's Ballybunion or Mount Juliet, and Royal Portrush (*below*) or Royal County Down in

BELOW *Golfers at the celebrated Royal Portrush course on the Ramore peninsula can enjoy a round in the bracing sea air, with wonderful views of the coast beyond.*

OUTDOOR PURSUITS (CONTINUED)

GAELIC SPORTS

IRELAND MAKES A STRONG showing in most of the major sports played in the world today: rugby, soccer, cycling, boxing and swimming to name a few. But the uniquely Irish games of Gaelic football and hurling are undoubtedly the most popular spectator sports in the country.

Gaelic football is a cross between soccer and rugby, but predates both of these games. It is played by two teams of 15, with a round ball, slightly smaller than that used for soccer. The object of the game is to get the ball through goalposts resembling a rugby crossbar. Gaelic football is a tough, physical game, with frequent disputes between participants. In one infamous incident in the 16th century, two quarrelling noblemen challenged each other to a duel; thankfully they were stopped by royal command before the appointed hour.

The connection between fighting and sport is an ancient one: indeed, young Gaelic warriors used the sport of hurling as preparation for

LEFT *As in rugby but unlike soccer, Gaelic footballers are allowed to run with the ball.*

ABOVE *Cork, in the red shirts, take on Clare at hurling in the All-Ireland championships.*

battle, employing, it is said, vanquished opponents' heads. Hurling is a high-speed game similar to hockey, played—again by two teams of 15—with a leather ball known as a sliotar, and a curved stick called a hurley. It is an extremely old sport, first being mentioned in a history of the Battle of Moytura in 1272 BC. But even before this, the legendary Irish hero of prehistory, Cuchulain, is said to have slain the hound of Cullen with a hurley and sliotar. Hurling was often a violent affair and it was proscribed by the Irish's English overlords in the 14th century. They were concerned that the game was a focus for Irish nationalism

and preferred the unruly masses to play gentler sports. Hurling retained its popularity, however, and was even taken back by the invaders to England, where it was eventually tamed into the game of hockey.

Hurling and Gaelic football are played on an amateur basis, mostly by Catholics, and culminate in the All-Ireland finals in September, when colourful, noisy, flag-waving crowds descend on Dublin's Croke Park for the highlights of the Irish sporting year.

Northern Ireland. Pitch-and-putt courses provide undaunting family entertainment.

Walking
(See page 158)

Water sports and fishing
Ireland's 3,000-mile coastline, together with innumerable lakes and inland waterways, makes it a paradise for water-babies. Coarse-, game- and sea-fishing possibilities abound, and many keen anglers vote it one of the best and least expensive destinations anywhere for their sport. Coarse fishing is available all year round in Ireland, and in the Republic no licences are required for the rich pickings of bream, roach, tench and pike which frequent many lakes and rivers. Game fish such as sea,

brown or rainbow trout and the legendary Irish salmon are available for much of the year, occurring mainly in unspoilt fresh water—best fished in May when the mayfly hatch. Sea fishing for bass, flounder, pollack and mullet is popular on piers and rocks all round the coast, while angling boat trips are advertised from many harbours, including shark-fishing expeditions. For information about permits, regulations, facilities and events, contact the Central Fisheries Board in the Republic or the Department of Agriculture and Fisheries in Northern Ireland. Both tourist boards publish detailed leaflets on fishing; several specialist tour operators offer Irish fishing holidays.

Clear, uncrowded inshore waters make sailing, surfing, windsurfing and scuba diving exceptionally pleasurable in Ireland, while

leisure boating on inland lakes and rivers has become a craze in recent years. Leisure cruisers can be hired by the week from a number of different points on the Shannon waterways or the Grand Canal. Most boats sleep up to eight passengers, and the more modern designs are very comfortable and well equipped. No previous experience is necessary, as full instructions are provided on arrival. Canoeing is popular on Lough Erne or on the Shannon and Barrow rivers, while sea kayaking can be arranged along the south Cork coast. Sailing is especially well catered for in the southwest too, where myriad islands and varied coastal conditions make boating especially interesting. Bare-boat or skippered charter are available at many different centres, along with tuition and specialist holidays.

THE FAME OF IRELAND

MANY OF IRELAND'S countrymen and women need no introduction. They have excelled themselves in music, art, sport and, of course, literature, among many others. For centuries Ireland has produced a wealth of accomplished individuals; and it is these people who are the inspiration for the young Irish talent bursting onto today's scene.

Francis Bacon
Painter
(1909–92, born in Dublin) This eccentric Irish artist left home at 16—reputedly thrown out for being homosexual—and drifted around Europe before settling in London. After working as an interior decorator, Bacon devoted himself to painting in 1930. His works are distinguished by the way they express hysteria and terror, contortion and distortion, one of his best known being the *Study After Velázquez's Portrait of Pope Innocent X*, a drastic reinterpretation of an already famous work. Bacon is widely regarded as one of the most important postwar artists, and his unusual life was recently the subject of the film *Love is the Devil*, starring Derek Jacobi.

Dr Thomas John Barnardo
Philanthropist
(1845–1905, born in Dublin) Dr Barnardo became a household name through the eponymous charity he established. Barnardo left Ireland as a young man to study medicine in London. His religious leanings led him to venture into the squalid East End to preach, where he discovered thousands of children sleeping rough. Such poverty spurred him to found the East End Mission for destitute children in Stepney in 1867. He went on to set up more than 90 homes for deprived and orphaned children. The good works continued after his death, and today Barnardo's is Britain's largest children's charity.

Samuel Beckett
Writer
(1906–89, born in Foxrock) Beckett was one of the founders of the 'theatre of the absurd'; a critic once said of his most famous play, *Waiting for Godot*, 'Nothing happened, twice.' He was educated in Enniskillen, and briefly taught French in Belfast before moving to Paris, where he met James Joyce and finally settled in 1937. He often wrote in French, including his acclaimed trilogy of novels *Molloy*, *Malone Meurt* and *L'Innommable*, which he later translated. During the Second World War he was an active member of the French Resistance. A recurrent theme in Beckett's work was his perception of the pointlessness of life, a theme he often explored with black humour. He writings were to prove a major influence in the development of 20th-century literature.

Brendan Behan
Writer
(1923–64, born in Dublin) Behan (*pictured right*) came from a strongly Republican working-class family. By the age of 10 he was a member of Fianna Éireann, the junior IRA, and by 16 he was in borstal for taking part in an IRA bombing campaign in Britain. He went on to serve another five years in an Irish prison for attempting to kill a policeman. He used his prison experiences to write

numerous highly acclaimed plays as well as prose; he also wrote poetry in Gaelic. Behan was a heavy drinker, and this contributed to an early end to his life at the age of 41.

LAND OF SAINTS

LEFT *The medieval manuscript* Voyage of Saint Brendan the Abbot *shows the Irish saint's boat being carried by a friendly whale.*

AFTER THE FALL of the Roman Empire, barbarian tribes plunged much of Europe into an age of darkness. Ireland, however, Christianised mainly by St Patrick, kept the twin candles of piety and scholarship burning. All over the country great monasteries were founded, and these became centres of learning. And, in time, large numbers of Irish monks felt impelled to leave their native soil to convert the heathen, in places as far apart as Scotland and Germany.

The embodiment of this questing spirit was St Brendan of Clonfert (c. 486–575), who set off into the Atlantic with companions in search of a holy island paradise. Others who emulated Brendan's spirit of adventure were Columba, or Columcille (c. 521–97), who converted the Picts of Scotland; and Columbanus (c. 540–615), who founded monasteries in Gaul and northern Italy.

In Ireland itself, the number of saints was legion, ranging from local saints such as Declan of Ardmore (who died early in the 5th century) to more famous figures such as St Brigid (d. 525), who founded the double monastery—for both monks and nuns—of Kildare. Some saints were renowned for their learning, for example Ciaran of Clonmacnoise (c. 512–45); others were better known for their devotion. Such was St Kevin (d. 618), who withdrew to Glendalough valley in the Wicklow Mountains to live a life of prayer and meditation. Kevin's discipline and devotion were so intense that a blackbird is said to have laid an egg on one of his outstretched hands as he prayed.

THE FAME OF IRELAND (CONTINUED)

George Best
Footballer
(Born 1946 in Belfast) Best is arguably the greatest footballer to have come out of Ireland. In the late 1960s he was one of the first celebrity players, winning the hearts both of football fans and love-struck young girls. His speed and balance earned him a place with Manchester United at just 17 years of age, and he won 37 caps for Northern Ireland. Best's career was relatively short: the pressures of world-class football and fame led to a drink problem, and his fitness consequently declined.

Dana
Singer
(Born 1951 in Belfast) Dana—the stage name of Rosemary Scallon (née Brown)—was still a teenager when she won the Eurovision Song Contest in 1970 with 'All Kinds of Everything'. The single went on to reach Number One in music charts all over the world, and several more Top 20 hits followed. In 1997 Dana made a reappearance in the media when she ran—unsuccessfully—in the Irish presidential elections.

Roddy Doyle
Writer
(Born 1958 in Dublin) Doyle went from teaching to become a popular novelist. The road to fame began with the highly successful film production of his first novel, *The Commitments*, which, like his subsequent novels, examines with both humour and pathos the trials and tribulations of working-class life in Ireland. In 1993 Doyle was awarded the Booker prize for *Paddy Clarke Ha Ha Ha*, which is told from the perspective of a 10-year-old boy.

James Galway
Flutist
(Born 1959 in Belfast) Galway was originally an orchestral player, but his impeccable tone and technique singled him out for a solo career. For more than 25 years he has brought the sound of the flute to millions through regular tours and numerous recordings of both popular and classical music. Galway prefers to call himself a flutist rather than a flautist, asserting emphatically that he does not play a 'flaute'.

Bob Geldof
Rock musician and philanthropist
(Born 1954 in Dublin) Before becoming a rock star with his band the Boomtown Rats, Geldof worked in Canada as a pop journalist. In the mid-eighties he turned his hand to helping famine-stricken Ethiopia by forming the charity Band Aid and organising Live Aid, the massive charity rock concerts held simultaneously in Philadelphia and London. He has written a best-selling autobiography, and in 1986 was made a KBE. Today he can be heard on the airwaves in his role as a radio disc jockey.

Seamus Heaney
Poet
(Born 1939 in Castledawson) Before becoming a Nobel prize winner and one of the 20th century's most respected poets, Heaney was a teacher in Belfast. An Ulster Catholic, he was so disturbed by the sectarian violence of Northern Ireland that he moved to the Republic in the early 1970s. By choosing Ireland's history and continuing political strife as the main subjects for his work, he has sometimes courted controversy.

James Joyce
Writer
(1882–1941, born in Dublin) Joyce was a Dubliner through and through, despite spending most of his adult life abroad. As a boy he lived in 14 different houses in and around Dublin, and he used this intimate knowledge of the city and the characters he met along the way in his novels. His writing ambitions began at the tender age of 10, and his works are now considered classics. (*See also feature on pages 104–5.*)

Barry McGuigan
Boxer
(Born 1961 in Clones) In his teens, as a bantamweight, McGuigan won a gold medal at the 1978 Commonwealth Games. He turned professional in 1981 and joined the ranks of featherweights. McGuigan's reputation for fair play and decency won the hearts of the public, and he became a national hero after he was crowned World Boxing Association Champion in June 1985. He has now retired from the ring, but keeps his hand in by commentating on television.

Brian Moore
Writer
(1921–99, born in Belfast) Moore lived on the Continent, working for the British government and as a freelance journalist, before emigrating to Canada. He wrote many novels, but is best remembered for the best seller *The Lonely Passion of Judith Hearne* (1955). Moore's writing often draws on his Irish background, and he is noted for his portrayal of women. In the 1960s he lived briefly in New York before settling in California, where he died.

Van Morrison
Singer/songwriter
(Born 1945 in Belfast) Van the Man, as his fans know him, was christened George Ivan Morrison. He left school at 15 with no qualifications, but his musical parents had educated him well in jazz and blues. He was the lead singer with Northern Irish band Them before embarking on a solo career. His eclectic style, combining jazz, rhythm and blues, folk, soul and gospel, has made him one of the most original and powerful figures in rock music. He is renowned for his impressive live performances, yet he limits his public appearances and eschews press interviews. He has made over 30 albums in the course of a long career.

Liam Neeson
Actor
(Born 1952 in Ballymena) The tall, muscular figure of Liam Neeson makes women go weak at the knees in cinemas all over the world. Before turning to the stage and screen, Neeson tried his hand at a variety of professions—boxer, architect's clerk and teacher. He started his acting career in the theatres of Belfast and Dublin, but moved to Hollywood in 1987. He has since made his name in blockbuster films such as *Schindler's List*, *Rob Roy*, *Michael Collins* and the new *Star Wars* movie, *The Phantom Menace*.

Edna O'Brien
Writer
(Born 1930s in Tuamgraney) Ireland's foremost female novelist settled in England in

A WOMAN'S PLACE

THE CHURCH HAS ALWAYS had a strong influence over the position of women in Irish society. 'Mother Church' has an ambiguous view of womanhood, holding the Virgin Mary in high esteem, while at the same time denying Irish women access not just to the priesthood, but to rights—divorce, contraception and abortion—that women in other European countries take for granted. It wasn't until 1973 that it became legal to import contraceptives—for the use only of married people aged over 18. In 1995 a referendum on divorce resulted in a tiny majority decision (by less than 1 per cent of the population) to end the ban, and led to its legalisation two years later.

Despite their traditionally lowly place in society, there have been some notably strong women in Irish history. Maude Gonne was born in England but became an agitator for Irish independence. One of the founders of Sinn Fein, she was sentenced to gaol for her involvement in the Easter Rising against the English in 1916.

Countess Constance Markievicz, married to a Polish count, was another early member of Sinn Fein; she too was sentenced—to death—after the Easter Rising, but was released in 1917. She went on to become Minister of Labour in Eamon de Valera's Dail (Irish Parliament) in the 1920s.

Fifty years later, as the fighting continued in the North, two Irish women,

ABOVE *Mary McAleese is sworn in as the Irish President in 1997. On her left is her predecessor, Mary Robinson.*

RIGHT *Betty Williams (centre) and Mairead Corrigan (left) collect the Nobel peace prize for their efforts to end Irish terrorism.*

LEFT *Irish politician Countess Constance Markievicz was a leading Sinn Fein member in the early 20th century.*

Betty Williams and Mairead Corrigan, formed a peace movement—the Peace People—to try to reconcile Protestants and Catholics and end the terror that was tearing their country apart. They were awarded the 1976 Nobel peace prize for their efforts.

Despite such influential early role models, the Dail today has few female members. All the more remarkable, then, that Mary Robinson, a campaigner for women's issues known for her radical views, was in 1990 elected the first female President of Ireland. Hot on her heels was her successor Mary McAleese, who in 1997 became the second woman, and the first person from Northern Ireland, to hold the post. The two Marys, with their high international profile, have shown the world the new face of Irish womanhood—self-assured, talented and independent.

---

the late 1950s, and started writing soon after. Her first novel, *The Country Girls,* was published in 1960. The sequel, *The Lonely Girl* (1962), was made into the popular film *Girl with Green Eyes.* The sexual candour of her writing caused her books to be banned in Ireland. O'Brien has also written for film and theatre. (*See also feature on pages 104–5.*)

Vincent O'Brien
Racehorse trainer

(Born 1917 in Churchtown) O'Brien has been acclaimed as one of the world's greatest trainers in both National Hunt and flat racing. His heyday was in the 1950s and 1960s, when he was champion trainer no fewer than four times. Between 1953 and 1955 he won all the major National Hunt races, including the Grand National, Cheltenham Gold Cup and the Champion Hurdle. He went on to achieve even greater success on the flat. His legendary partnership with jockey Lester Piggott led to many great wins. O'Brien retired from horse training in 1994 to enjoy his leisure pursuits of golf and fishing.

THE FAME OF IRELAND (CONTINUED)

Sinéad O'Connor
Singer/songwriter

(Born 1966 in Glengeary) A huge vocal range and shaved head made Sinéad O'Connor one of the most distinctive performers in the pop world in the late 1980s and early 1990s. She courted controversy when she ripped up a picture of the Pope on television, but later apologised—and went on to be ordained as a priest, though in a French ceremony unrecognised by the Catholic Church. She became even more of a controversial figure shortly afterwards, on becoming Ireland's first pregnant priest.

Mary Robinson
Politician

(Born 1944 in Ballina) In 1990 Mary Robinson, a lawyer and women's rights activist, won the Irish presidential elections to become the country's first ever female President. She brought vibrancy and youthfulness to the position—traditionally one held by retired politicians—and was widely respected both within Ireland and beyond its shores in Europe. During her seven-year term she helped to make women an accepted force in Irish politics, a legacy she has passed on to her successor—another woman—Mary McAleese. Robinson went on to become the United Nations High Commissioner for Human Rights in September 1997. (*See also feature on page 165.*)

Stephen Roche
Cyclist

(Born 1959 in Dundrum) In 1987 Roche enjoyed an exceptionally successful year in the world of professional cycling, winning first places in the Tour de France, the Tour of Italy and the World Road Race Championships. This hat trick had only ever been pulled off once before. In honour of his outstanding contribution to the sport, along with that of fellow Irishman Sean Kelly—who was ranked number one in the world for five consecutive years—the opening stages of the 1998 Tour de France were held in Ireland.

George Bernard Shaw
Writer

(1856–1950, born in Dublin) Shaw left his job as a cashier in Dublin in 1876 to try to establish himself as a novelist in London. There he established strict personal ethics, becoming both a socialist and a vegetarian. He joined the newly founded Fabian Society, and soon had a high profile as a controversial commentator on social issues. His career as a playwright took longer to establish, but by 1925 he had received recognition and was honoured with the Nobel prize for literature. His plays dealt with Victorian prudishness, and revelled in the exposure of hypocrisy. His best-known works include *Mrs Warren's Profession, St Joan, Man and Superman* and *Pygmalion* (later made into the acclaimed musical *My Fair Lady*).

Shaw lived in London until his death.

Jonathan Swift
Writer

(1667–1745, born in Dublin) Jonathan Swift, author of *Gulliver's Travels*, was a renowned satirist, and to avoid libel he took care to keep his personal identity separate from his writings. He also used his literary talents to express his right-wing views and to defend the Anglican Church. As Dean of St Patrick's Cathedral he devoted much of his time and salary to the poor of Dublin. (*See also feature on page 104.*)

J. M. Synge
Writer

(1871–1909, born in Rathfarnham) John Millington Synge had intended to be a musician, but his shy nature and nervous disposition made public performances difficult. Instead he devoted himself to literature. He lived for a time on the Aran Islands, and incorporated his experiences among the islands' isolated rural people into his works. Ireland had produced many famous playwrights, but Synge was the first to write about Irish matters for an Irish audience. He led a solitary life and died young from Hodgkin's Disease. (*See also feature on pages 104–5.*)

U2
Rock band

(Formed 1978 in Dublin) For more than 20 years U2 have enjoyed phenomenal success. Their ability to develop their music in line with changing pop trends has kept them at the top of their field. Unusually, the line-up has remained the same since the band first started playing at school. They are famous for their vibrant live performances and regularly make international sell-out tours. As a band they are politically aware: the Troubles that besiege Ireland have been the subject of several of their songs, and they have played numerous benefit concerts for Amnesty International.

Arthur Wellesley, Duke of Wellington
Professional soldier and politician

(1769–1852, born in Dublin) Wellington proved his military prowess in India and Denmark as well as on the shores of France and Spain. In June 1815 he participated in the final routing of Napoleon at the Battle of Waterloo. He had dabbled in politics as Member of the Irish Parliament for Trim in the late 1790s, and after 40 years in the army he became Prime Minister, but he became unpopular in England for accepting Catholic emancipation and refusing political reform. His nickname, the Iron Duke, was probably based on his strict disciplinarian attitude to his troops. Yet in his retirement he was remembered fondly by the public for his efficiency, honesty and dignity.

Oscar Wilde
Writer

(1854–1900, born in Dublin) Wilde excelled at both Trinity College, Dublin, and Oxford, winning the Newdigate prize for poetry in 1878. He married and had two sons, yet went on to adopt an unconventional way of life which led ultimately to social disgrace. The themes of his writing reflected his own character: homosexuality, individualism, and indifference to authority, and his most successful plays were those in which he mocked the morality and behaviour of the English upper classes, such as *A Woman of No Importance* and *The Importance of Being Earnest*. In 1895 he was imprisoned for two years for his homosexuality. After his release his only publication was *The Ballad of Reading Gaol*, and he left England for the Continent, where he later died. He is buried in Père Lachaise cemetery in Paris.

Terry Wogan
Broadcaster

(Born 1938 in Limerick) Wogan entered the media as an announcer on Radio Telefis Éireann in 1963. He became a household name in the 1970s and 1980s as the host of BBC

HISTORIC HOTELS, INNS AND PUBS

Radio Two's *Breakfast Show* (a position he returned to in 1994). He hit the television screen with the comic game show *Blankety Blank*, and went on to host his own chat show. His Irish blarney has endeared him to the public, and he has won numerous awards over the years, including an OBE in 1997.

Jack B. Yeats
Artist
(1870–1957, born in London) Jack Yeats was sent to school in County Sligo at the age of eight. He followed in his father's footsteps and became a painter, choosing scenes of

Irish life and Celtic mythology as the subject of his works. Like his brother, William, Yeats contributed to the Irish struggle for independence in the early 20th century; during this period he started using oils and his work matured. Unbeknown to many, Yeats was also, like William, a writer, producing a number of novels, plays and volumes of poetry.

W. B. Yeats
Writer
(1865–1939, born in Dublin) As the driving force of the Irish literary revival William Butler Yeats brought Ireland to the forefront of the literary world. His writings—poetry, prose and plays—encompassed his knowledge of Irish history and literature, as well as his own personal brand of spiritualism and mysticism. Yeats was involved in political controversy just before the outbreak of the Second World War, when his reputation was tainted by his involvement with fascism. (*See also feature on page 104.*)

Ballynahinch Castle Hotel
near Recess **B5**
Ballynahinch Castle has a history as rich as its Connemara surroundings. The original castle was once home to the pirate queen Grace O'Malley. Much later, in the 18th century, an inn was built on the site. It is from this building that the present castle grew, becoming a private home in the early 19th century. One master of the house, Richard Martin, or 'Humanity Dick', was famous for his role in the foundation of the Society for the Prevention of Cruelty to Animals. In the late 19th century the house was sold to the Indian Maharajah and cricketer Ranjitsinji, who used his immense wealth to transform the grounds. The Irish Tourist Board purchased the property in 1946, and it escaped the fate of negligence that many other stately homes in Ireland suffered.

Cashel Palace Hotel Cashel **D7**
In 1730 Archbishop Theophilus Bolton built this attractive Queen Anne house. It remained Church property until 1959, soon after which it underwent a radical change of use and opened as a luxury hotel. The palace saw action during Wolfe Tone's insurrection of 1798, when several rooms were damaged. They were renovated during the Regency period, introducing a new style to the property. The hotel has its own private walk to the Rock of Cashel, ancient seat of the Kings of Munster, where there is a 13th-century church. Arthur Guinness's father worked in the palace, and the gardens

contain the descendants of the original hops used by the Guinness family to brew their now-legendary stout.

Clontarf Castle Hotel Clontarf **F5**
Clontarf, near Dublin, was the scene of a famous battle fought by the High King of Ireland, Brian Ború, in 1014. The area's strategic importance demanded a castle, and in 1172 one was established as part of an inner circle of defence protecting Dublin. The building seen today, however, was completed in 1837, after the original was declared unsafe. The castle became a hotel in 1957, and was a leading entertainment venue until 1997, when the last cabaret show was staged.

The Cock Tavern Gormanstown **F4**
It would be easy to doubt the veracity of this tavern's claim to being the oldest in Ireland, as the modern building belies the old thatched whitewashed cottage that once stood on this site. The tavern did incredibly good business one night in particular, when Oliver Cromwell and 13,000 soldiers are said to have stopped there for refreshment. It was also the scene of great excitement in 1807, when Ireland's most famous highwayman, Mick Collier, was captured; on earlier occasions he had reputedly taken refuge here. Today, good food and beer, with occasional impromptu music sessions, maintain the tavern's popularity.

The Crown Liquor Saloon Belfast **G2**
This gin palace flourished in 19th-century industrial Belfast. Much of the extravagant decoration—a gem of real Victoriana—was

BELOW *Ballynahinch Castle Hotel's spectacular location overlooking Ballynahinch River rewards guests with tranquil and relaxing views. More active visitors can enjoy superb fishing.*

HISTORIC HOTELS, INNS AND PUBS (CONTINUED)

allegedly introduced by the architect son of a former landlord. There are snugs which suit the weary or lazy: once seated, no further strenuous movement is necessary thanks to the presence of gunmetal plates for striking matches and a bell system for alerting bar staff to your thirst. It is said that Italian craftsmen working on Irish churches executed the tiling, glasswork and ornamental woodwork in the 1880s. The Crown has been lovingly restored to its original glory by the National Trust, which, encouraged by the late Poet Laureate Sir John Betjeman, purchased it in 1978.

Davy Byrne's Dublin F5

James Joyce in *Ulysses* described Davy Byrne's as a 'moral pub', perhaps because in the novel the landlord opposed gambling. The connection is good enough for fans of Joyce, who stream through the doors on Bloomsday to eat Gorgonzola sandwiches (Leopold Bloom's favourite snack) by the plateful. Some regard Davy Byrne's as a good example of a Victorian pub, but the murals that adorn the walls in fact date only from the 1950s.

Hargadon Bros Sligo C3

This property was licensed to sell liquor in 1864. Patrick and Tom Hargadon bought the pub in 1908, and it has remained in the family ever since. The old features of stone floors, dark wood, cosy snugs and a turf fire make it

an archetypal Irish pub, so much so that the makers of the film *The Field* chose to replicate the interior for one of their sets. As with many traditional Irish pubs there is no jukebox, television or slot machine, and Hargadon Bros has a reputation as a 'talking pub', serving a superb pint of Guinness and good conversation.

Matt Molloy's Westport B4

The famous landlord of this atmospheric pub, Matt Molloy of music group the Chieftains, ensures excellent traditional music can be

heard every night. The local McGing family ran the pub-cum-shop for just over a century, from 1896 to 1989, until Matt bought it. The old grocery store section has now been integrated into the bar, but little else has changed. The authentic, lively and intimate atmosphere attracts locals and tourists in abundance.

Morrissey's Abbeyleix E6

Morrissey's is one of the few pubs in Ireland that still operates as both grocery shop and public house. Entering the establishment is like entering a time warp. While waiting for your Guinness to settle you can buy some of Morrissey's own blend of tea or coffee, and then settle down by the warm iron stove. But

what makes Morrissey's utterly unique is the proprietor, Paddy Mulhall, for, in true rural style, in addition to running the pub he is also the local undertaker, auctioneer and valuer, and newsagent.

Shelbourne Hotel Dublin F5

In the 1820s Dublin needed a hotel that would cater for the wealthy Anglo-Irish gentry, and the Shelbourne took on this role. It underwent major renovations in the 1860s and emerged as one of the world's most opulent and luxurious hotels, worthy of the patronage of the Empress of Austria in 1879. During the Easter Rising and subsequent Troubles it maintained a cool professionalism, with staff working unflinchingly during bomb attacks. The Shelbourne achieved legendary status when, in 1922, the constitution for the Irish Free State was drafted in one of its rooms. In 1993 it re-entered the political scene when it agreed to host several secret meetings that contributed to the Irish peace process.

Waterford Castle Hotel near Waterford E7

Waterford Castle is situated in splendid isolation on an island near Waterford, accessible only by ferry. Over 800 years ago Maurice Fitzgerald (one of whose descendants, Edward, translated Omar Khayyam's *Ruba'iyat*) occupied the island and built a Norman keep; the island remained in the Fitzgerald family until 1958. The castle dates back to a 15th-century tower which was enlarged several times in the 19th century. It is only since 1987 that the general public have been able to enjoy the magnificent building as a hotel.

USEFUL INFORMATION

Listed below are the details of Tourist Information Centres for a selection of destinations. Please note that these details may be subject to change.

BELFAST
St Anne's Court
59 North Street
Belfast
Tel. (028) 9024 6609

CORK
Grand Parade
Cork
Tel. (00 353 21) 273251

DUBLIN
Dublin Tourism Centre
Suffolk Street
Dublin 2
Tel. (00 353 1) 605 7700

GALWAY
Victoria Place
Eyre Square
Galway
Tel. (00 353 91) 563081

LIMERICK
Arthur's Quay
Limerick
Tel. (00 353 61) 317522

LONDONDERRY
44 Foyle Street
Londonderry
Tel. (028) 7126 7284

WATERFORD
The Granary
The Quay
Waterford
Tel. (00 353 51) 875823

For general information from mainland Britain, contact:

THE IRISH TOURIST BOARD at:
150 New Bond Street
London
Tel. (020) 7493 3201

THE NORTHERN IRELAND TOURIST BOARD at:
Britain Visitor Centre
1–3 Lower Regent Street
London
Tel. (0870) 155 0077

The following websites may also be of interest (NB website addresses can change):

Ireland at a Glance
http://web.one.net.au/~silverback/ireland/

Irish Tourist Board:
http://www.ireland.travel.ie/home/index.asp

Heritage of Ireland:
http://www.heritageireland.ie

Destination Ireland:
http://www.lonelyplanet.com/dest/eur/ire.htm

Northern Ireland Tourist Board:
http://www.ni-tourism.com

CALENDAR OF FESTIVALS AND EVENTS A SELECTION

IRELAND PROVIDES *a year-round programme of sporting events, fleadhs (festivals), ceilidhs or seisuns (concerts) and other happenings. The majority of these take place during the holiday season between Easter and October, obviously with an eye to the tourist trade. Most, however, are local, community-based events reflecting the Irish love of getting together and making merry which is typical both north and south of the border. The following events are regular annual fixtures, but may be scheduled slightly differently from year to year. Check dates with the tourist boards.*

JANUARY
BELFAST NORTHERN IRELAND OPEN FENCING CHAMPIONSHIPS The UK's top fencers compete at this major event.

FEBRUARY
BELFAST MUSICAL FESTIVAL This long-running festival showcases the best of Belfast's youthful musical talent.
ENNIS ALL-IRELAND DANCING CHAMPIONSHIPS

MARCH
DUBLIN FEIS CEOIL Music festival held at different venues.
GALWAY SET DANCING FESTIVAL
THROUGHOUT IRELAND ST PATRICK'S DAY (March 17). Ireland's patron saint's day is celebrated in parades and festivals, especially in Dublin, Downpatrick, Limerick and Londonderry.

APRIL
CORK INTERNATIONAL CHORAL FESTIVAL Held in churches and other venues.
DUBLIN FILM FESTIVAL Celebrating the best of Irish and international cinema.
FAIRYHOUSE IRISH GRAND NATIONAL This demanding steeplechase is a highlight of the racing year.
TRALEE PAN-CELTIC INTERNATIONAL FESTIVAL

MAY
ADARE MAY FAIR Carriage driving, clay pigeon shooting and other events.
ATHLONE ALL-IRELAND DRAMA FESTIVAL Featuring drama groups from all over Ireland.
KINSALE VINTAGE CLASSIC INTERNATIONAL RALLY Car rally round west Cork.
SLIGO ARTS FESTIVAL
WICKLOW GARDEN FESTIVAL

JUNE
BELFAST GARDEN FESTIVAL
CORK ARTS FESTIVAL
THE CURRAGH IRISH DERBY

DUBLIN (JUNE 16) BLOOMSDAY Marking the setting of James Joyce's *Ulysses*, walks and trails follow Leopold Bloom's perambulations around Dublin.
DUBLIN GARDEN FESTIVAL
KILDARE GOFFS BLOODSTOCK SALES One of several similar events at intervals through the year.
LISTOWEL WRITERS' WEEK Irish literature is celebrated in readings, music and dance.
PORTAFERRY GALWAY HOOKERS REGATTA A colourful boat procession to Strangford Lough.
THROUGHOUT IRELAND FESTIVAL OF MUSIC IN GREAT IRISH HOUSES Classical concerts in stately surroundings.
TRALEE SIAMSA TIRE Show by the National Folk Theatre, staged throughout the summer.

JULY
ARAN ISLANDS CELTIC SPIRIT Traditional singing, dancing, boat trips, etc.
BELFAST ULSTER SENIOR HURLING CHAMPIONSHIP
CARRICKFERGUS LUGHNASA FAIR Traditional Irish event with costumed entertainers.
DUBLIN JAMES JOYCE SUMMER SCHOOL
DUN LAOGHAIRE AMERICAN WEEK Celebrating American Independence.
GALWAY FILM AND ARTS FESTIVALS
PORTRUSH NORTH OF IRELAND AMATEUR OPEN GOLF CHAMPIONSHIP
THROUGHOUT NORTHERN IRELAND (JULY 12) ORANGE DAY Marches celebrate the victory of William III over King James II's army at the Battle of the Boyne.
WICKLOW MURPHY'S IRISH OPEN GOLF CHAMPIONSHIP

AUGUST
ARMAGH ULSTER PIPE BAND CHAMPIONSHIP
ARMAGH WORLD ROAD BOWLING FINALS International teams compete in this ancient Irish game.
BALLYCASTLE OULD LAMMAS FAIR A traditional event famous for its edible seaweed.
CLIFDEN CONNEMARA PONY SHOW
DUBLIN HORSE SHOW A major horse-jumping event and social gathering.
FEAKLE INTERNATIONAL TRADITIONAL MUSIC FESTIVAL
GALWAY RACES Held in July and August.
KILLORGLIN PUCK FAIR *(see page 125)*
SLIGO YEATS INTERNATIONAL SUMMER SCHOOL
STRADBALLY ANNUAL STEAM RALLY
TRALEE ROSE OF TRALEE INTERNATIONAL FESTIVAL

SEPTEMBER
CAPE CLEAR ISLAND INTERNATIONAL STORYTELLING FESTIVAL
CLARENBRIDGE/GALWAY OYSTER FESTIVALS Feasting and fun with the bivalved molluscs.
DUBLIN ALL-IRELAND FOOTBALL AND HURLING FINALS

ABOVE *Galway ladies tempt visiting gourmets with the region's speciality shellfish at the annual Oyster Festival in September.*

Croke Park comes alive with noise and colour when it plays host to these popular events.
LISDOONVARNA MATCHMAKING FESTIVAL
WATERFORD INTERNATIONAL FESTIVAL OF LIGHT OPERA

OCTOBER
BALLINASLOE INTERNATIONAL HORSE FAIR AND FESTIVAL
CORK GUINNESS CORK JAZZ FESTIVAL
CORK INTERNATIONAL FILM FESTIVAL
DUBLIN THEATRE FESTIVAL
KINSALE INTERNATIONAL GOURMET FESTIVAL A chance to experience memorable meals in local restaurants.
LONDONDERRY TWO CATHEDRALS FESTIVAL
WEXFORD FESTIVAL OPERA *(see page 141)*

NOVEMBER
BELFAST FESTIVAL Artists and performers converge on Belfast for a feast of drama, dance, cinema and every type of music from pop to classical.
KEADY BARD OF ARMAGH FESTIVAL Humorous poetry competition.

DECEMBER
BELFAST WINTER AGRICULTURAL FAIR Royal Ulster Agricultural Society dairy cattle show.
DUBLIN NATIONAL CRAFTS FAIR OF IRELAND
WOODFORD MUMMERS FEILE Traditional music, song, dance and mime in costume.

INDEX

and acknowledgments

Note: page numbers in **bold** refer to captions for illustrations

ACKNOWLEDGMENTS

The editors gratefully acknowledge the use of information
taken from the following publications during the preparation
of this volume:

AA Essential Explorer: Ireland by Lindsay Hunt, The Automobile
Association 1994
AA Leisure Guide Ireland, edited by Susi Bailey, The Automobile
Association 1993
The Armada in Ireland by Niall Fallon, Stanford Maritime 1978
Blue Guide: Ireland by Ian Robertson, A & C Black 1992
Cadogan Guides: Ireland by Catharina Day, Cadogan Books 1991
Chambers Biographical Dictionary edited by Magnus Magnusson,
W & R Chambers Ltd 1990
Companion to Irish History by Peter R. Newman,
Facts on File 1991
The Dictionary of National Biography, Oxford University Press
The Encyclopaedia Britannica
Eyewitness Travel Guide: Ireland by Lisa Gerard-Sharp and
Tim Perry, Dorling Kindersley 1995
Fodor's Ireland 90 edited by Richard Moore, Fodor's 1990
The Great Irish Famine edited by Cathal Poirteir,
Mercier Press 1995
History of Ireland by Desmond McGuire, Hamlyn 1987

A History of Ulster by Jonathan Bardon, The Blackstaff Press 1992
Insight Guide: Ireland edited by Brian Bell, APA Publications 1998
Ireland: The Rough Guide by Margaret Greenwood and Hildi
Hawkins, Rough Guides 1994
Irish Pubs by Barrie Pepper, Eric Dobby Publishing Ltd 1998
The Literary Guide to Ireland by Vivien Igoe, Methuen 1994
The Oxford Companion to Irish Literature edited by Robert
Welch, Oxford University Press 1996
The Oxford History of Ireland edited by R.F. Foster, Oxford
University Press 1989
Reader's Digest Illustrated Guide to Ireland Reader's Digest
Association Ltd 1992
The Shell Guide to Ireland by Lord Killanin and Michael V.
Duignan, Irish Shell Ltd 1989
The Shell Guide to Reading the Irish Landscape by Frank
Mitchell, Country House 1987
A Short History of Ireland by John O'Beirne Ranelagh,
Cambridge University Press 1994
Vanishing Country Houses of Ireland by The Knight of Glin,
David J. Griffin and Nicholas K. Robinson, The Irish
Architectural Archive and the Irish Georgian Society 1989
The Wreck of the Girona by Laurence N. W. Flanagan,
Ulster Museum 1973

PICTURE ACKNOWLEDGMENTS

T = top; *C* = centre; *B* = bottom; *L* = left; *R* = right

Front Cover V. K. Guy Ltd/Mike Guy **Back Cover** *T* Christopher Hill Photographic/Jill Jennings *B* Tony Stone Images/Paul Wakefield **2** Robert Harding Picture Library/Roy Rainford **4** Reader's Digest/Neil Holmes **6–7** Slide File **10** Woodfall Wild Images/David Woodfall **12** *L* Reader's Digest/Neil Holmes *R* Slide File **13** Christopher Hill Photographic **14** Robert Harding Picture Library/David Lomax **15** *T* Slide File *B* Christopher Hill Photographic/Jill Jennings **16** Gateway **16–17** Slide File **18** Reader's Digest/John Vigurs **19** National Maritime Museum, London **20** Don Sutton International Photo Library **21** *L* Geray Sweeney *R* Katz Pictures/Alan O'Connor **22** Woodfall Wild Images/David Woodfall **24–5** Network/Georg Gerster **26** Robin Neillands **27** Collections/Alain Le Garsmeur **29** *T* Magnum Photos/Peter Marlow *B* Collections/Geray Sweeney **30** *TL* Collections/Image Ireland/Bill Kirk *TR* Bombardier Aerospace-Shorts *CL* Irish Linen Centre/Lisburn Museum Collection *B* Harland & Wolff Photographic Collection, © National Museums and Galleries of Northern Ireland, Ulster Folk and Transport Museum/Negative: HI561A **31** *T* Christopher Hill Photographic/ Jill Jennings *B* Collections/Image Ireland/David Barker **32** Hulton Getty **33** By permission of the British Library **34** Robert Harding Picture Library/Roy Rainford **35** Christopher Hill Photographic **36** *L* Collections/George Wright *R* Christopher Hill Photographic **37** *T* The Old Bushmills Distillery Co. Ltd *L* Christopher Hill Photographic *C* Collections/George Wright *R* Christopher Hill Photographic **38** *L* National Geographic Society *R* Reproduced by kind permission of the Trustees of the National Museums & Galleries of Northern Ireland **39** Images Colour Library **41** Robert Harding Picture Library/Roy Rainford **42** *T* Bridgeman Art Library, London/Private Collection *B* Bridgeman Art Library, London/Lambeth Palace Library, London **43** Coleraine Times/Paul Nash **44** *TL* Trevor Jones Thoroughbred Photography *TR* Collections/Image Ireland/Alain Le Garsmeur *C* Board of Trustees of the National Museums and Galleries on Merseyside/Walker Art Gallery, Liverpool *BL* Kit Houghton *BR* Robert Harding Picture Library/Liam White **45** Christopher Hill Photographic **47** *L* Magnum Photos/Donovan Wylie *R* Hulton Getty **49** *T* National Museum of Ireland *B* Reproduced by kind permission of the Trustees of the National Museums & Galleries of Northern Ireland **50** *TL* Woodfall Wild Images/David Woodfall *TR* Woodfall Wild Images/Paul Hicks *C* Slide File *BL* Julian Cotton Photo Library *BR* NHPA/Martin Wendler **52** Pacemaker Press **53** *T* Dorling Kindersley/Alan Williams *B* Atlas Van Stolk, Rotterdam **54** Michael Diggin **56–7** Slide File **57** Northern Ireland Tourist Board **58** *T* Irish Stock *B* Collections/Bob Brien **59** Slide File **60** Pacemaker Press **61** Christopher Hill Photographic/Jill Jennings **62** Slide File **63** Slide File **64** Collections/Michael Diggin **65** Slide File **66** Irish Stock **67** Tony Stone Images/Paul Wakefield **68** *T* Bridgeman Art Library, London/Manchester City Art Galleries *B* National Museum of Ireland **69** Collections/Alain Le Garsmeur **70** *T* Images Colour Library *B* Robert Harding Picture Library **71** Julian Cotton Photo Library **72** *L* Mary Evans Picture Library *C* Don Sutton International Photo Library **72–3** Photo AKG, London/Eric Lessing **73** *L* Mary Evans Picture Library *R* Collections/Images of Ireland/Geray Sweeney **74** Mount Falcon Castle **76** Mary Evans Picture Library **77** *L* Irish Stock *R* Courtesy of the Director, National Army Museum, London **78** *TL* Mary Evans Picture Library *TR* Science Photo Library/Astrid & Hanns-Frieder Michler *C* Department of Irish Folklore, University College Dublin *BL* Robert Harding Picture Library/K. Gillham *BR* Magnum Photos/Bruno Barbey **80** *L* Bridgeman Art Library, London/ Bradford Art Galleries & Museums *R* Mary Evans Picture Library **81** Courtesy of the Allen Library, Dublin **83** *T* Slide File *R* Collections/Michael St Maur Sheil *B* National Museum of Ireland **84** *T* Magnum Photos/Abbas *CL* Don Sutton International Photo Library *C* Topham *BL* Collections/George Wright *BR* Collections/Ashley Cooper **86** *L* Mary Evans Picture Library *R* National Museum of Ireland **86–7** Katz Pictures/Mansell Collection/Time Inc. **87** Dúchas, The

Heritage Service **88** *L* The Board of Trinity College, Dublin *R* Christopher Hill Photographic **89** *TL* By permission of the British Library/Roy.13.B.VIII folio 26 *TR* Christopher Hill Photographic *B* Images Colour Library **90** *L* Collections *R* Slide File **91** Anthony Mason **92** Tony Stone Images/Paul Wakefield **93** Bridgeman Art Library, London/Private Collection **94** Michael Diggin **95** Slide File **96** *T* Slide File *C* Woodfall Wild Images/Mike Powles *BL* Christopher Hill Photographic *BR* Oxford Scientific Films/Deni Bown **97** Robin Neillands **98** Geray Sweeney **99** Tony Stone Images/Joe Cornish **101** *T* National Museum of Ireland *B* Hulton Getty **102** Collections/Image Ireland/John Lennon **103** *T* Fionnbar Callanan *B* The Royal Irish Academy **104** *L* Slide File *R* Rex Features/Richard Gardner **104–5** Courtesy of the Irish Tourist Board **105** *L* Courtesy of the Irish Tourist Board/Brian Lynch *R* The Abbey Theatre/Amelia Stein **106** Geray Sweeney **107** *T* Skyscan/Kevin Dwyer *B* Christopher Hill Photographic **108** *L* Collections/Image Ireland/Geray Sweeney *R* Magnum Photos/Eve Arnold **109** Don Sutton International Photo Library **110** Slide File **111** Reader's Digest/John Vigurs **112–13** Woodfall Wild Images/David Woodfall **114** *TL* Christopher Hill Photographic/Jill Jennings *TR* Woodfall Wild Images/David Woodfall *CR* National Museum of Ireland *BL* NHPA/John Hayward *BR* Joe Cornish **115** Slide File **116** Courtesy of the National Gallery of Ireland **117** *L* Don Sutton International Photo Library *R* Skyscan/Kevin Dwyer **118** Woodfall Wild Images/David Woodfall **119** Collections/Michael Diggin **120** Alpha Photographic Press Agency Ltd/Dermot Murphy **120–21** Pictorial Press/Polygram **121** *T* The Ronald Grant Archive *BL* Pictorial Press/ Polygram *BR* The Ronald Grant Archive **122** Hulton Getty **123** V. K. Guy Ltd/ Vic Guy **125** Slide File **126** Collections **127** Paul Wakefield **128** Robin Neillands **129** Robin Neillands **130** V. K. Guy Ltd/Vic Guy **131** Geray Sweeney **132** *T* Robin Neillands *B* Irish Stock **133** Robin Neillands **134–5** Christopher Hill Photographic **136** *T* Christopher Hill Photographic *C* Slide File *B* Slide File **137** *T* Dorling Kindersley/Ulster Folk and Transport Museum *C* Slide File *CR* Robert Harding Picture Library/Peter Ryan *B* Collections/Michael Diggin **138** *T* Robert Harding Picture Library/Roy Rainford *B* Geray Sweeney **139** Bridgeman Art Library, London/Trinity College Library, Dublin **140** *T* V. K. Guy Ltd/Mike Guy *B* Christopher Hill Photographic/Jill Jennings **141** Wexford Festival Opera **142** *TL* Slide File *R* The Abbey Theatre *B* Don Sutton International Photo Library **143** *T* National Museum of Ireland *B* Robert Harding Picture Library/Duncan Maxwell **144** *T* Reader's Digest/Neil Holmes *CL* Slide File *CR* Tony Stone Images/Third Eye Design Ltd **145** *T* The National Trust Photo Library/Matthew Antrobus *BL* The National Trust Photo Library/ Patrick Prendergast *BR* Images Colour Library **146** *L* The Irish Picture Library *R* Slide File **147** V. K. Guy Ltd/Mike Guy **148** *T* Slide File *B* Robert Harding Picture Library/Philip Craven **148–9** Irish Museum of Modern Art **150** *T* Julian Cotton Photo Library *B* Collections/Image Ireland/Alain Le Garsmeur **151** *L* Slide File *C* Reader's Digest *R* Reader's Digest/Neil Holmes **152** Slide File **153** *T* Collections/Michael St Maur Sheil *R* Waterford Crystal Ltd *BL* Waterford Crystal Ltd **154** Woodfall Wild Images/David Woodfall **155** *L* Slide File *R* Collections/John Tordai **156** Christopher Hill Photographic **157** *R* The National Trust Photo Library/Joe Cornish *L* Collections/Michael Diggin **158** Michael Diggin **159** Slide File **160** Christopher Hill Photographic/Jill Jennings **161** *T* Slide File *C* Don Sutton International Photo Library *B* Christopher Hill Photographic **162** *T* Don Sutton International Photo Library *B* Northern Ireland Tourist Board **163** *T* Hulton Getty *B* Universitätsbibliothek Heidelberg **164** *T* Redferns/David Redfern *B* ALLSPORT/Steve Powell **165** *T* PA News/Brian Little *BL* Hulton Getty *BR* Associated Press **166** *T* Fionnbar Callanan *B* Topham/Sean Dempsey **167** *T* Hulton Getty *B* Slide File **168** *L* The National Trust Photo Library/Will Webster *R* Slide File **169** Slide File

SEPARATIONS Studio One Origination Ltd, London
PAPER Périgord-Condat, France
PRINTING AND BINDING Printer Industria Gráfica SA, Barcelona, Spain